Birgit Bock-Luna

The Past in Exile

Forum Europäische Ethnologie

herausgegeben von

Dorle Drackle, Thomas Hauschild,
Wolfgang Kaschuba, Orvar Löfgren,
Bernd Jürgen Warneken und Gisela Welz

Band 9

LIT

Birgit Bock-Luna

THE PAST IN EXILE

Serbian Long-Distance Nationalism and Identity in the Wake of the Third Balkan War

LIT

Gedruckt auf alterungsbeständigem Werkdruckpapier entsprechend
ANSI Z3948 DIN ISO 9706

Umschlagbild: Birgit Bock-Luna

Bibliographic information published by the Deutsche Nationalbibliothek
The Deutsche Nationalbibliothek lists this publication in the Deutsche Nationalbibliografie; detailed bibliographic data are available in the Internet at http://dnb.d-nb.de.

ISBN 978-3-8258-9752-9
Zugl.: Frankfurt (Oder), Europa-Universität Viadrina, Diss., 2005

A catalogue record for this book is available from the British Library

Chausseestr. 128 – 129
D-10115 Berlin

Auslieferung:
LIT Verlag Fresnostr. 2, D-48159 Münster
Tel. +49 (0) 2 51/620 32 - 22, Fax +49 (0) 2 51/922 60 99, e-Mail: lit@lit-verlag.de

Distributed in the UK by: Global Book Marketing, 99B Wallis Rd, London, E9 5LN
Phone: +44 (0) 20 8533 5800 – Fax: +44 (0) 1600 775 663
http://www.centralbooks.co.uk/acatalog/search.html

Distributed in North America by:

Transaction Publishers
New Brunswick (U.S.A.) and London (U.K.)

Transaction Publishers
Rutgers University
35 Berrue Circle
Piscataway, NJ 08854

Phone: +1 (732) 445 - 2280
Fax: + 1 (732) 445 - 3138
for orders (U. S. only):
toll free (888) 999 - 6778
e-mail:
orders@transactionspub.com

Table of Contents

Part II. Living in the Past: The Role of the Second World War

Part III. Conspiracy theories, future visions, and the International Community

Acknowledgements

I want to thank a number of people who made this book possible: family members, colleagues, institutions, and interviewees. My family has lived with this book. For their moral support and intellectual contributions, I would like to thank my life-time anthropological companions: Nora-Christine Braun, Tilman Lanz, and Kerstin Veigt. Jeremiah Luna and Klara Luna have accompanied me on my fieldwork stays in California and provided me with the energy needed to write this book.

Intellectual support has been offered by the many insightful research discussions in the "Institutskolloquium" at the "Department of Vergleichende Sozial- und Kulturanthropologie" at the European University Viadrina at Frankfurt (Oder). I am grateful to my first doctoral advisor, Prof. Werner Schiffauer, who offered encouragement and contributed intellectually to the research process and writing up of the material. Support has also been provided by Prof. Andrei Simić whose inspiring comments on my fieldwork and writing at various stages in the research process helped shape the contents of this work.

Financial support has been provided by the "Graduiertenkolleg Repräsentation, Rhetorik, Wissen" of Prof. Anselm Haverkamp, chair of the department of Western European Literatur at the Viadrina University. Between October 2000 and March 2004 I received a research grant of the "Deutsche Forschungsgemeinschaft" (DFG), without which this dissertation would not have been possible. The Graduiertenkolleg also generously financed my three fieldwork stays in California.

My warmest thanks go to the numerous Serbian immigrants in the San Francisco Bay Area whom I interviewed and who willingly shared their life stories, precious time, coffee, and food with me. I enjoyed their hospitality and trust immensely. I would prefer to acknowledge them directly, but since I use pseudonyms at all times it seems best to protect their privacy. *Hvala ljepo!*

Introduction

In the Shadow of the Balkan War, on the Shore of California Orchestrated Solidarity?

Belgrade in early August. It seems that we came here for the hottest and stickiest week of the year. We are sitting in a crowded apartment filled with smoke, located in the center of the city. There are cars honking on the street underneath the window,and people wandering the sidewalks, meeting friends in cafés and apparently enjoying themselves as usual. As usual?! It's the year 1999, the NATO bombing has only ceased a few weeks ago, at the end of June, and the ruins of the ministry buildings in the government section of town are still fresh. At eight o'clock in the evening we watch the television news. The state-sponsored television station delivers triumphant messages about the successful restoration of electrical systems and other public infrastructure; images of torn down bridges, and talks with bombing victims flicker on the screen. Then a journalist reports on a "diaspora congress," where hundreds of "Yugoslavs," settled outside Serbia come to meet President Milošević who officially thanks them for "helping rebuild the country": "I am grateful for the millions of dollars we received in these dark times from our comrades in Western Europe and the United States to help us endure and rise up again." [Fieldnotes]

What at first seemed to be a random newscast about a crowd of people, all emigrants and exiles, meeting under the Serbian flag and the SPS (*Socialistička Partija Srbije)* logo, later raised numerous questions. Who were these people? Which ties did they keep to their homeland? What was their impact from abroad on the former Yugoslavia and the wars that ripped it apart? Was their role really that significant? What motivated their actions and which feelings did they have for Milošević's Serbia? What was exaggerated and myth in this news piece, and what was fact? How significant was the NATO bombing of Yugoslavia in 1999 for the national consciousness in the diaspora and in the wider context of the Third Balkan Wars?

The orchestrated act of global solidarity, I suggest, only pretended that the socialist president's shaky regime had the ex-patriates' support on its side. In fact, the diaspora's relationship to Serbia has never been as harmonious as Milošević would have liked it to be, but as the scene demonstrated, he was well informed how crucial a factor diasporas are today. In this work, I will analyze the diaspora's role in the recent Balkan Wars, as seen retrospectively by Serbian exiles[1] in the United States at the beginning of the new millennium. I will try to answer a number of questions: 1) if and how displaced Serbs living abroad had an impact on the tragic political events in the homeland, 2) how the war impacted them and 3) why their relationship to Milošević's Serbia was foremost factionalized and ineffective. However, my main interest does not concern Serbia or Yugoslavia as such, but Serbian migrants living thousands of miles away from their homeland. In specific, I am interested in how the Yugoslav disintegration influenced political practices as well as discourses on national and personal identity, nationalism, and memory in exile.

Diasporas and ethno-national conflicts in the homeland

In the wake of the latest Balkan Wars[2] a plethora of academic and journalistic studies have focused on the violent unmaking and remaking of nation(s) as well as the underlying ethnic antagonisms and historical underpinnings involved in the breakup of Yugoslavia.[3] The dismemberment of Yugoslavia was portrayed more or less as a local phenomenon, putting aside the immense role that global agents, such as Croatian and Serbian diaspora communities, played in providing ideas, propaganda material, money, and personnel to incite the conflicts. Very few studies have paid attention to the role of these émigré circles in the violent wars[4] that

1. Serbs in the United States can be described by many terms, such as exiles, diaspora, displaced persons, immigrants, migrants, American Serbs, and the like. These terms basically range from meaning that someone has been banned forcibly from his native land, to leaving voluntarily and in the search for a better professional career. Often the categories are overlapping, since for example all the displaced persons (DP) of the Second World War later became immigrants. There are also immigrants who entered the United States as professionals or students and at the same received visas on the basis of political asylum and are thus officially refugees. Many scholars have written articles which solely focused on the problems of definition. However, as is the case with most academic categories, they are rarely used by the people we work with in the same way, often they are not used at all. My task is not to indulge in the typification of the people I conversed with, which is always a very shaky endeavor. In my work I will refer to all of them as "exiles" and "displaced," i.e., not living in their homeland, and specify according to the individual case.
2. By "last Balkan Wars" or "Third Balkan War" I mean the various violent conflicts on the territory of the former Yugoslavia starting in 1991 in Slovenia, spanning to war in Croatia (1991-92), in Bosnia-Herzegovina (1992-1995), and finally to Kosovo and Metohija (1998) and Yugoslavia (1999) (see also Glenny 1996).
3. From the vast amount of literature on the topic, see for instance Glenny 1996, 2000, Halpern and Kideckel 2001, Ramet 1996, Silber and Little 1995, Thompson 1993, Woodward 1995a.
4. The following works are the only ones on the topic which have been published and that I know of: Hockenos 2003, Procter 2000, Skrbis 1999, Winland 1995.

engulfed the former Yugoslavia. But what, if the politics of "nation-building" and "nation-destruction"[5] have their origins in part in Western countries with traditionally large "Yugoslav"[6] immigrant communities? How could one explain the prevalence of exiles that came back to the help of their country of origin, if as volunteer soldiers, for private visits, or on political missions? Is an active and highly interactive relationship between the ethnic homeland and the diaspora population necessary for intense ethno-national sentiments to develop in the diaspora? How does external threat, e.g. war, influence the nature and extent of these feelings? How do situations of conflict impact on the way that the personal and national pasts are viewed? Or, how is history being reconfigured and represented in the shadow of war? These and other questions deserve our intellectual curiosity, because they provide one of the important keys to an understanding of the global societal processes in conjunction with migration in contemporary modernity. They are of particular importance for countries with a large intake of diverse groups of migrants (United States, Canada, Australia, Germany, Sweden, Israel, et al.).

Loring Danforth, in *The Macedonian Conflict* (1995: 7), claims that many conflicts are "cultural wars," that involve ethnic minorities, diaspora communities, and international organizations like the United Nations and the European Union. With regard to the former Yugoslavia, however, there has been very little study concerning either effective diaspora-homeland relations or unsuccessful ones as part of a "cultural war". The involvement of former Yugoslav exiles has long been overlooked, but their contributions to the evolving nationalisms in the Yugoslav republics have proven crucial and even dangerous. It seems timely to take a closer look at the phenomenon of Balkan "exile patriotism" (Hockenos 2003) or "long-distance nationalism" (Anderson 1992). Borrowing an argument from Mary

5. Walker Connor (1994: 4) remarks with regard to the prevalent term "nation-building," that it is inappropriate, since most nation-states are multination-states, and most nations are not also states. It would be therefore more adequate to speak of state-building. However, concerning Croatia nation-building coincides with the strict semantics of the term, since the new independent country is more or less ethnically homogeneous. This is a little different in Serbia, where the population is still highly mixed and comprises of approximately 26 ethnic groups, although Serbs are the clear majority population at app. 86% (see Hayden 1996).
6. I use the term "Yugoslav" when addressing the historical period between 1917 and 1991, when the multination-state Yugoslavia existed. Moreover, whenever I speak of all the different national groups and not one specific one, I choose to employ "Yugoslav" as well, similar to Halpern's and Kideckel's decision to title their book *Yugoslavs at war* 2000. I am aware that many people, esp. Croats, would not be content with this use of the term, but I believe that it is the only short term for including all the different ethnic groups, instead of listing them all. Of course, the term is also employed, when the question of a "Yugoslav" identity, before or after the actual existence of the Yugoslav state is addressed. On paper Yugoslavia existed until the year 2002, when Serbia and Montenegro substituted the shrinking rump state of Yugoslavia.

Kaldor's *New and Old Wars* (1999: 17, 52 ff.), I suggest that the civil war in Yugoslavia cannot be sufficiently understood by focusing only on the local. Instead, these "new wars" are "world wars," insofar as global and transnational actors such as diasporas intersect with events on the national scale.

This study sets out to explore long-distance nationalism in the United States where Serbian nationalism has historically been a strong factor within Serbian communities. More specifically, this book is not about migration, nor does it deal with Yugoslavia, Serbia, and the wars of disintegration, but throughout my writing I will touch upon these issues as they are contextually relevant for the interlocutors who participated in my research. The work centers on the phenomenon of long-distance nationalism and an analysis of Serbs in United States with a particular focus on "first generation"[7] individuals. In order to understand the sentiments that Serbs in America feel for their homeland, I will investigate identity politics and memory, the relationship between life historical narratives of exiles, their transnational practices, and the political and global context that frames their stories.

The belief that modernization processes would eventually bring about the demise of nationalism, could be partially held responsible for the lack of attention to the 'new' nationalisms of today (Hobsbawm 1990, Harris 1991). Closely related are the widely shared assumptions about the impact of globalization, leading to a weakening of national cultures in favor of global cultural streams and supranational connections between people, such as the European Union, are also to blame for this lack of attention. These overtly optimistic assumptions about the attractiveness of global culture and the descendancy of nationalism ignore what A.D. Smith calls "the continuing development of the nation-state and a revival of ethnicity" (1995: 160). It appears that ethno-nationalism has successfully adapted to the new "global flows," such as 'media-scapes' and 'ethno-scapes', to borrow from Appadurai (1996: 33).

In light of the all too optimistic expectations about the gradual demise of nationalism the global resurgence of nationalism since the 1980's and the question of the persistence of ethno-nationalism seem all the more challenging and interesting.

7. There are different understandings of "first generation." To some, it means "the migrating generation," to others "the first generation born in America." Based on the fact that the former was mentioned to me much more frequently than the latter, I decided to apply the term to those who have been mainly socialized in the former Yugoslavia and emigrated as adolescents or adults. Those Serbs who entered the United States as children or were born in the U.S. as children to "first generation" immigrants, and therefore have been mainly socialized in the U.S. I call "second generation."

Long-distance nationalism defined

"Long-distance nationalism" is a term authored by Benedict Anderson (1994), drawing on Acton's aphorism "exile is the nursery of nationalism" (ibid.: 315). There is often an assumption that migrants cut their ties to the homeland as soon as they arrive in the host country, when in reality they continue to care for their country of origin for many years after their emigration. In contrast to this assumption, it has even become commonplace to believe that migrants are more conservative and more nationalistic than their fellow nationals at home. The insight, that exile is a space where strong sentiments for the nation are cultivated is drawn from the knowledge that many great nationalist leaders of the past, going back as early as the 17th century, lived outside their homeland for long periods of time. According to one of Anderson's examples, English settlers to the United States "are in a way, getting ready to be 'English' exactly because they are in Massachusetts, not in England" (Anderson 1998: 61). To be English, not only in England but especially in Massachusetts, speaks to the significance of concepts such as the "deterritorialized nation-state" or the "transnational nation-state" (Basch, Blanc, Glick Schiller 1994), concepts that try to help disentangle the complexities that ensue once scholars take notice of the mistake inherent in the image of the world as divided into separate, sovereign states, each representing a nation.

The ultimate example of a deterritorialized nation which developed its national consciousness in and through exile is the Jewish diaspora. The idea of "the Jewish people," a religiously defined nation that was for centuries scattered in the world, started with the biblical flight into the desert and ended with the Zionist project of the establishment of the Jewish state of Israel, which is still closely connected to its global diaspora.[8] Figuring as the paradigm for a diasporic consciousness that is based on suffering and persecution, Serbs and other diasporic people have made claims to a 'kinship in suffering' with Jews to undermine their own political claims. However, examples such as the Jewish diaspora, testify to the significance of exile in the development of national or ethnic consciousness. The major theorists of nationalism (Anderson 1983, Gellner 1983, Hobsbawm and Ranger 1986) have done their part to ignore the issue of nationalism that stretches beyond and across nation-state borders.[9] Thus, migration confronts us with the paradox that migrants, though physically loosening their

8. See Assmann (2000: 83f.), Tölölyan (1991: 6).
9. Ernest Gellner (1983: 6) employed the image of Chamisso's figure of a French émigré, the "Man without a Shadow," to point to the underlying meaning of the "Man without a Nation." For Gellner, this allusion implies the necessity of national sentiment. But the issue of the place where this national sentiment is uttered, exile, is treated as a mere coincidence. What it means that this longing for the nation is embodied by an émigré deserves no explanation.

ties to the homeland, at the same time engage in the imaginary process of approaching it from the distance. Leaving home and becoming enmeshed in the society of a new country does not only lead to 'mixing' or "hybridity" (Bhabha 1994); it is also characterized by the imagination of national 'purity' despite (or due to) being away from the homeland. As Anderson further states "[n]ationalism's purities (and thus also cleansings) are set to emerge from exactly this hybridity" (ibid.: 62). Anderson (1992a, 1992b, 1994, 1998) charts the way for further exploration into the intersections of migration studies and nationalism. He establishes a close link between the capitalist world order, mass migrations, and global communications.[10]

Following Zlatko Skrbiš' (1999: 2) proposition in *Long-Distance Nationalism*, the conventional understanding of the concepts distance, isolation, space, and time require thorough re-evaluation. Migrants relativise time and space, and go beyond passive feelings of compassion with family and friends back home; they actively participate in the political struggles in the homeland, as if distance didn't exist, or 'as if they were there'.[11]

Many cases, e.g. Irish Americans' successful lobbying for the IRA struggle, indicate that large-scale political manipulation from the safe heavens in the West help produce a new category of nationalist, the long-distance nationalist. In Anderson's words he is described as follows:

> "For while technically a citizen of the state in which he comfortably lives, but to which he may feel little attachment, he finds it tempting to play identity politics (via propaganda, money, weapons, any way but voting) in the conflicts of his imagined *Heimat* – now only fax-time away. But this citizenshipless participation is inevitably non-responsible – our hero will not have an answer for, or pay the price for, the long-distance politics he undertakes. He is also easy prey for shrewd political manipulators in his *Heimat*." (Anderson 1992a: 13)

---

10. Anderson argues, for example that the role of a wealthy Armenian diaspora in finding the funds and weapons to assure Yerevan's military triumph over Baku was decisive (Anderson 1998: 74).
11. To note, in using the notion "homeland" I am referring to the place that my informants come from, be it Croatia, Bosnia, Serbia, or Yugoslavia. However, I do not treat the homeland as a real entity that reflects concrete life worlds. In the words of Skrbiš (1999: 38): "Instead homelands are spatial representations which are influenced by political and cultural factors, rather than a simple fact of geography. It is important to view the homeland as a constructed and imagined *topos* rather than a clearly definably entity." The rather presumptuous statement made by a Greek Consul in Melbourne: "Australia is the first line of defense over the battle of Macedonia" (Danforth 1995: 7f.) not only points to the significance that Australia had for the political conflicts in the wake of Macedonia's independence, but to the suspension of spatial distance thought to divide Macedonians in Australia from Macedonians in Macedonia.

Anderson's quotation delineates the interest and scope of this study. The figure of the long-distance nationalist hero illustrates that migrant groups *are* affected by events in their homelands and they actively take part in them, without having to live with the consequences of their actions.

Certainly, Anderson's contribution is ground breaking in that it carves out a new field of interest. In practice, however, Anderson does not pay attention to the nature of the migrants' participation, because he does not employ fieldwork, nor does he analyze texts in order to underline his claims. He simply points to the "non-responsible" political behavior underlying their transnational activities, without providing ethnographic material and analysis thereof.

In contrast to Anderson's work, David Bruce MacDonald's *Balkan Holocausts?* (2002), is a treatment of Croatian and Serbian victim-centered propaganda and the war in Yugoslavia, and is a brilliant example of an analysis that includes an examination of the writings of what we might call 'armchair' nationalists. MacDonald defines these 'armchair' nationalists as "believers throughout the world who promote their own interpretation of history and current events on the Internet, and in the popular press." He further states, "such people formed a crucial base of support for Croatian and Serbian nationalist regimes [...]" (MacDonald 2002: 12). Like MacDonald, Paul Hockenos also reaches out to questions that Anderson's thought-provoking but aborted exploration of the world of long-distance nationalism had left unanswered. In *homeland calling. Exile Patriotism and the Balkan Wars* (2003: 218f.), Hockenos investigates closely the paradoxical relationship between the émigrés to the hostcountry. Doing research among Serbian, Croat, and Kosovo Albanian exiles[12], Hockenos notes that the realm of diaspora politics doesn't necessarily reflect the democratic and pluralistic values which have developed in the societies of the host countries:

> "The world of diaspora politics itself is a no-man's-land with few written rules, one in which basic democratic concepts such as ac-

12. I know of no other ethnographic research which has been undertaken among Kosovo Albanian exiles. Kosovo Albanians lack a diaspora with historical roots, for they have not been politically active abroad before the 1990's. However, during the 1990's their diaspora engagement has been remarkable. Kosovo Albanians in Germany, together with Bukoshi's government in exile in Stuttgart mainly financed the health infrastructure in the rebel republic (Hockenos 2003: 213 ff.). In general, the focus on Serbian and Croatian migrants, to the exclusion of Slovenian, Bosnian Muslim or others, is made, because the two main Yugoslav ethnic groups have held the most decisive historical antagonisms; and their emigration and diaspora activism through exile organizations is characterized by a great temporal depth, reaching back to the middle of the 19th century. As for Bosnian Muslims, they organized very little politically abroad, both before and during the Yugoslav wars of disintegration.

> countability, checks and balances, term limits, representation, and pluralism are meaningless. [...] He who shouts the loudest or raises the most money or both carries the mantle until someone louder and wealthier appears on the scene."

To Hockenos, the insight that exiles betray the democratic traditions of their respective host countries comes across as the biggest setback, frustrating the author's high expectations of Western democratic principles. But maybe, this failure is intrinsic to the political system of the United States itself? Perhaps, the exile nationalists described above have taken a lesson from so-called democratic political practices in the United States where access to financial wealth, not "democratic values" is regarded a basic prerequisite for running a political campaign? As Glick Schiller (2001: 12f.) contends:

> "Not only does it appear that transnational migration is as American as an apple pie, but it is also becoming clear that long-distance nationalism has been an important, although little noted, aspect of political history of the United States and emigrant-sending countries."

Long-distance nationalism in action

During the 1980's the main authors of nationalism, Ernest Gellner (1981), Eric Hobsbawm (1981), and Benedict Anderson (1983) had convincingly argued that the spread of European nationalism in the 19th century was made possible by the printing press. The production and consumption of books on a large scale enabled the imagination of simultaneity and homogeneity among populations that had hitherto rather identified with each other on a face-to-face level (Anderson 1996: 44). Twenty years later, theorists of transnationalism and diasporas do not focus as much on books as a medium of nationalism, but on the new media, satellite telephones, and the world wide web. In *Modernity at Large* (1996: 9) Arjun Appadurai, e.g., has pointed to the relevance of "mobile texts" that "create implosive events that fold global pressures into small, already politicized arenas." MacDonald (2002: 114) describes the use of these novel means of global communication that also influenced nationalism in the Balkan as follows:

> "That Serbs and Croats basically saw each other's history as a mirror image of their own should come as no surprise. A great deal of debate occurred between these two nations during the war, in newspapers, in magazines, and most importantly, on the Internet. The use of the world wide web as a medium of communication opened many new avenues for propagandists. While it is both expensive and

> difficult to print and circulate propaganda in large quantities, it was relatively cheap and easy to scan and paste Serbian and Croatian propaganda on a variety of websites. Those who agreed with the government position benefited from links to official websites. This allowed for a continuous stream of new information and publications, designed to rebut arguments advanced by the other side. This new medium of expression allowed for the spread of a great deal of information within a very short time."

For various reasons, Croats were much more successful in their capacity to link the homeland with the diaspora by using the Internet but also through return visits, political networking and the like. In this context, the career of Gojko Šušak deserves mention. Šušak, a Toronto-based Croat from Western Herzegovina who emigrated in 1968, was heavily involved in Canadian-Croatian affairs and some smear campaigns against the communist regime in Yugoslavia. In 1990, the pizza-baker rallied massive financial and political support for Croatian independence and came back to his native Croatia to help Franjo Tudjman's political party, later taking part in political and even military actions.[13] In 1991 he became minister of defense and in 1993 the vice-president of the leading HDZ (*Hrvatska demokratska zajednica*). Until his death in 1998 he was considered to be the right hand of the Croatian president Tudjman. While some characterized Šušak as the mythic hero of Croatian independence, others saw in him one of Croatia's "ugliest strongmen" (Skrbiš 1999: 8).

In support of the argument that the homeland does matter to immigrants and that in the extreme diasporas are more nationalistic and conservative than their home-based co-ethnics, Daphne Winland, in her study on Croats in Canada, states that in terms of ideology, the HDZ in North America was even more radical than Tudjman's party in Croatia (Winland 1995: 20). And, according to Misha Glenny (1992: 63), four million dollars were raised by the emigrant Croatian community abroad toward the HDZ political campaign in 1990, a financial support that was believed to have been decisive for Tudjman's electoral victory, which was mainly based on nationalist aspirations.

The 'Serbian side' failed to provide such successful "long-distance heroes," but nevertheless it did not lack in equally significant returnées who influenced the political landscape of Serbia. The wealthy American Serb, Milan Panić, manager of a pharmaceutical company in Los Angeles, went back to his parents' homeland to become elected as Prime Minister of Serbia in 1991, although he had no political experience and was at first insecure when speaking his mother tongue. The millionaire stayed in office

13. See Tanner 2001: 222f., 250.

only for half a year due to internal political competition in Belgrade, for which the *connoisseur* of American business strategies found himself unprepared. Panić quickly left the harsh political landscape in Serbia and re-returned to his more amiable Southern California. His former protégé and later competitor, Slobodan Milošević, worked in a New York bank in the 1980's before enmeshing himself in Serbian politics and holding on to presidential power in Yugoslavia until 2000. And Zoran Djindjić, Prime Minister, reformer, and fierce opponent of Milošević's political networks had lived in Germany and earned his doctorate in Konstanz, before returning and acquiring political power, which he held until his assassination in spring 2003. In 1991 Crown Prince Aleksandar Karadjordjević, born in 1947 in a London Hotel room which was subsequently declared Serbian territory, began rallying for the return of the monarchy in Serbia, although in his lifetime the would-like-to-be king didn't even make an effort to learn Serbian. What motivated these individuals to turn their backs on their adopted home countries where they spent most of their lives, and engage in the politics of a faraway homeland?

That these "long-distance nationalists" are not only found among Croatian and Serbian émigrés is amply illustrated by the many examples offered by Lithuania, Israel, or Greece. At the beginning of 1998, Valdas Adamkus of the United States was elected president of Lithuania, although he lacked any political experience. The former prime minister of Greece, Andreas Papandreou, started life as a Greek citizen, became an American citizen, and then, when opportunity beckoned, became again a Greek citizen to enable his long-time political career in Greece (Anderson 1998: 71). Another player in the long-distance game is Joe Gutnick, an Australian billionaire who may have decided the 1996 Israeli election by mobilizing the ultra-orthodox Jewish vote with his one million U.S. dollar donation to support Netanyahu (Skrbiš ibid.: 9). Indeed, most scholars of diaspora, transnationalism, and long-distance nationalism (Glick Schiller and Fouron 2001, Ong 1999, van de Veer 1995 et al.) agree upon the fact that migrant communities maintain a considerable impact on the politics, society, and economy of the homeland.

The intimacy of long-distance nationalism

In all the above mentioned examples long-distance nationalism is rightly understood as a *political* principle. As the range of names revealed, the political nature of long-distance nationalism can be discerned most easily in the figure of the politician who returns to the homeland in order to become a statesman. Nevertheless, in this study I shall use a rather different approach, focusing not only on outstanding, politically prominent leaders, but on 'ordinary' individuals, local diaspora organizations and their key figures. This broader focus is useful as it reveals that long-distance nationalism is not something that only well-known individuals take part in. It is – most often so – a group-based phenomenon which pervades both public and private spheres of life. The cases of Sri Lanka and Haiti, both sharing an extraordinary high number of emigrants and providing excellent case material for the study of long-distance nationalism, illustrate that more than prominent political figures are of concern for the student of long-distance nationalism.

Of course, not every migrant necessarily becomes a long-distance nationalist. According to Øivind Fuglerud in his study *Life on the Outside* (1999: 1), of an estimated 700, 000 Tamil refugees worldwide, that is one-third of Sri Lanka's entire pre-war Tamil population, only a few turn into leading nationalists, successfully bridging the distance between their exile and the politics in the homeland. And of the hundreds of thousands of Haitians who by sending remittances provide a central component of Haiti's national income (Glick Schiller and Fouron 2001) certainly not everyone is necessarily a long-distance nationalist, as Glick Schiller's text seems to suggest. But what is the difference between a long-distance nationalist and somebody who 'simply' identifies with his homeland, but who is not a long-distance nationalist? Is somebody who frequently visits his homeland and sends remittances already a long-distance nationalist? In which ways do processes of identitification or transnationalism and long-distance nationalism interrelate?

In contrast to the political focus in Anderson's and MacDonald's works, Glick Schiller and Fouron (2001: 17f.) define nationalism (and long-distance nationalism) "as a set of beliefs and practices that link together people of a nation and its territory." In my view, this definition is far too broad, leading the authors to state "that almost everyone spoke to us as nationalists, as persons who idenfitified and loved Haiti" (ibid.: 15). This very inclusive conception of nationalism lays risk to leaving the concept of nationalism too vague. Whereas a pronounced national identity or "expressive identity" (Safran 1999) seems to be a prerequisite for being a nationalist, not everyone who has a strong national consciousness is necessarily a nationalist: in other words, national identity is not equivalent with long-distance nationalism. Transnationalism is a broader category, denoting all social practices linking people in the homeland and in migration through family ties, letter writing, visits, the sending of remittances and the like, practices that cross national borders. In contrast to this, long-distance nationalism connotes a strengthening of the perception of national borders, the emphasis that identity is not hyphenated, accompanied by political agency or "instrumental identity" (Safran 1999) which is directed toward the homecountry. As the Serbian case reveals, long-distance nationalism occurs in times of crisis and war and is specifically characterized by a discourse on historical injustice and violence. Thus, in this work, I regard long-distance nationalism as a political principle with underlying *political and historical claims*, not just a marker of national identity.

Not everybody who feels for the homeland and people s/he left behind should be understood and categorized as a nationalist, meaning that s/he holds nationalist aspirations for his/her land of origin.[14] Developing a nationalistic attitude towards one's nation and homeland is only one way of coming to terms with the manifold experiences of distance and migration. But many migrants, especially those whose homeland is in conflict, are constantly renegotiating their identity not only with regard to the homeland but also vis-à-vis the host society. Or, following Becker (2001: 38, my transl.), "the reflexive autobiography becomes the experience of migration per se" – exile heightens the awareness of Self. Expanding on Becker, I argue that the increased awareness of Self and the nation in exile is one of the major factors shaping the specific forms of nationalism in migration, or long-distance nationalism. The ramifications of this assumption form the core of this study.

This book is not so much to prove the existence of long-distance nationalism, but rather to show some possible ways in which the genealogy and manifestations of the phenomenon of long-distance nationalism can be looked at. I agree with Kapferer (1988: xvi) that theories of nationalism, by employing a macro-systemic view of the nation and nationalism, "remain committed to a linear and too homogenized conception." They are oblivious to people's practices, discourses, and actions. Partha Chatterjee (1986: 21) formulates a similar critique when he argues that Anderson's work eliminates agency and the potential for dispute and that "instead of pursuing the varied, and often contradictory, political possibilities inherent in this process, Anderson seals up his theme with a sociological determinism." According to Herzfeld (1997: 6), Anderson looks at nationalism as a process that functions from the top to the bottom: "[H]e does not tell us why this works so well and so often, nor does he tell us whether the actions of the converted exert a reciprocal effect on the cultural form of the state." Herzfeld proposes to delineate the impact of ordinary people on local nationalisms, the "idealized virtues," "little acts" of essentializing, and bina-

14. According to Gellner (1983: 1) "nationalism is primarily a political principle, which holds that the political and national unit should be congruent." He continues that "nationalist *sentiment* is the feeling of anger aroused by the violation of this principle, or the feeling of satisfaction aroused by its fulfillment" (Gellner ibid.). In contrast, the principle of nationality is emotionally more neutral, someone who feels English does not necessarily pursue the goal of Irish and Scottish to bow to the English national idea. However, any definition of the nation, nationalism and nationalist is problematic, but the most common ground is the conviction which can be based on the choice to belong to a nation. This conviction is neither static nor natural and two brothers can hold loyalties and solidarity for two different nations (see Danforth 1995: 222-231).

risms people employ in everyday life. Formulating the concept of "cultural intimacy" is thus an attempt to direct the phenomenon of nationalism away from the political and historical macro-narratives about the nation's past, present and future, and towards "the social uses" in ordinary people's lives.

Moreover, a problem arises out of the common belief that Western nationalism is "good nationalism," or patriotism, and non-Western nationalism "bad nationalism." It seems prudent to understand nationalism in terms of the morality it is imbued with. Nationalism does not necessarily have to be dangerous, as Kapferer claims. And Glick Schiller and Fouron (2001: 271) state: "The political agendas of subaltern populations translated into contemporary long-distance nationalisms represent a crucial component of global movements for social and economic equity and justice." This highly optimistic outlook on long-distance nationalism remains questionable, but I regard the claim interesting, if one tries to go beyond the claim that nationalism, especially in non-Western countries, is bad. It seems to be worthwhile to investigate closely the specific claims underlying nationalist endeavors.

In a similar vein, Serbian American anthropologist Andrei Simić (2002: 144) views Southslav nationalisms not as opposed to Western democracies but to a capitalist American popular culture, so that "despite the capacity of nationalisms to generate widespread terror and destruction, the nation and nationalisms provide the only realistic socio-cultural framework for a modern world order." Insofar as it is the anthropologist's task and strength to understand and to interpret the voices of the people he works with, his effort is to make visible their moral universe. That nationalisms are not only dangerous but most of all attractive and empowering in the modern world, characterized by fundamental transitions and far-reaching shifts in the economic, social, and political, underscores that the task ahead, to study Serbian nationalism not only in Serbia but as a global phenomenon is even more timely.

One needs to consider the multifaceted nature of nationalisms and the sense in which they are always a part of a broader and heavily symbolic discursive field. Nowhere is this heterogeneous nature of nationalism more obvious than in the study of migrants who through the spatial and temporal distance they acquired have the freedom to assemble an image of the "lost land" independent of the physical reality of living there. Like the *bricoleur* (Lévi-Strauss 1962) the long-distance nationalist assembles an image of the nation out of small and big bits and pieces of information, experiences, facts, fiction, and ideas. He does not have to test his hypotheses about the nation and what he imagines to be the "real" truth about it, nor does he face directly the tragic events which, however unanticipated, may partly be the consequence of his bricolage. The assemblage of the longed for nation in theory is prone with ambivalence, contradictions, forced coherences, and creative new beginnings -- an imagination of community of special quality. The cultural issues which the long-distance-nationalist draws upon are old, and yet they are new.

One of (long-distance) nationalism's biggest assets is the past and the historicity of the nation in the present. Explaining the homeland's present troubles through the prism of the past serves as the long-distance nationalist's main tool for formulating political and historical claims. Considering the significance of the past for Serbs abroad, below I will outline some key events in Serbian history which Serbs in the U.S. regard as crucial for their nation and which will be touched upon frequently in this study.

The Serbian diaspora and the Balkan wars in historical perspective

There was no Yugoslavia before 1918. Until then, Serbs and Croats had never lived in the same state. Until then, Slovenes and Croats had for centuries been politically attached to Austria; in cultural terms, they looked north to Vienna rather than to Belgrade in the south. Kosovo, remembered by Serbs today as the heartland of the medieval Serbian kingdom, was ruled for some 500 years by the Ottoman empire, and by 1913, when the Serbs regained control over the province, it already had an Albanian majority. The Illyrian movement in the early 19th century inspired the idea that the various South Slav groups belonged to the same nation. The 'Illyrians,' named after "Illyricum," the name of the western Balkans of classical antiquity, were comprised mainly of pan-Slavic, pro-Yugoslav Croats from Dalmatia (Glenny 1999b: 42). Only with the rebellions at the beginning of the 19th century, the wars of liberation against Turkey at the end of the 19th century, until the 1912/13 Balkan war, did the South Slav nations move towards independence and the crucial national question. Without delving into the complex history of the Balkans, which is an extra topic of study, below I will point in short to a few events in the 20th century which were and are of crucial importance for the recent history of the former Yugoslavia and Serbian migrants abroad.

Two wars were extremely relevant for the South Slavs, both in the homeland and in the exile communities; these were the First World War and the Second World War. The dream of a united, multiethnic state, freed of foreign rulers, was on the rise in Yugoslavia when World War One began. On Vidovdan, June 28, 1914, a day revered by all Serbs, during a visit to Sarajevo, Gavrilo Princip of the nationalist organization "*Mlada Bosna*" (Young Bosnians) assassinated Archduke Franz Ferdinand, under circumstances that are still unclear (Glenny 1999: 304). Austria used the assassination to declare war on Serbia, the only country that resisted the imperial expansion of Germany, Austria and their allies to the south. Subsequently, there were tremendous wartime casualties for both the Serb army and civilian population during the war; more than a million people were killed, which amounted to a quarter of the population and two thirds of its male population between the ages of fifteen and fifty-five (Judah 2000: 101). No other warring party had such high toll per capita of the population.

In a way, Yugoslavia started in exile. In the winter of 1915-16 some 150.000 troops, a government with Prince Regent Alexander and his ailing father King Peter I as heads, together with fleeing civilians from the eastern flank, were forced to withdraw from Serbia. They made their way through Montenegro, over the Albanian mountains, and finally reached the Greek island of Corfu, where the army regrouped and returned to the Saloniki front in the spring of 1916. During the war, Croat and Serbian émigrés began diplomatic talks concerning the foundation of a multiethnic state, but the declaration of Corfu in 1917 was unable to achieve such a state, due to diverse political ambitions. In February 1919 Yugoslavia was founded as the Kingdom of the Serbs, Croats, and Slovenes (SHS) through the diplomatic efforts of President Woodrow Wilson of the United States. Yugoslavia was created in order to appease the various ethnic groups and to grant the Serbs, who had been on the allied victors' side, a federal state where the power of each ethnic group was kept in balance. Serbs of the diaspora also had an impact on the politics surrounding the creation of Yugoslavia through lobbying efforts in their respective locations. Throughout the First World War Serbs in the United States marched for Yugoslav independence, sent aid to the Red Cross of Serbia and Montenegro, formed a Serbian Relief Committee, and urged notable Americans to support the Serbian cause. About 15, 000 Serbian volunteers returned to fight as troops in the war. The distinguished Serbian scientist and professor at Columbia University, Michael Pupin headed the Serbian National Defense (SND), which boasted approximately one-third of the total Serbian population in the United States as members. Pupin was also a personal friend of Woodrow Wilson and was particularly successful at collecting money and influencing American public opinion during the war (Vucinich 1983: 66f.).[15]

The interwar period (1919-1941) did not live up to the expectations for a period of peaceful coexistence amongst the various ethnic groups. Rather, political conflict along ethnic lines simmered in the multiethnic monar-

15. To note, the above mentioned examples of Serbian migrants' political lobbying for their homeland reflect what authors of long-distance nationalism have underlined in their works. By emphasizing the development of national consciousness and the relations of the Serbs with their homeland, Vucinich's way of describing the Serbian community clearly resembles what would later be called a transnational or diaspora approach. In doing so, Vucinich implicitly supports Anderson's point, namely that transnational political practices are not 'new' but a much older, previously overlooked phenomenon.

chy where Serbs had a distinct political advantage (Banac 1992). In 1929, the parliamentary experiment and its hope for integration failed. The political rivalries that existed between the numerous parties escalated, leading to assassinations in the parliament and eventual dictatorship when King Alexander dissolved the parliament and prohibited all political parties (Sundhaussen 1993: 57). The dictatorship was de facto Serbian by its composition and its expressed goals of a "Greater Serbia." This resulted in the reactionary, if understandable, nationalistic fervor amongst the Croatians, who began to articulate their own dream of establishing a Croatian nation-state. In 1941, Stjepan Radić, founder of the Croatian National Peasant Party and most important proponent of Croat nationalism, was assassinated and Ante Pavelić set up the Ustaša Croatian Liberation Movement in Zagreb[16] (Tanner 2001: 125).

During the period of the Second World War Yugoslav territory was divided into two separate territories: one, an occupied one under the German Nazis, comprised mostly of the territory of Serbia, and a separate territory consisting of Croatia and parts of Bosnia controlled by the fascist Ustaša NDH (*Nezavisima Drzava Hrvatska*) with the help of the Germans. The Ustaša drew substantial support from many frustrated Croats who felt that Serbs had taken over Yugoslavia and suppressed the Croatian drive for national independence. With this support the Ustaša state pursued a brutal campaign of conversion, expulsion, and massacre of its Serbian population, primarily in the Croatian provinces of Slavonia and Krajina.

Many Serbs, as well as some Croats and Muslims, followed militant groups known as the Royalist Chetniks[17] into the mountains of Herzegovina and Montenegro. There they engaged in guerrilla warfare under the leadership of Draža Mihailović. The Chetnik movement received broad support from British and American allies, who saw in the Greater Serbian movement a potential ally for defeating the Germans in the West and communism in the East. But in 1942 another resistance movement arose, the communist Partisans under Josip Broz Tito. A bitter civil war ensued between the two movements and eventually Tito was able to wrest the allies' support from the Royalist Chetniks. With the allies' support Tito won the war and then established the Socialist Federal Republic of Yugoslavia (SFRJ).[18]

Following their defeat by Tito's Partisans, many Chetniks fled to the United States via Austria, Germany, or Italy. As Skrbiš (1999: 29f.) documents, of the twelve million DPs in Europe at the beginning of 1945,

16. An *ustaša* is one who takes part in an *ustanak* – an uprising.
17. *Chetnik* is derived from *Chetna* and was the name of an army unit operating in the forefront of the Serbian army.
18. Like the First World War, the Second World War brought death to incredibly many people in the former Yugoslavia: at least half a million Serbs, 192,000 Croats, and 103,000 Muslims (a total of over one million) (in Judah 2000: 134).

about 229, 000 of them were 'Yugoslavs' who stayed in prison camps for several months or even years, before returning to Yugoslavia or emigrating further. More than 17, 000 were granted American visas for immigration, based on their acceptance for labor-market goals. Among my informants, some influential persons belonged to Chetnik organizations or had experienced victimization as Chetnik fighters during the Second World War.

On July 17, 1946, the much revered Chetnik leader Draža Mihailović, who is still the hero to many diaspora Serbs, was executed in Belgrade, after a special commission found him guilty for collaboration with the Axis powers. In the United States the Serbian and American public, led by the "Committee for a Fair Trial for General Mihailovich," protested vigorously against what they perceived as political and unfair proceedings.

> "The fingers of history, rustling through the pages of the Second World War, may provide an ironic postscript to the scene that took place at dawn yesterday, somewhere in the vicinity of Belgrade when General Drazha Mihailovich crumpled before the bullets of a Yugoslav firing squad... History may decide that it is not Tito – who was in safety while Mihailovich was fighting in the hills those early days – but the executed Chetnik leader whose statue should stand in Red Square in Moscow. But Mihailovich fell yesterday in Belgrade." (from the *New York Times* in Martin 1978: xii)

Following the Mihailović execution the Chetnik movement in Yugoslavia was essentially dead, surviving only in "hidden histories" (Hayden 1994: 169),[19] but in the United States the Chetnik movement was just beginning, coinciding with the arrival of the first political exiles or displaced persons (DP) from Yugoslavia.[20] The particular history that the Chetniks brought with them and their vision of the Yugoslav/Serbian nation proved to have an enduring impact on the diaspora consciousness.

Whereas a certain level of unity in the Serbian diaspora had developed over the course of the First World War, the Second World War led to a process which Gregory Bateson (1972) has called "schismogenesis," a pattern of increasing oppositions[21] amongst Serbs in the United States. Fol-

19. About the continuing relevance of the memory of the Chetnik movement and Ustaša cruelties during the Second World War among Serbian villagers in central Bosnia, see also Simić 2000.
20. Hockenos (2003: 119) states, "the royalist exiles dispersed across the world, often following the path of their former field commanders. The Chetniks of western Bosnia and Croatia in "Duke" Momčilo Djujić's Dinaric division ended up in the United States and Canada. In 1990, from his California headquarters, the elderly Djujić took it upon himself to bestow the highest Chetnik title, Vojvoda (duke), on Serbia's ultra-right leader Vojislav Šešelj, a man whose killer commando units operating in Croatia and Bosnia carried on the very worst of the Chetnik tradition."
21. See also Denich 2000: 47f.

lowing the war both Ustaša émigrés and Chetnik exiles settled in Northamerica, Australia, and to a lesser extent in Western Europe, where they founded new organizations and continued to fight for their respective causes.[22] But the Serbian pre-World War One immigrants and their offspring didn't share the militant visions of these nationalistic political exiles, former soldiers and victims of the Ustaša. Furthermore, their predominantly peasant background was not comparable to the more educated, urban background of the DPs (Vrga 1975: 63). In 1963, the already fragmented Serbian immigrant community underwent a further split, with the *raskol,* or church split dividing the church into two separate Serbian Orthodox Churches. Due to the significance of the Serbian Orthodox Church in Serbian community life, this divide led to increased strain between the two immigrant communities, the "unity faction" and the "autonomy faction" (Buchenau 2003, Padgett 1979, Vrga 1975). Not only was this event detrimental to the financial rescources of the church, but it also resulted in further fractionalization of an already small Serbian community. This schism in the church only ended in 1993 following the dismemberment of Yugoslavia. With the end of the Cold War the internal fighting between "communists" and "anti-Communists" had become obsolete, making way for a re-unification of the two churches.

When war erupted again in 1991, the Serbian community, which under Tito's regime had lost some of its incentive for political struggle, began another era of political mobilization. This time a new wave of Serbian immigrants to the US, refugee families from Bosnia and young "braindrain" émigrés from Serbia, transformed the landscape of diaspora politics once again. As Vucinich rightly foresaw a decade earlier: "As the Second World War and its aftermath showed us, the history of the Serbian community in the Bay Area could be changed that were totally unforeseen previously" (Vucinich 1983: 84). This unforeseen change was brought about by the Third Balkan War.

Sample characteristics and methodology

In order to provide background information on Serbs in the United States I will now summarize the ethnic makeup of the former Yugoslavia and data about Serbian immigration to the United States.

Serbs were numerically the largest group of the various ethnicities (Croats, Slovenes, etc.) united under monarchic Serbian rule (1918-1941) and later constituted a large portion, along with these same ethnic

22. As Denich (2000: 52) points out, there is considerable literature in English on the Chetniks, of which Tomasevich 1975 represents the most comprehensive scholarship. Curiously, there is no equivalent body of work on the Ustaša or its wartime Independent State of Croatia.

groups,[23] of the population of the unified socialist state of Yugoslavia (1945-1991). In 1981 the predominant Yugoslav nationality was Serbian, comprising 36.3% of the total population and therefore representing the largest national group (*narod*)[24], numbering about 8.1 million out of a total 22.4 million persons. Serbs were historically scattered most throughout the Balkan Peninsula, inhabiting areas of Macedonia to the East as well as Bosnia, Croatia, and Slovenia to the West (Ninić 1989: 9). Croats were the second largest group with 4.4 million or 19.7 % of the population. Ethnic Muslims numbered 2 million or 8.9 % of the population. The Slovenes were the fourth largest group in 1981 (1.8 million or 7.8 %), followed by the Albanians (1.7 million or 7.7 %). Other groups, including Macedonians, Montenegrins, Hungarians, Gypsies, and Turks numbered less than 1.7 million persons (Ramet 1996: 1). Regarding national homogeneity, the census of 1981 indicates that 85.4% of the population in Serbia was Serbian, whereas 75.1% of the Croatian population was ethnic Croatian (Skrbiš 1999: 11). The latter had a substantive Serbian minority in the provinces of Slavonia and Krajina, numbering at about 270, 000 before the outbreak of war in 1991. Yugoslavia was also a multi-religious country. The three largest religious groups were the Serbian Orthodox community, the Catholic community, and the Islamic community. Serbs were mostly Orthodox and Croats were primarily Catholics.

It is difficult to know how many Serbs have migrated to the United States, since immigration records before World War One either categorized them with other South Slavic groups or identified them in terms of their regions and countries of origin. Thus, during the period of peak immigration around 1900[25], they were variously recorded as "Bulgars, Serbs, and Montenegrins," "Dalmatians, Bosnians, and Hercegovinians," "Croats and Slovenes," or "Austrians and Hungarians." Today, because ethnicity and country of origin do not necessarily overlap, immigration figures are

23. Usually Serbs, Croats, and Slovenes are mentioned as the constitutive groups in the former Yugoslavia. However, to state only these three numerically largest groups obscures the fact that about 26 different ethnic groups lived together on the territory of the former Yugoslavia.
24. The term *narod* means 'Volk' or people and lies in the middle between ethnic group and nation. Only the constituent groups in the former Yugoslavia, Serbs, Croats, Slovenes and since 1974 also Bosnian Muslims, were *narodi*, whereas the other ethnic groups did not acquire the official status of narod. Serbs, Croats and the other ethnic groups living in the former Yugoslavia are also called *nacija* which in turn is not to be understood as nation but rather as ethnic group, in a religious sense. Thus a Croat belongs to the Roman Catholic *nacija*, and a Serb to the Serbian Orthodox *nacija*. See Bringa 1995: 20f.
25. The peak of Serbian immigration lasted from 1890 to 1913. Some areas in Herzegovina were basically depopulated, as Vladimir Nicholas Vucinich underlines in his study *From the Adriatic to the Pacific* (1983: 13): "From the 2,500 Orthodox homes in the Trebinje district there were by 1903 over 2,000 immigrants in America, many of whom left illegally to escape the draft."

equally inaccurate. According to the Immigration and Naturalization Service (INS), officially some 60, 000 "Yugoslavs" entered the United States between 1991 and 1999, with a peak from 1991 to 1996. Over the last 180 years (between 1820-1999) roughly 200, 000 Yugoslav immigrants have been recorded in total (US Department of Justice: Immigration and Naturalization Service 1999: 22). Therefore, compared to other immigrants in the United States, the Serbs comprise a relatively small ethnic group. Andrei Simić and Joel Halpern (1997: 786) estimate their numbers between 175, 000 to 300, 000 in 1981. However, as the authors point out, far fewer are actively involved in the cultural and religious life of the community. Active involvement in community life has been most effectively preserved in the major centers of Serbian settlement, in such places as Chicago, Pittsburgh, Milwaukee, San Francisco, and Los Angeles.

For the present study it is important to emphasize that while most Serbs do not participate in diaspora activism, a great many try to downplay their ethnic background, and only a very few individuals have turned into long-distance nationalists. But the active few have a much greater impact on diaspora politics than the 'silent' majority.

This work is based on ethnographic fieldwork, the core of which comprises 52 narrative interviews. These interviews resembled "friendly conversations" (Spradley 1979: 43), which means that they took the form of open, unstructured and semi-structured talks with 31 individuals living in the San Francisco Bay Area, California. The interviews were conducted between November 2000 and August 2002, and my fieldwork stay covered an entire year, consisting of three sessions ranging from three to five months of length. The people I interviewed were between twenty and eighty-two years of age. A snowball technique was used in the selection of respondents, but I used as a starting point contacts I had with a few immigrants from my year of study in American universities in 1996/97, and as well as contacts in the Serbian Orthodox church, which serves as the center of religious, cultural and social diaspora life. The sample consists of 18 men and 13 women, whereby 19 persons were interviewed once, and 12 individuals were interviewed more than once and up to four times. The interview sessions lasted between one hour and four hours, with an approximate duration of two hours. Of those 31 persons four belong to the second- and even third-generation of immigrants, and two of these are leaders of diaspora politics. Eight persons, many of whom I interviewed more than once, are DP's (displaced persons) from the Second World War, three migrants came in the 1960's and 70's, eight left Yugoslavia in the 1980's and another eight emigrated during the 1990's. The latter are mainly categorized as "brain drain" migrants, meaning that they were university-educated and emigrated to the U.S. for professional and occupational reasons.[26] This reflects of the substantial migratory movement during the 1940's and 1950's, the following decrease of immigration to the United States beginning in the 1960's, and a subsequent increased out-migration from the crisis-ridden Yugoslav state in the 1980's onward. Overall, semi-structured interviews were mostly used in follow-up sessions only. I took great care to develop the theory out of the material I gathered, instead of deductively interpreting the narratives along the lines of an already formed theoretical approach. In doing so, I was inspired by Anselm Strauss and Juliett Corbin's (1990: 23) concept of "grounded theory" that "begins with an area of study and what is relevant to that area is allowed to emerge."

In other words, the research consisted of long periods of time where I tried to understand what was important to the participants in my study, instead of directing informants according to my already formed assumptions and hypothesis. As H. Russell Bernard states (1994: 151), "the temptation is to ask a lot of questions in order to learn as much as possible as quickly as possible." But the problem, as Bernard points out, is that due to the constructedness and artificiality of the interview situation, answers are not likely to be given freely, and if they are, they may consist of evasions. Anthropology, which in my narrative approach could be called the 'science of listening' requires time, and often it takes a lot of listening before fieldwork questions evolve and informants actively participate (Verne 1999: 10)[27]. In the case of my Serbian interview partners' 'the passion to speak' impacted on the interviews in a significant way, often disabling any questioning and

26. Although I did have contact to recent refugees from Bosnia and also conducted interviews with several families, this group of migrants is certainly underrepresented in my work, for various reasons. First, relatively few Serbian refugees in comparison to Bosnian Muslims immigrated to the U.S. Due to the political situation the American government did not grant visas to Serbian refugees before 1997. Second, most of these families were extremely busy with making a living, so it was hard to set up interviews with them. During my fieldwork many also moved away from the costly Bay Area to live in more affordable inland areas, such as Sacramento. Third, personal experiences in the recent war were a very touchy subject that people would delve in at great pains, since the memory of violence was still fresh. In many cases I obtained from using their narratives simply out of respect, and because I felt that they were told to me 'involuntarily' in order to do me a favor.
27. Some anthropologists might disagree in this point and instead call their discipline the 'science of observing,' emphasizing more the visual component and 'participant observation.' In my approach, participant observation is certainly second-place to interviewing and the gathering of narratives. This choice is based on the nature of emigrant life which is characterized by a high degree of narrative reconstructions of the homeland and, what I would call, a "talking culture" among the migrants. Besides, cultural practices which can be observed by the fieldworker often take place on weekends only, so that the people I worked with can also be called "weekend Serbs." In contrast to this, daily life is mainly characterized by work and other social practices in the host country which are more or less unrelated to Serbian culture and difficult to observe.

relegating me to the position of the 'pure listener,' leaving dialogic ideals astray.

In addition to interviewing, I spent many hours doing participant observation or as Bernard (1994: 152) calls it, "hanging out." I attended divine liturgies in the Serbian Orthodox churches in the Bay Area, met people for coffee without using the recording machine, went to music festivals, concerts, cultural congregations, and major celebrations such as Christmas, the New Year's Eve party, and Easter. I was also invited to *Krsna Slavas*, celebrations of the Serbian patron saint, in people's homes. A field diary was used on a daily level in order to trace the given meetings and experiences.[28]

Theoretical approach

In this work I shall focus on "first generation" individuals who arrived at various historical times and from diverse geographical places. In order to clarify the significance of the first generation I will shortly outline the differences between first generation migrants and second (or subsequent) generations. I agree with the assumption made by Zlatko Skrbiš (1999: 1) that the particular focus on "second generation" individuals is a "real test of the strength of ethno-nationalism." This adheres to Werner Schiffauer's (2000) choice of second generation Turks living in Germany. Certainly, questions of the "imagination of communities" are the most obvious among people who have no or very little actual experience of living in the homeland. Nevertheless, I suggest, that persons who have emigrated ten years or even fifty years ago engage in imaginative practices of a very similar kind. In contrast to second generation individuals their imaginations draw on memory and biographical narratives of a life far away that are based on 'real' lived experience. Since I am interested in exactly this relationship between narrative of past experiences and imaginative processes that are at work in these narratives, it seems far more fruitful that, in my case, I focus on first generation individuals. Considering the crucial role that past violence plays in the stories of the old and in Serbian long-dis-

28. A note on the method I employed for the writing-up of the material: I transcribed all the interviews completely, not leaving passages out that at first seemed to be of little relevance, and did so solely by myself. This time-consuming practice enabled me to get to know my material fairly well and access it in a more systematic way, e.g. by finding out roughly which topics were of central importance to my interlocutors. Before entering the writing stage, I followed Anselm Strauss' 1994 methodology of "coding" the narratives, interviews as well as field diary notes, according to major themes, e.g. history, national identity, or nationalism. This way I could assure that the themes and issues were developed out of the material, say that my work centered on what people said and what was important to them, and not on my already formed assumptions.

tance nationalism, an analysis of the first generation generates a better understanding of the specific makeup of Serbian diaspora politics.

One theoretical insight or one theoretical 'school' did not guide the present study, but throughout my writing I have introduced various possibilities of reading the extensive material, constantly opening up new theoretical angles, instead of limiting myself to a single way of reading. In doing so I have been animated by Roland Barthes' contention that a text consists of "a tissue of quotations drawn from innumerable centers of culture" and that its meaning lies "not in its origin but in its destination" (in Clifford 1986: 51ff.).

My theoretical focus concerns 'the life' of stories, not as they are lived but how they are told and how they are used to form an image of the nation. By focusing on narrative I am inspired by Anthony Kerby's study *Narration and the Self* (1992). Drawing from hermeneutics, phenomenology, and postmodern philosophy Kerby emphasizes the storied nature of human experience. According to Kerby (1992: 45) "we are 'story-telling animals' precisely because we are already caught up in a story, and already committed to meaning." Of course, individuals do actually experience the events told in their life stories, but often the significance of telling their life story is that it is a mode of comprehension that necessarily takes second place in relation to the experiences comprehended (Kerby 1992: 41).

The interviews and narratives that I gathered can be understood as "discursive acts" following Michel Foucault's (1973: 40ff.) elaboration of discourse analysis. According to Foucault discourse is not comprised of the grammatical sentence, the speech act and descriptive statements that are often assumed to be "discourse" in contemporary academic jargon. Discourse applies to specific connections of statements (spoken or written) that are successive and, in the abundance of their events and facts make for a constructed discursive field. Thus, discourses themselves are not real, but as people try to make sense of society, they produce a reality in discourse through their representation. As Demirovic (1996: 101) explains, discourse analysis aims at delineating the relations of power in the social production and distribution of meaning, it lays open the ways that people negotiate understanding, truth and consensus, and finally, it reveals breaks and ambivalences in these processes.

Serbs in the U.S., I suggest, participate in a discourse of negotiating the nation from afar, whereby they draw on various intersecting local and global sources, stemming from memory about life in Yugoslavia and in the U.S., as well as written and spoken diaspora knowledge, Western media representations, Internet publications, and accounts from relatives and friends back home. Despite the heterogeneity of views and expressions there are culturally set norms for what is regarded as meaningful representations of reality and what is not. I chose to include only those statements that were representative, meaning those belonging to an interconnected discursive field. If, for example, there was a person that seemed completely disconnected from other Serbs and uttered statements that were singular, I would not regard his/her statements as belonging to the discursive field. On the other hand, if the speaker was generally respected in the Serb community, enough so that his opinions would not be seen as disconnected from the wider public, a singular statement could still belong to the discursive field. Throughout this work I aim for transparency when it comes to how a discursive act is situated and how credible an individual is to other participants in my study.

When dealing with oral histories or life stories in this work I am interested in the "politics of narration" (Feldman 1991: 10). Drawing from insights by theorists on memory and narrative I do not focus on the actual memory of events, or as they *really* happened, but how these memories are narrated (Ricoeur, in Kerby 1991: 40). Narratives draw on experiences in the past that are always already narrated. Oral histories, although derived from events in the past also belong to the present in which their telling is embedded. The politics of narration is also a story of the power of narratives and I claim that the production of narratives forms a highly crucial aspect of life for migrants living in a setting far remote from events in the homeland.

Unlike Liisa Malkki (1995) and Allen Feldman (1991) I have chosen not to rely on composite narratives of which I am critical for their homogenizing drive, but to examine individual stories and their speakers, because it makes it easy to ascertain who claims to speak for the Serbian exiles and how gender, generation, and personal background figure in such accounts. This is especially crucial for my analysis, since I do not focus solely on memory and self-narration but also on how long-distance nationalist practices are grounded in the memory of violence.

The narratives chosen underwent minor editing on my part, mainly where it seemed important for readability and what I understood was most important to the speaker him/herself.[29] As Feldman (1991: 12) points out, editing is a practice inherent in any reading of a text and forms a core aspect of anthropological work.

> "Editing, in the field, is the construction, reconstruction, and simulation of context. Yet, editing is often portrayed in recent theoretical discussions as the betrayal of the "dialogical ethic." In this approach the dialogical is reduced to the positivist model of face-

29. For example, I erased filling words like „ah," because I found these frequently uttered words to be irrelevant for understanding the narratives. Moreover, I occasionally formed composite narratives out of interview sections which had originally included questions that I asked in between the sentences.

> to-face encounter with the other, which is deformed by writing and editing as practices that subtract from the originary mis-en-scène."

Liisa Malkki notes, "rather than be silent or apologetic about the editing process, a theoretically principled ethnography must be both self-conscious and explicit about the motives and justifications for its editing strategies" (Malkki 1995: 57). I am aware that the narratives I use were produced in a specific situation and are now presented in a way that is reflecting not only the narratives but also my understanding of them. There are ample possibilities for interpretation and the one presented here reveals my own interpretive choices.

Throughout this work I will make use of multiple methodological devices, such as interviews, participant observation, theory, and "thick description," since my conception of anthropology is grounded in the belief that discourse has to be analyzed in connection with the social practices in which it is embedded.

This research attempts to surmount the methodological difficulties arising from treating ethnic groups as organic homogeneous communities, rather than as groups stratified by power, and composed of individuals with different interests. The focus on the first generation does not leave aside generational differences, since people leaving at very different times, and thus belonging to different life cycle generations, are subsumed under the same category. I wish to analyze, how the varying circumstances of time of migration, age, and stage in the life cycle form the ways along which national identities are negotiated and long-distance nationalism is fostered or contained.

Reflections on the fieldwork setting

"Everyone is an ambassador of his own
people in these hard days."
(Budimir Pesić[30], eighty-year-old)

The fact that I am a German from Germany (not an American of German origin) and a foreigner in the United States impacted my work in a number of ways. To a certain extent this was therefore a reflexive ethnography in which the prominence of myself as a researcher within the research context was interrelated with interpretation of social processes and narratives (Fischer 1986, Marcus 1986, 1995).

To many Serbs I was an outsider in a double sense, first, because I did not have any family ties to Serbia, which puzzled a great many over the

30. In order to ensure anonymity of the participants in this study I do not mention the real names of my informants but use pseudonyms at all times.

motivation for studying 'them,' and second, since I was not myself an American. The fact that I had never lived in Serbia and didn't speak Serbo-Croatian fluently[31] helped to consolidate my position as an outsider. I was understood to be in need of a lot of 'lecturing' and story telling to make up for my social distance to Serbia and Serbs. And it was these stories and hours of monologues that produced the narratives I will analyze in this study. Any fieldwork and interview situation is an artificial arrangement and is subjective, with the fieldworker's "I" influencing in various ways what is said or done. Therefore, I do not refrain from using the first person singular throughout the text. For instance, following an interview I was sometimes asked: "*So, did you hear what everybody else has told you before?*" or „*Have I told you what you wanted to hear?*" These rhetorical questions make crystal-clear that discourses were produced for me, in turn mirroring the personal nature that makes ethnographic research so singular.

To many informants my relationship to American society and the state was assumed to be similar to theirs. "We" were both "Europeans" in a foreign land; "we" shared speaking a foreign language[32] on a daily basis. I was in the know of what it meant to immigrate to America and the hardships it implied, and "we" shared a 'distant view' of the homeland, even if in relation to two different countries, Germany and Serbia. Borrowing from feminist theorist Gloria Anzáldua (1987: 21), we shared the dual perspective of a "consciousness of the Borderlands." According to Anna Lowenhaupt Tsing (1993: 21), the image of the border turns attention to the creative projects of self-definition of those at the margins." Residing entirely remote from the continent we both called a home, San Francisco almost resembled what Tsing calls an "out-of-the-way-place," where I was linked to the people I worked with by the imaginations about the world and the countries we came from that were produced by distance. This 'complicity in distance' was obvious when I asked a young woman how she felt towards her homeland Bosnia and the difficulty of her decision to immigrate and she responded: "*Well, you can ask yourself, how it is right?*"

Another important detail about my position as a researcher was that I am married to an American and during my research I lived with or close

31. Since 1999, I attended several university classes for Serbo-Croatian and studied and practiced the language with tutors both in Germany and the U.S.. Unfortunately, I never lived in the former Yugoslavia, so that paired together with the predominant use of English by Serbian exiles I did not have enough opportunity to acquire fluency in the language. Nevertheless, my efforts at learning their language was usually met with appreciation and praise.
32. Here I need to stress that my interviews were conducted in English only, not Serbian. Since speaking English implied that we were on the same level of not speaking our 'mother tongue,' the outcome of this study is also special in a linguistic sense. Certainly, since I spoke mainly with first generation individuals, talking English meant communication on equal terms, with all the insufficiencies and innovations that conversations in a second language involve.

to his family. As family values among Serbs are strong, and this includes Serbs in exile, my status as a married woman (and later expectant mother) certainly helped me to be seen in a more favorable light.[33] Nevertheless, objections against being interviewed, due to the precarious situation 'back home,' fears for personal safety once they revealed details about their lives and immigration and even the suspicion that I may be a spy were no singular cases. The title of Barbara West's (2002) work on life in postsocialist Hungary captures the atmosphere of my fieldwork quite well: *The danger is everywhere!*

At the time of my writing Serbia's former President Slobodan Milošević and the leader of the Radical Party, Vojislav Šešelj, stood trial in the International Criminal Tribunal in the Hague, Netherlands (ICTY), while Bosnian Serb leader Radovan Karadžić and military commander general Ratko Mladić have been indicted as war criminals and are wanted men. Throughout the last decade Serbia proper and Bosnian Serbs, in particular, were considered by the United Nations and world community as the main perpetrators in the Balkan conflict. In 1993 an Amnesty International report argued that:

> "Deliberate and arbitrary killings, torture and ill-treatment continued on a horrifying scale and largely by Bosnian Serb forces. They repeated and extended patterns earlier seen which appear to be aimed at intimidating the civilian population, most frequently Muslims, into leaving their home areas or being compliant when forcibly expelled." (AI INDEX: EUR 63/03/93, in: Procter 2000: 2)

Therefore, positioning myself vis-à-vis the war in the former Yugoslavia and international interventions against Serbs was no minor detail, and I was asked about my opinion over and over again. How I positioned myself influenced the interviews profoundly.

As Halpern and Kideckel in *Yugoslavs at War* (2000: 5) point out, scholars writing about the war in the former Yugoslavia often share partiality in political terms. In focusing on one group only or even when trying to include various groups, foreign and native anthropologists hold diverse, conflicting viewpoints that are often necessarily biased. No author can escape political biases of one sort or the other, especially not in such a politically charged atmosphere that surrounded the disintegration of Yugoslavia, where the matter of guilt and basic facts concerning the nature of the war, whether it was "genocide" by Serbs or a civil war involving the three main ethnic groups, were and are not generally agreed upon.

33. My situation very much resembled that of Linda A. Bennett (1978: 14) who undertook fieldwork among Croats, Serbs, and Slovenes in Washington D.C.

In German and American literature the war was predominantly viewed as Serbian aggression against Bosnian Muslims and Croats (see e.g. Banac 1991, Meštrović 1993, Ramet 1996 et al.). I personally believe that Serbian military and paramilitary forces have contributed the most to the terrible atrocities and deaths that occurred in the first half of the 1990's in Croatia and Bosnia and throughout the decade in Kosovo. However, if one looks at the statistics of wartime casualties, simply considering the deaths of 145,000 Muslims, 95,000 Serbs, and 23,000 Croats[34] the declaration of genocide appears exaggerated, to say the least. While some are outraged at those who reject the one-sided view of Serbs as sole aggressors in the wars (Bieber 2001), I personally agree with the contention of Hayden (1992, 1995, 1998), Halpern and Kideckel (2000), Woodward (1995a), and Simić (1993, 1996) that the Yugoslav wars were indeed civil wars involving all three parties and that the International Community's inconsistent diplomatic moves and attribution of blame on the Serbian side only contributed to the violent course of events.

Holding these viewpoints implicitly meant that I leaned towards "the Serbian side," not only because I studied 'them,' but also since I had traveled to Belgrade, Dubrovnik and the Bay of Kotor, Montenegro, and not to Bosnia or Croatia. More importantly, in 1999 I had participated in protests against the NATO bombing, both in the Bay Area and in Germany. Before people would consent to tell me their stories, these facts of my life were generally addressed – I had to give "political support."

In fact, through most of the 1990's I had not felt competent enough to form an opinion about the complex ethnic conflicts. My later political engagement at the time of the NATO bombing was not 'for Serbs,' but against the dangers involved in undertaking international military interventions in the name of human rights, what Hayden calls "humanitarian rightism" (Hayden 2000). That the Balkan conflicts were not as one-sided as they were portrayed to be has been underlined by Halpern and Kideckel (2000: 7): "The lack of decisive victories or defeats by the Serbs or their opponents has thus contributed to an atmosphere in which wounds, both real or imagined, fester. Clearly any foreigner venturing to examine such matters can expect hostility from one group or another". In my mind, the political bias Halpern and Kideckel regard as problematic is a more general phenomenon which is intrinsically tied to anthropology, where loyalties to the group under study are the prerequisites for the establishment of intimate relationships necessary for a deeper understanding of 'culture' and individuals. As Becker (2001: 22f.), in referring to recent works by Gupta and Ferguson (1992) and Schiffauer (1997), claims, the anthropologist himself participates in the construction of cultural boundaries, or 'Other-

34. According to Udovički in Udovicki and Ridgeway (eds.) 1997: 304.

ing.' Critics may dislike my viewpoints and call them politically biased or not, but I simply aim at analyzing and understanding the ways in which Serbs in exile feel about the nation, including victimization, which to my knowledge has not been analyzed so far.

My German background also had an impact on what people told me and what they disclosed. Critiques of American foreign policy and ambivalent relationships to American society were possibly mentioned more freely than they would have been to an American researcher. However, in light of Nazi atrocities against Serbs committed during the Second World War, my German background was problematic. Once an old Chetnik migrant who had difficulties hearing, and therefore did not catch my foreign accent, told me his turbulent story of struggles, massacres, and fights in the Second World War. In his narrative he mentioned somewhat proudly, as a minor detail, how he "*shot a few Germans.*" When, in the course of the conversation I revealed that I was from Germany, his surprise was mixed with protestations of how he never had anything against "us" and how today all enmities belonged to the past. This was, of course, only part of the truth. His narrative was a presentation of Self and the nation that mistakenly pointed to the polishing work inherent in any production of stories. People try to avoid inconsistencies, and often address the interlocutor following rhetorical norms of political correctness.

For the young educated migrants, the past didn't loom nearly as large as to the older exiles. Germany was one European country which was geographically close to Serbia and was relatively rich and therefore economically attractive. Some Bosnian Muslim and Bosnian Serb migrants I met had fled to Germany in the 1990's and lived there for some years, but due to the Dayton accords were prohibited to stay permanently in Germany. Many of them went back to the former Yugoslavia, but thousands of them further migrated from Germany to the United States. Upon getting acquainted, my nationality almost always necessarily invoked the enthusiastic remark: "*Oh, Germany! It was nice there, we would have liked to stay, life was good there.*"[35] Generally, people avoided complaining about immigration restrictions in Germany. Thus, "what I was" obviously influenced how they came to terms with "what we are."

Finally, in the wake of the recent Yugoslav wars that were widely seen as having been caused by Milošević or even by "Serbia" and "the Serbs," my Serb interviewees shared something else: the issue of historical guilt. Politicians, journalists, and academics widely employed the comparison

35. To understand this statement one should know that the German government provided financial and material help for the refugees, who received an apartment and didn't have to worry about survival. But they neither acquired a residence status, nor did they get work permits. In the Bay Area it is the opposite, welfare is hard to attain, apartments are expensive, and refugees are forced to start working right from the spot, often under difficult conditions and with only the minimum pay.

between 'Serbian aggression' in Bosnia, best exemplified by the massacre in Srebrenica[36], and the Holocaust. Many Serbs I talked to were aware of this negative image and were quite upset about what they believed was a totally 'unjust' equation.[37]

The study of long-distance nationalism necessarily involves the interlocution of one's own, the anthropologist's 'national identity'.[38] Migrants, in their stories about the nation, constantly evaluate their nation's role in the "national order of things" (Malkki 1995). In doing, so they implicitly refer to other nations, especially those with historical significance to their own nation. Therefore, it seems important that I discuss the concepts of nationality, nationalism, and long-distance nationalism within common fields of power and knowledge.[39]

Chapter Review

This book starts with an exploration of identity-politics among Serbian exiles in the United States. Drawing from a broad spectrum of statements, part one, *Identity in Exile,* is both an overview of the major themes of the whole study and a discourse analysis of a variety of these central topics, e.g. history, national identity, and 'Otherness' in relation to the semantics of being "Serbian" or "Yugoslav" in the wake of the Third Balkan War. Chapter one, *Being Serbian in the United States,* is informed by a number of theorists on Serbian identity, such as Ivan Čolović (2002), and focuses on

36. In 1995, the town of Srebrenica became known for one of the worst massacres during the Third Balkan War. Although the area in and around the town had been declared a UN-'safe area,' controlled by Dutch forces, on 6th of July Bosnian Serb forces began an all-out drive to capture it. About 1,200 men were executed on a single day. Srebrenica became a symbol for Serbian "ethnic cleansing" in Bosnia and Muslim suffering in the four years of war. A few major commanders and generals were sentenced at the Criminal Tribunal at the Hague, Netherlands (Glenny 2000: 239-241).
37. About the relevance of the Holocaust-debate for Yugoslavia see part three, chapter five.
38. For an in-depth study on long-distance nationalism, which in addition to including the views of the people studied, also analyzes the prejudices against nationalism on the side of the American researcher, see Glick Schiller and Fouron 2001. What is most interesting in their joint study *Georges Woke Up Laughing* is how the foreign, American researcher, Glick Schiller, and the Haitian born immigrant researcher, Fouron, engage in a lively debate about the pros and cons of (long-distance) nationalism, thereby reflexively laying open the divergent subjectivities that not only inform but produce the outcome of the research.
39. Here I implicitly refer to the reflexive turn in anthropology that started with the "Writing Culture" 1986 debate and since then informs a "self-conscious" anthropological writing. It involves questions about the asymmetrical relationship between researcher and informants, first world and third world, and the production of knowledge. Many of these issues have been derived from Michel Foucault's work, but some are also inspired by Derrida, especially post-colonial studies and feminist approaches.

the essentializing narratives which dominate much of Serbian long-distance nationalist thinking. Yet, I attempt at pointing to the heterogeneity of discourses and viewpoints, characterizing the highly factionalized and loose "community" of Serbian immigrants. Ranging from nationalist to non-nationalist, Serbian to Yugoslav, and Serbian American declarations of identity, and including also those who do not interact with the Serbian "community" at all, my focus lies on differences, binarisms, and conflicts that lay at the core of the negotiation of identity. After all, identity is not a static concept, but fluid, in the making, situated, and often based on "personal choice" (Bennett 1979) as people try to come to terms with what means to be Serbian in the shadow of the Balkan War.

In chapter two, *The Unmaking of the Yugoslavs*, I analyze this dynamic nature of identity with regard to discourses concerning "Yugo-Nostalgic" viewpoints, a minority within my total sample. Curiously, these non-nationalist, highly ambiguous statements similar to the writings of Dubravka Ugrešić (1995), have mainly been uttered by women, and I inquire why that may be so.

In chapter three, *Creating One Voice*, I look more closely at one of the most influential Serbian diaspora organizations world-wide, the *Serbian Unity Congress*, striving to unify Serbs abroad. From its base in San Francisco, the SUC has been vocal throughout the Third Balkan Wars by distributing information via the Internet, lobbying for politicians in Washington in order to influence U.S. foreign policy toward Serbia, or sending money to politicians in the homeland. Analyzing one of the key figures of the organization I attempt to understand the personal motivation and historical underpinnings of Serbian long-distance nationalist politics.

Part two, *Living in the Past: The Role of the Second World War*, is designed to go deeper into a topic already discussed in part one: the relevance of the past in identity construction and long-distance nationalism. More precisely, this part has been animated by versions of the past and life histories centering on World War Two as told to me by several participants of my research. In contrast to the preceding chapters, this part of the book is less concerned with a plethora of discourses than with the detailed stories of a few selected elderly individuals. Chapter four, *Remembering War and Displacement*, is inspired by theories on memory (Connerton 1989, Gillis 1994, Halbwachs 1992, Meyerhoff 1992, et al.), and discusses the connection between "worlds made" in the narratives of my interlocutors and transnational practices in the present. At the core of the chapter lies the argument that in the diaspora, the recent wars of disintegration were often seen as a mirror image for reliving World War Two. The stories of the old teach us that the experience of past violence is *the* crucial component for understanding Serbian long-distance nationalism. Thus, "unsettled accounts" of the past in a way led to new "unsettled accounts" in the present, underscoring the necessity to take serious the claims to the past that various peoples from the former Yugoslavia hold.

Chapter five, *The Architecture of Memory*, is based on the same life accounts as the preceding chapter, but interprets the stories from another angle which has been rarely taken into consideration by anthropology so far, that is the material 'art' of memory. Drawing from insights of Bachelard (1992), Bahloul (1996), Ballinger (2003) and others I am interested in how my interlocutors fashion their homes with paintings, photos, flags, awards, or little items taken from their former houses. This side to memory, I suggest, cannot be understood as illustrative description of interior decoration, but as another form of laying claim to "lost" houses and a "lost" landscape.

The third and last part of this study, *Conspiracy Theories, Future Visions, and the International Community* is concerned with historical explanation of a specific kind: conspiracy theories. In chapter six, *Conspiracies in the Age of Globalization*, I will mainly analyze two conspiracies and relate them to the wider body of conspiracy theories, e.g. Groh (1992), Hofstadter (1952), Marcus (1999), and Todd and Sanders ed. (2003). My guiding questions are: What does the striking prevalence of this phenomenon among Serbian exiles teach us about conspiracy thinking in general and in the specific case of former Yugoslavia? Which is the role of the Cold War in narratives centering on conspiracy theories?

Finally, chapter seven, *Imagining the Future in the Light of a Violent Past*, analyzes conspiracy thinking in relation to visions of the future and the images of the International Community. What comes next, after the tragic breakup of the homeland? As opposed to the focus on history in the anthropological literature dealing with the violent dismemberment of Yugoslavia, Serbs in the U.S. were strikingly eager to unfold to me their future oriented "geostrategic imaginations" about Serbia and the world. Uncovering the realms of lived experience that inform the informant's claim that visions of the future are indeed important for understanding the transnational context of the wars in the Balkans, inspired by Malkki (2000), Ricoeur (1998), and Wachtel (1998), I explore the theoretical implications of this changed outlook on temporal dimensions. Interestingly, the future visions my informants draw point to a conciliatory and optimistic outlook on the former Yugoslavia, indicating that long-distance nationalism, instead of consisting of radical political viewpoints only, can comprise reconciling voices as well.

In chapter eight, *Conclusion*, I draw the main themes discussed in the previous chapters with a view to exploring the implications of the argument of this study. This chapter begins with a discussion of substantive issues emerging from the study and concludes with an outlook for further research.

Part I. Identity in Exile

"Is that really you when you say 'we'?" – Lena's story

> If one is at home with and immersed in this life, then the question of "who?" need not arise. We are supported by our ongoing practices, our established meanings. It is often in light of a possible or impending future, or a problem in the present that the question of "who?" is seriously raised. (Kerby 1991: 38)

Lena Milenković, a 42-year-old artist and trained psychologist from Belgrade, has been a resident of the United States since 1988, when her husband Zoran was offered a job in a computer company through friends in Serbia. Given that the political and economic situation in Yugoslavia was already tensed, the decision to leave was not a hard one, considering that the accelerated job developments were very promising in the Silicon Valley, where Zoran earns a high salary today. Inhabiting a studio apartment in the "Clock Tower" on Second Ave in downtown San Francisco, right by the Bay Bridge, Lena and Zoran have a splendid view of the billboards along the crowded freeway linking the East Bay with San Francisco. Her home is also her workplace where she paints on large oil canvasses, applying oil as well as computer parts, newspaper articles, and yarn. Furnished with antiques, a long table with benches in the middle of the room, wooden boxes, Persian carpets, pressure meters and other old ship equipment the room itself appears like a piece of art: "*We have moved so much that our apartment now is like a ship. I like wood and steel, the wooden box used to be a suitcase of the early immigrants*," she explains.

But the most striking objects are Lena's newspaper-oil-collages, in which she expresses her deep-seeded feeling of pain about the Third Balkan Wars. In the cooking area I notice a threefold painting, in the middle a black blurry figure like a martyred Christ on a dark brown colored background, to the right several pieces of crumpled newspapers from the local *San Francisco Chronicle* in a light brown with English letters, reading about the fierce battle of Serbian military for the town of Vukovar in 1992, and the "ethnic hatred of the Serbs" based on their "Second World War revitalizations." To the left side of the painting the barely readable, oil soaked newspaper articles contain Cyrillic letters from the Belgrade daily *Politika*, telling of "NATO aggression". From the high ceiling hang three gray bar chairs, also in newspaper-collage-style, which she made for an art school project during her graduate studies at the San Francisco Art Institute: "*I taped newspaper clips on the seat and tied a rope around the bottom. These seats have to be uncomfortable and simple, not pretty. That's how I felt, I sat uncomfortably in this country, my body literally hurt.*"

During our interview session Lena tells me about her life in Yugoslavia, where nationality was a minor issue and being Serbian (or Croatian or Muslim) was taken for granted. She always knew that she was Serbian and did not declare herself Yugoslav, as did so many other young people in the 1970's and 1980's, but this did not mean that she refuted Yugoslavia. As a youth, her parents cautiously told her about the family's Second World War experience – her grandfather was a Chetnik –, making sure that she would not get in trouble with the Partisan inspired official socialist ideology. Therefore, she tells, she was never exposed to nationalism, and enjoyed that she didn't think about which nationality her friends had. As a young woman she frequently visited her father, who had emigrated to California at the end of the 1970's, where she got a glimpse of both Republican and Chetnik diaspora circles, which she rejected equally. "*When I visited my father and uncle in Chicago I went to a Chetnik picnic, where they held speeches. It was a completely different tone from the one in Yugoslavia, very intolerant against anything in the homeland. They would ask me if we had typewriters in Yugoslavia. Isn't that amazing? I laughed, yes we do.*" During the ten years of war she undertook serious introspection into her own life and realized how much she had changed over time. "*I was always oppositional and suddenly I found myself in the situation that I talk like Milošević. I critique him when I am among Serbian people, but when I discuss the war with Americans I have to defend myself and the Serbs. And I discover that I use short phrases and arguments that are from Milošević! To them I am the nationalist, but for myself I critique nationalism.*" Neither a member of the church, which she doesn't even visit for the major celebrations, nor participating in any diaspora organization, Lena is what one could call "a non-active Serb." And yet she participated in political action during the Balkan Wars, especially during the NATO bombing in 1999, an event she experienced as the "major war."

One of her most exciting recollections of that time concerns the protest marches against the bombing of Yugoslavia in 1999 in downtown San Francisco. While walking through the neighborhood she carried a big Serbian flag attached to a broom -- without adding an American flag, thereby violating U.S. law. From March, 24th till June, 19th Lena and her husband spent an abundance of time and money to communicate with people over the Internet, to read Serbian news, and to make numerous phone calls to check on family and friends who were living under the bombardment. "*One month we spent a thousand dollars on the phone bill, but we didn't care.*" The Balkan Wars did not only shatter her view of the United States, that as an immigrant she had "idealized a bit" in order to feel at home, but, to her, waged a war against Serbia from the very beginning in 1991. The war especially upset her vision of the homeland and herself: "*Once an American asked me, when talking about the war: 'What is that when you say 'We'. Is that really 'you'? And I replied to him: 'Yes, somehow that is 'me', bodily I feel that something happens to me, too. As if my identity dissolved and my body fell apart. I had to express that in my art. [...] Meanwhile, I started painting whole figures and bodies again, because I thought I would need that after all these events.*"

I have chosen Lena's story to open up this chapter about identity-politics and being Serbian in exile, because I suggest that her narrative epitomizes many central themes dealing with the diasporic experience of the Third Balkan Wars. Other stories and other individuals could have been selected as well, but I find that the above example elucidates some crucial aspects of the complex dynamics involved in long-distance nationalism.

Lena and her husband belong to an estimated 20, 000 "braindrain" émigrés, or professional, university educated people, who left the country around the beginning of the war and 2000 (Grečić 2002: 2). She and her husband were lucky that they received visas to enter one of the fastest growing industries of the 1990's, profiting from the computer boom in California. Being able to afford a second study, while her husband is the male breadwinner, like so many other immigrants the couple represented a societal strata that "went to America to make money." To Lena, who had traveled there with her father already six times, the United States were never like paradise, but the final decision to immigrate followed clear economic reasons. While still in the process of settling down and adapting to the "American way of life," the violent dismemberment of her homeland, that she had left but nevertheless felt very attached to emotionally, created, what she calls "nostalgia," and set in motion a painful process of reflection.

Media and the long-distance experience of war

What Nicholas Procter (2000) in *Serbian Australians in the Shadow of the Balkan War* by recurring on theorists of globalization calls "long-distance devastation," may be of relevance here, too. Focusing on the mental health of his Adelaide informants, Procter underlines the simultaneity of what was happening in Yugoslavia and in Australia. Arguing that the global, the Yugoslav wars of disintegration, had a huge impact on the local, the Serbian community in Australia, Procter analyzes "what life is like for people who see themselves under attack" by the public of the host country which (wrongly) views them as the group to blame in a terrible war (Procter 2000: 8). The feeling of being under attack is indeed crucial for Serbian identity-politics, memory, long-distance nationalism, and conspiracy.

In Procter's study, long-distance devastation is enhanced through biased media reporting, for which Lena's collection of media articles and their transformation into art is a prime example. The artist's illustrative descriptions of "falling apart," "dissolving," and "hurting" correspond closely to the Australian findings, demonstrating how the news coverage of Serbian atrocities affected the well-being of émigrés all over the world. Lena's narrative reflects what it was like for her to be 'under attack,' and how her personal well-being and identity have been affected and changed over time. The representation of the war through media reporting is of central relevance for how émigrés experienced the war from afar.

Ten years after the war started I still came across stories of young men stripped naked, skewered on a spear and burnt alive[40], pregnant women whose stomachs have been ripped open, and little babies that got shot in the head or neck[41], stories that attest to the significance that "pornographic" modes of reporting had in influencing public opinion. Especially during the Bosnian wars, cruelties had been televised at an unprecedented rate, whereby my Serbian informants univocally voiced that the brutalities reported were unfairly attributed to having been committed by Serbian perpetrators only. Images of "Muslim" burials, with crosses on the gravestones, and other examples, with the Markale massacre[42] ranking highest in importance were seen to "prove" that the media reports were false and mere "propaganda," downplaying to which degree Serbs, too, were brutally massacred. While being perturbed by the intensity of the suffering "back home," Lena was also confused with the divergent media accounts she received from both sides, American as well as Belgrade news sources.

Lena's artistic newspaper projects display a deep ambiguity of feeling like a Serb and an American, a split Self, who internalizes and personalizes a bloody political conflict. Literally sensing that she is sitting in-between the stools, with her art, she expresses an identity dilemma which many other Serbs in the diaspora know all too well: the news they received about the tragedy in the homeland, talks they got involved in, and brutal images that flickered on the TV screen produced an immediacy of suffering that

40. See Dorich 1994: 20f.
41. See Dorich 1994: 53.
42. In February 1994, sixty-nine people were killed by a shell in Sarajevo's Markale market (Glenny 2000: 300). The massacre was also called "breadline massacre," because most of the victims had been waiting in a line to buy bread. Right after the event Western journalists and politicians held the Bosnian Serb forces responsible for the deaths. According to later analysis, however, the massacre has not been univocally attributed to Serbs. Especially in Germany and Austria, there arouse a fervent critique against media reporting based on judgments which jumped at conclusions much too fast. Among those, authors referred to a UN-report from August 1995, which claimed that the shell was fired by Bosnian Muslim government troops (Hofbauer 1999: 103-109). From these and other examples a radical media critique developed, claiming for example that the Muslim military had shot its own people in the bread-line on Markale market in Sarajevo to influence global public opinion and to provoke a military response against Serbs by the International Community. See Bittermann 1996, Bogdanich 2002, Dorich 1994 et al.

sharpened collective identity abroad. I suggest, that her narrative elucidates a contradiction which is an overall theme throughout my sample.

The artist's narrative is important in a number of aspects. First, narrating her daily life during the bombing of her hometown, Lena describes common social practices of transnational interaction, ranging from calling her loved ones excessively,[43] sending money, being glued to the television, to consuming Serbian and local Californian newspapers. Second, referring to her prior visits to the United States she testifies to the long tradition of migration and return migration linking the Serbian diaspora with the homeland. Her experience in Chicago Chetnik circles elucidates the generational and ideological differences that persisted not only between inhabitants of the former Yugoslavia and its émigré citizens, but also led to schisms within the "Serbian community," pointing to the heterogeneity and fragmentation of Serbs in the United States. This heterogeneity is mainly derived from the divergent social, political and historical contexts of the societies in the homeland and in the diaspora.

In fact, the notion "community" that emphasizes commonality and coherence has increasingly come under scrutiny, as Daphne Winland undermines in her study *We are now an actual nation* (1995), dealing with the impact of national independence on the Canadian Croatian diaspora. Lena testifies to the relevance of regional background, time of emigration, and family history (mostly in regard to political affiliations in World War Two) for making identity claims and delineating intra-group difference. Whether descending from a communist Partisan family or a family that leant towards the Royalist Chetnik side also impacted on how not only Yugoslavia but also the renewed ethnic antagonisms were understood. Moreover, stating that the bombing of Belgrade was to her "the major war," Lena, who comes from Belgrade, demonstrates how much the perception of war is tied to regional origin. Whether a migrant originates from Krajina, Serbia, or Herzegovina, the place of origin often determines how events in the homeland are viewed.

In contrast to Procter's approach which favors the presentist view of mental health, what I regard most crucial not only in Lena's story but in many of my interviews is the significance of history, memory, and collective/national identity that spans the globe. History, memory, and identity

43. Interestingly, many informants told of extended phone calls home, sometimes even at the same time that NATO bombs fell on Belgrade. While they univocally voiced extreme fear and depression, they emphasized that relatives and friends in Belgrade were relatively relaxed, made jokes, or calmed them down. This discrepancy suggests, that in exile identity and sorrow are emphasized in their own ways, not despite the distance to the homeland but because of it. But in the homeland ways of coping with a hard reality are much more based on "having to go on" and make life bearable. Procter 1999 who focuses on the mental health of his informants introduces the term "long-distance devastation" for describing the grave mental distress of Serbian Australians during the Croatian and Bosnian wars.

are not homogeneous, coherent *topoi*, instead, histories and counter-histories, memories and counter-memories compete with each other, as is hinted at in Lena's recollection of competing Chetnik and Partisan memories in the former Yugoslavia.

Lena is aware of the attractiveness of long-distance nationalism in a time of crisis, which she critiques at the same time that she complies with it, thus posing a stark contradiction in her narrative. When she wholeheartedly contends: "*Somehow that is 'me'. Bodily I feel that something happens to me, too,*" while watching the Balkan Wars from the distance, the process of identification with a 'people,' an epic 'we' far away that she left years ago, seems to be at the core of Serbian identity politics in the wake of the Third Balkan Wars. Interestingly, Lena made this statement upon an inquiry by an American, indicating how crucial external ascriptions are for claiming a certain identity.

My hypothesis for understanding long-distance nationalism is the following: at the time of war, Serbian migrants in the U.S. experienced a strong sense of feeling under attack, thus strengthening their non-hyphenated Serbian "expressive" identity (Safran 1999), making an in-betweenness (whether as Serbian-Americans or Yugoslavs) often impossible. The eruption of war meant an "identity-building"[44] event, fundamentally changing people's perception of Self and the nation – a change that often started with the questions, "Who am I?" or "Who are we?"[45] (chapters one and two). Due to an unreconciled, violent historical past the sense of Serbian identity could easily be transformed into "instrumental" identities, with a few political activists and long-distance nationalists instrumentalizing the expression of resentment of the many (chapters three and four).

Nationalism and non-nationalism

The variety of statements on Serbian identity which are to follow, far from revealing any homogeneity and closure, display huge differences which can be largely attributed to either nationalistic or non-nationalistic attitudes. Exploring what being Serbian means to the participants in my study, I was constantly confronted with the tension between nationalist and anti-nationalist discourse, creating divisions within the "Serbian community" and laying open fissures and ambivalence even in one and the same person, as the example of Lena indicated. In the present part of the book I will ana-

44. I derive this notion from "nation-building" in the classical literature on nationalism, where crucial events, such as wars, are used as a template on which to elaborate on the vision of the homogeneity of the nation (Gellner 1983: 9).
45. Interestingly, Evgenija Krašteva-Blagoeva in *Who are We? Types of collective identities in contemporary Bulgaria* 2003 poses the same question and describes similar identity discourses, thus showing how similar Bulgarian and Serbian or Southeast European identity discourses are in the time of transition.

lyze a plethora of statements by a number of people, keeping in mind the strong attraction of both positions, which for the sake of clarity I call "nationalist" and "non-nationalist" discourse.

What does it mean for a person to utter nationalist or non-nationalistic attitudes? And how is one to distinguish between the two? In his ethnography *The Past in Question* (2003), dealing with the uncertainty of the modern Macedonian nation, Keith Brown underlines that the Federal Republic of Yugoslavia, although having been the result of a national movement and representing a nation-state, was not fostering nationalism. In Yugoslavia, he states, "there was no rhetoric of an ancient Yugoslav past" (Brown 2003: 24). The author further explicates: "In so far as Yugoslav nationalism existed, then, it did so in a form which drew attention to its own novelty and its own volition – in short, to its own constructednes, rather than its naturalness" (ibid.: 25). From the viewpoint of globalization theory the non-aligned, socialist country represented a model of multiculturalism and hybridity, with Arjun Appadurai euphorically claiming: "Federal Yugoslavia could be said to have represented an attempt by its leaders to think beyond the nation in ways that anticipated later scholarship urging theorists to do the same" (1993: 411).

Oscillating between ethno-national identities and the supranational Yugoslav idea, Yugoslavia provided a singular example of multinational coexistence. In this vein, notwithstanding the political and social problems that were inherent from the very beginning, I use the term non-nationalistic broadly for those statements that are in favor of Yugoslavia, as opposed to nationalistic, pro-Serbian viewpoints claiming primordial, natural essences of Serbdom. In contrast to Skrbiš (1999) and Procter (2000) who almost exclusively focus on those who claim to be Serbs, Croats, or Slovenes, and very rarely mention the designation "Yugoslav," thus zeroing in on long-distance nationalism by zeroing out on 'non-nationalism,' I believe that it is important to also include those who defy or try to defy ethno-national categorizations. I regard the use of counter-designations, as which "Yugoslav" is sometimes used, crucial, since most people I talked to refer to both Serbian and Yugoslav identifications, often in order to set themselves apart from each other. Therefore, to hold that "[b]eing a Yugoslav is more than just being a person with mistaken past political affiliations ... [but] anyone who breaks the rules of conformity" (Skrbiš 1999: 134), underscores the significance that "Yugo-Nostalgia" still possesses – if only in the interrelatedness that bind the two juxtaposed concepts, or the Serb-Yugoslav binary, together.

Binaries or the contrastive use of identity designations, as Herzfeld has pointed out, is a key ordering principle of political identities, often including Manichaean pairs as well as subversive meanings (Herzfeld 1997: 15).

Caution is needed on the part of anyone writing about nationalism. According to Herzfeld

> "social life consists of processes of reification and essentialism as well as challenges to these processes. ... Distrust of essentialism in social theory should not blur our awareness of its equally pervasive presence in social life. *Essentializing essentialism is pointless.* ... [r]ecognizing the essentialisms shared by nationalism and anthropology provides both historical insight and critical distance." (ibid.: 26, italics mine)

In my mind, one of the key challenges is to explore the essentialisms and uses of stereotypes at work, while not "essentializing essentialism," in other words not taking part in them in the process of writing. But how do I refrain from processes of reification and the creation of even more fixity to identity claims by writing about them? Is not the mere choice of describing them already an act of reification? With the choice to depict the rather stereotypical, nationalist claims of Serbdom, first, I hope to shed light on essentialism at work, while an analysis of non-nationalist, Yugoslav discourse will show the tension, conflict, and fluid nature of identity in the diaspora.

Like Lena, many Serbian migrants in the U.S. did not simply give up one identity (Yugoslav) for the other (Serbian), as the homeland stood in flames, but they were confronted with various positions of identification which were influenced by events back home (and their reporting), opinions of relatives and of the "Serbian community," and personal stories that often put in motion changes in identity claims. To label these multi-stranded and heterogeneous modes of identification simply nationalistic and non-nationalistic is a choice to mark the two poles in-between which the negotiation of identity in the diaspora appears to take place. Thus, in the following section, my analysis will foreground a broad variety of discourses that, as I suggest, are situated in the tensed relationship between nationalism and non-nationalism, sometimes in very clear-cut, essentialized ways, and at other times crisscrossing each other, as people are trying to make sense out of the complicated meanings of Yugoslavia, the Balkan wars and what it means to be Serbian abroad.

Chapter 1. Being Serbian in the United States

> "In Serbia you are a Serb, that's a simple fact, you cannot change it. But in the U.S. you have to do something for it, here you must do something in order to be a Serb."
> (Milan Vukić, San Francisco)

Let us be what we are!

"*Do you know what it takes to get to know a Serb?*", seventy-two-year old Zoran Dušić asks me in an interview at the beginning of my fieldwork. "*If you want to get to know a Serb, you have to eat 300 kg of salt with him, did you know? That takes time, to share 300 kg of salt.*" While in the process of establishing a network of people who would work with me, either through friends or when visiting the church on Sundays and meeting with the parishioners after the divine liturgy, people were often generous with "fatherly" advice or discouraging remarks concerning my fieldwork. The above statement reveals the temporal dimension of getting to know a Serb, or the impossibility of an outsider to ever know a Serb. Therefore, as the proverb suggests, Serbs are different, they are "obstinate Others," whose encoding of difference is so absolute that it cannot likely be decoded, at least not by an outsider. Or: "It needs a Serb to know a Serb", as the Dutch anthropologist van de Port (1999: 8) phrases it:

> "The 'obstinate others' that I met in Serbia, those people who told me in a thousand different ways 'No way! You are not going to penetrate our Otherness! We are different!' were not interested in intercultural dialogue. They were up for exclusivity, for being essentially different. Over and over again they told me that I should not expect to be able to grasp everything about them, insisting that some differences between Serbs and people from the West are for *real.*"

Disbelieving the existence of such an absolute and impenetrable difference, I asked myself, what *do* I find out about being Serbian when spending time with 'them'? What is communicated as the essence of being Serbian by Serbs themselves? In keeping true to van de Port's observations, one of my first attempts at establishing contact with Serbs in the San Francisco Bay Area comprised of a major setback, which in a few moments of despair convinced me of the frustrating impossibility of accomplishing my fieldwork. In order to illustrate the situation at hand, I will quote from my field diary where I comforted myself with the dilemma experienced by writing:

I call Mira to arrange a meeting, but she isn't home. Her sister answers the phone, Ljubica, whom I have never heard of. With utter skepticism she inquires who I am, what I want, and what my profession is. Almost interrupting my shy answer – I explain to her in a few sentences that I was an anthropologist and that I knew Mira and do a research on the Serbian diaspora – she says authoritatively: "My sister is an old woman and doesn't have much time!" In the next second she already condemns my work and doesn't give it any chance. She advises me in an unfriendly way to go to the university library if I wanted to learn about her country – which by the way is very open and friendly. Her way of talking, the tone and unfriendliness in her voice make me feel awkward, like a failure, as if there is no way I could see her sister again, although Mira was so nice and helpful to me before. Considering how this conversation goes, the talk could have ended here, but she continues talking without interruption – my comments appear superfluous. Her voice tells me through the telephone wire, what a scandal The Hague is, how difficult her flight from Yugoslavia more than forty years ago was, she talks about her status as foreigner and refugee in the U.S., and especially the suffering of her family, with special emphasis on her sister Mira and brother Budimir. "The heavy burden of history, that's something you could study, but not waste time and try to talk to people here." Such a bitterness! She could have brought the conversation to a halt, but instead she continues further for about half an hour, like a strict elementary school teacher who kicks me out of the classroom, because I violated the school rules. Besides, she insists, that the Serbs have a developed European culture. I am not getting at why she tells me all this and in this devastating way. From there her monologue jumps to the concentration camps in the Second World War in the Croatian Krajina where Tesla and she were born. She mentions numbers: numbers of concentration camps and numbers of the dead in order to clarify a history to me, as if I haven't ever heard about the Ustaša state of Croatia. Finally and surprisingly, she closes her warning by wishing me luck and informing me when it is convenient to reach her sister. I feel like a spy and a loser." [Fieldnotes]

Here I was, forced to understand "that Serbs are not interested in intercultural dialogue." Some time after this devastating talk I was told by Ljubica's seventy-nine-year-old and extremely agile sister, Mira Connor Pesić, whom I did reach soon after and was later able to establish a relationship with, that her younger sister is "not normal," that she gets "nervous attacks" and doesn't behave like a normal person does. Although I can retrospectively see that this explanation could be true, especially when taking into consideration her aggressive and hysterical tone, I did not forget her emotional telephone 'curse.' Instead, the verbal attack she made nevertheless remained alive in my memory. Perhaps, Ljubica's monologue did matter to me, because it did open up significant discourses about being Serbian that were of relevance in a wider sense. Reading it again I discerned some major topics that could not be projected to her traumatized "state of mind" alone, but were mentioned with great frequency in many conversations and interviews I conducted later.

Ljubica's talk is prone with a collectivizing rhetoric. Take for instance the equaling of the country with the people, when she tells me that I should get to know Serbia, although I communicated to her my intentions of getting to know Serbs in the Bay Area. Serbs are often seen as an intrinsic part of Serbia, as indistinguishable from the (history of the) nation. Moreover, in the statement "the Serbs have a European culture," it is emphasized that Serbia belongs to Europe – thus foregrounding that this not an uncontested fact which is taken for granted. This claim reveals nothing about that culture per se, but much about the multilayered, conflictual discourse of "Europe," prevalent in most Southeast European countries at present.[46]

Another collectivizing strategy for claiming the uniqueness of the ethno-nation was given by Ljubica in her allusion to the famous Serbian physician and inventor, Nikola Tesla (1856-1943), who arrived in the United States in 1884. The "scientific superman" (Tomashevich 2000: 71), as the inventor of the "Tesla coil" – a patent of electro-magnetic motors, he secured some forty other patents, among them the discovery of electric light. Like other outstanding Serbian immigrants to the U.S., the best known being Mihailo Pupin, Serbs took great pride in claiming the "Serbianness" of Tesla.[47] Some went even so far as to hold congregations on the famous immigrant ancestor: one of my first events with Serbs in the Bay Area was a public talk by a Serbian professor of Nuclear Science at UC Berkeley, preceding the show of a new BBC documentary on the inventor from Yugoslavia. Curiously, the professor seemed to stress as much his scientific achievements as his *Serbian* biography, although according to the literature Tesla's social contact with the Serbian community must have been sparse. George Tomashevich's *Portrait of Serbian Achievers* (2000) makes a similar

46. The "imagination of Europe" takes many forms, not only in the middle and Western European countries that are part of the EU. In Southeastern Europe, marking the traditional border between "East" and "West," "Asia" and "Europe," the continent is often seen as having its cradle in Greece and the Balkans, thus juxtaposing the dominant versions of a "backward" Southeast that is not really part of Europe, and an "advanced" Western Europe (see Todorova 1999). Ljubica in using the allusion to the "cultured" Europe hints at exactly those meanings, by self-consciously declaring Serbia Europe (as opposed to viewing it as its antipode) and alluding to its "culture" (as opposed to viewing it as 'barbarian'). See also Herzfeld 1987, Roth 1988, Bakić-Hayden and Hayden 1995.
47. Interestingly, because Tesla originated in the Croatian *Krajina*, or military frontier, Croat historians were busy trying to reassert the Croatianness of the physician, albeit with little success, since it is widely accepted that Tesla's parents were both Serbs. See Skrbiš 1999: 93f.

point in trying to project the uniqueness of the man's accomplishment on his ethnic group. Including short overviews of Vuk Karadžić, Petar Petrović Njegoš, Mihailo Pupin, and Nikola Tesla, Tomashevich's work has appeared on the verge of the NATO bombing in order to provide a positive image of "the Serbian people [who] gave the world a considerable number of notable figures in all fields of human creativity" (ibid.: xi). Curiously, the book's publisher, the "Serbian Literary Company" in Toronto, like the literary journal "Serbian studies," seem to share the same goal: to link the individual accomplishments of famous Serbs with a collectivizing representation of the group as a whole.

Prominent in Ljubica's talk is the central importance of history, the bitterness of cruelties committed against Serbs in the Second World War,[48] an unjust treatment of Serbs with regard to the violent disintegration of Yugoslavia, and the aversion against any outsider's representation of "them." These are themes already discussed in van de Port's work on Serbs in Novi Sad, based on his fieldwork beginning in 1991: Serbs and Serbian history are impenetrable to outsiders, thus everything written about "them" or spoken of "them" was necessarily wrong. In short, there was nothing new for me when talking to Serbs, I should consult the history books – and yet, despite the fear of espionage and misrepresentation, she wished me luck. This was one extreme example for the many other voices that while feeling the need to talk to me, rejected any representation by outsiders, and while claiming their obstinate Otherness so strongly, nevertheless opened up angles from where to understand what being Serbian might be about.

Plainly speaking, in the year 2000, being Serbian was prone with conflict on a personal, political, international, and historical level. People like Ljubica were personally disturbed, traumatized, and confused, as well as militantly self-righteous and defensive. After all, did she not point in a subtle way – if one views it from the angle of an anthropologist schooled in postmodernism – to an aspect of anthropological work that had been central in the last two decades of theory-building and radical postmodern critique, that is the "crisis of representation"? Was it not true that representation is always a construction, with inherent political dangers and embedded in knowledge/power that made it so urgent for anthropologists in the 1990's to retain from ethnography (for a while) and instead to indulge in analyses of self-reflexivity and the power of representation? (see Marcus and Clifford 1986) If she tried to prevent me from getting to know Serbs, however, in her conversation she certainly made a first step of opening up discourses of being Serbian. How Serbs characterize themselves and how they per-

48. The relevance of the Second World War in Serbian life historical accounts and for long-distance nationalist activism will be discussed at length in part two of this work.

ceive themselves vis-à-vis Big Powers and the International Community; these were all issues Ljubica's "not so normal," but also 'not so unusual' narrative indicated, issues which were to become central in the research and will be discussed in detail throughout this book. But first, take another example of Obstinate Otherness, before discussing representations of the essence of being Serbian.

The retired priest of San Francisco's Serbian Orthodox church, Father Dimitrije Aleksandrović, who seemed to be as involved in politics as in religion, confronted me one day with another riddle about being Serbian, albeit in a less dramatic one than Ljubica had done before. Sitting in his apartment overlooking the city, high on top of Diamond Heights, making me feel as if I had a view of San Francisco from the sky, he laid out his future vision of Serbia to me by referring to the present state of Serbs: "*And that's what we are, most of us: patriots without illusions. We see the situation, we know when we have to do it, we try to make Serbian people what they are. They are not what most Serbs think – that they are number one. When some simple Serb talks he thinks that Serbia is number one, everything is around Serbia, most small people think that. [my emphasis]*"

Father Dimitrije certainly points to the ultimate uniqueness of Serbs, as had Ljubica done, by taking into consideration the nation-state order of things. In his view, Serbs are proud and think that Serbia is geographically located at the center of the world. But what are Serbs? What is "it" that "we have to do"? What do most Serbs think they are and why is that wrong? And what does the tautology mean, to make Serbian people what they are? Remaining entirely vague in his allusion to Serbdom, it appeared that I was confronted with obstinate Otherness again, if only in a more comfortable way and couched in more positive contents. While intended to express ultimate uniqueness, the phrase reminded me of Skrbiš' observation that "to be a Slovenian is to be a Slovenian" (1999: 120). Maybe, a great many people in the world take part in such tautologies, thus inherently defying their own claims? Father Dimitrije's statement only left questions, not answers, thereby communicating an absolute difference beyond words.

In order to understand the tautological phrase the priest employs it is helpful to consult Ivan Čolović who in *Politics of Identity* (2002) analyses recent intellectual and poetic Serbian texts on being Serbian. The Belgrade anthropologist refers to a strikingly similar phrase, "Let us be what we are!" which as he argues, epitomizes the meaning of Serbianness (Čolović 2002: 64). Čolović interprets this identity rhetoric as based on the fundamental idea of the stableness and self-evidence of the ethno-nation, which is expressed in a clear, specific difference. Relevant here is the essentializing assumption that "it is so deeply rooted in every Serb that it is unchanged regardless of the circumstances and places in which Serbs live."

> "'But a Serbs remains a Serb', says Gojko Desnica, 'wherever he is born and wherever he lives. For little Serbs can be born in a foreign state, but their consciousness of belonging to their people surpasses everything.'" (Čolović ibid.: 64f.)

Therefore, it doesn't matter if Serbs are born abroad, in Serbia, or in one of the other former Yugoslav republics, since Serbianness is spiritual, as the quote reveals, it isn't bound to territory, and not even to language, or religion. To be Serbian entails a certain consciousness, and that consciousness can even be pushed in the very background, so that a Serb may not even feel Serbian. In this vein it is possible to understand, for example, a statement made by Ljiljana Cvetković, a Serbian woman living in Southwest Germany, whom I met again during a visit to her thirty-year-old daughter in the U.S. who was born in Belgrade, raised in Germany and now lives in Los Angeles, California. Tamara, the mother to a one-year-old daughter herself has hardly any contact to Serbs, partly due to her husband's grandmother's Croatian background, does not practice any Serbian tradition, does not speak the language, nor talks about anything Serbian. Ljiljana, upon complaining about her daughter's lack of Serbdom describes her identity as follows: "*Tamara's Serbian identity is slumbering, but it is there.*" When uttering the last words she moves one hand to her breast, indicating that the heart is the place where Serbian identity rests. This bodily gesture adheres to a statement that I heard repeatedly: "*My body and life are here, but my heart is there, in Serbia.*"

The assumption that a Serb remains a Serb, pointing to the rootedness of Serbdom, is indeed crucial. It helps explain why Serbian identity in the U.S. is believed to prove so resistant to change, and why even second and third generation Serbs still identify with, or at least know, some concrete details about their ancestor's place of origin. As a second generation Serbian woman in the Moraga church proudly confessed: "*Many of my American friends envy me for knowing so much of my native land. They often only know the simple fact that their grandparents came from Germany or Ireland, but I know in which town my grandparents and great-grandparents lived, I have even visited, and I know a lot about the history of my family and my nation.*"

In this view, being Serbian is represented as being entirely different from a belonging to any other ethno-national category. Serbs are tied to Serbia and preserve the history of the family and the nation that makes them automatically different from Americans. Although being American is based on being an immigrant and through immigration Serbs are similar to other (immigrant) Americans, they are claimed to differ in the important aspect of homeland ties. Whereas other immigrants forget and 'melt' into American society, thus losing their national identity without acquiring any new one – since an immigrant American identity is not really a national identity at all – only Serbs remain "what they are." As Čolović remarks, "Let us be what we are ... is transformed into a dream of complete separation from the world ...the Serbian nation, its 'spirit-people', becomes a 'guarantee of the salutary separation of the Serbian world from the whole rest of the world" (Čolović ibid.: 66).

Even as Americans they are separated from other immigrant Americans and yet they appear to be similar, especially to classic American diaspora groups, such as Jews and Armenians. Basing their absolute difference and superiority on the diasporic history of persecution, they claim to be like the "chosen people," or "heavenly people" according to Serbian mythology (Anzulović 1999). The violent events in the former Yugoslavia during the twentieth century seem to have furthered the construction of a diasporic identity that is in line with *the* emblematic diaspora group, the Jews. Serbian difference, couched in historical revisionism attests for the strenuous efforts made in Serbia and abroad to fix the image of the suffering, heroic, and misunderstood people. "We try to make Serbian people what they are," lies at the center of that revisionism, specific enough in its manifestation of stableness, and vague enough in its semantic emptiness, which can be filled with a plethora of meanings suitable for (exile) nationalist endeavors. But again, what is that "we," that should be what "we" are? And, what are 'spirit-people'? I will now search for less opaque statements Serbs make about themselves and try to understand the cultural semantics of what it means for my informants to be Serbian.

There, far away

There, far away, far away from the sea,
there is my Serbia, from there I am.
Why did she have to come, that sad night?
When you, my beloved, went to the bloody battle.[49]

In order to 'prove' to me the uniqueness of Serbs, Milan Gajić, fifty-year-old electrical engineer employed at NASA in the Silicon Valley, explained that Serbs are very emotional and committed, they are proud, quite concerned about their outer experience and they make something out of every situation, usually at the same time implying the lack of all these characteristics in others, such as Americans or Croats. Most importantly, they don't give up but struggle, even when life seems unbearable, or when they are,

49. My translation from the Serbian. This part of the folk song *Tamo daleko* is only one version of it. Further below I will quote another version.

as anthropologist Marko Živković phrases it, "living in bearable evil" (Živković 2000: 58). Rambo Amadeus, a famous Rock'n Roll singer in Serbia, states: "I suffer from strong emotional ups and downs: I feel normal when I am crazy!" (in Seierstad 2001: 285, my translation). This suffices to say that the word "crazy" or *lud* is to be understood more in the positive context of youth language, crazy meaning extraordinary, great, not normal, but special and unusual, than in it's negative or psychological context, whereas the latter can in a subtle way be inferred as well, if only to make the term more thrilling. Craziness, as one more variation of the absolute difference of being Serbian, is not the only state of mind that Serbs associate themselves with (or the situation they find their homeland in).

Miša Gajić, Milan's son and eighteen-year-old second-generation Serb studying electrical engineering at UC Berkeley, upon meeting in the University library and talking about literature on Serbs in the U.S. tells me that he loses his Serbian language ability quickly when he doesn't frequently travel back to the land where his parents were born and lived for 30 years. When asking him if he feels more American than Serbian he doesn't need to think long: "*Spiritually I am Serbian.*" But what does it mean for someone who lived his entire life in the U.S. to not *feel* like an American, but like a Serb? How does one belong 'spiritually'? Interestingly, Čolović observed a recourse to "the spiritual" in Serbia, too. In the 1990's words like "spiritual property," "spiritual movement," "spiritual suicide," and "Serbian spiritual space" were abundant in Serbian public discourse. "This endless spiritualization of things," encompassing amusement in cafés, says the author, has even found contributions of clerics, who one might suggest could be more wary of the banalization of the sacred" (Čolović 2002: 127). The inflation of "the spiritual" then is another catchphrase for clothing contemporary Serbian nationalism in the fashion of the old. With Miša at least, the spiritual message arrived. While believing that he expressed his innermost sacred belonging he lay pray to the 'spiritomania' in his homeland, not leaving even him, "the lost son" abroad untouched.

From these examples it appears that a discourse of sentiment and emotions is at play, or more precisely when it comes to "feel crazy" a general emotional excitability. Following the track of emotions and sentiment Milan advised me to go to the festivals and major celebrations in the church in San Francisco, "*that is where you feel the energy, that is where the young kids from Bosnia go whose fathers fought in the [recent, B. B.-L.] war. They bring that fighting mentality, that natural energy, that mentality with them, you can feel it!*" Milan inferred that a warrior mentality from Bosnia had traveled to the U.S., infusing the Serbian community with new power, or maybe 'spirit'? Actually, I did make use of every occasion and attended the parties in the church. In a sense then I did 'eat as much salt as I could' with Serbian people. And what did I find?

At a "Music Benefit Festival" in the hall of the San Francisco Serbian Orthodox Church in June 2002, over a hundred people gather together, listening to various musical contributions on the stage: a folklore band playing traditional Tamburica music, the Orthodox songs of the church choir, and the classical incantations of a Serbian opera singer who is employed at the San Francisco Opera. Except for the Tamburica band which is a professional group of musicians, flown in from the Serbian community in Phoenix, Arizona, all the music is "home-made," presented by the "gifted" members of the San Francisco/Bay Area parish. A High School boy plays Mozart on the piano, followed by *narodna muzika* (folk music), *starogradska muzika* (music of the old city) and Byzantium church songs. Glasses with the Serbian national drink *rakija* pass freely from person to person, before a musician announces the singing of the melancholic song *Tamo daleko* (There, far away): "*zajedno,*" together. Talks that went on before while listening to the musical contributions come to a halt. At once the folk song arouses the feelings of young and old, who stand up and wholeheartedly sing and embrace each other, as if they sang their national anthem.

Tamo daleko, daleko od mora, tamo je selo moje, tamo je Srbija.	There, far away, far away from the sea, there is my village, there is my Serbia.
Tamo daleko, gde cveta beli krin tamo su život dali zajedno otac i sin.	There, far away, where the white lily blooms, there their lives laid down father and son together.
Tamo daleko, gde cveta limun žut, tamo je srpskoj vojsci jedini bio put.	There, far away, where blooms the yellow lemon tree, there was to the Serbian army the only open way.
Tamo daleko, na Korfu živjeh ja, ali sam uvek klic'o "živela Srbija!"	There, far away, I lived on Corfu – but I always cried out "long live Serbia!"

This folk song, like the Yugoslav national anthem 'Hej, Sloveni' ('Hey, Slavs'), is World War One vintage, commemorating the ghastly winter withdrawal over the Albanian mountains in 1915, escaping from German and Austrian troops. Hunger, disease, cold and bandits decimated the Serb army, who regrouped in Corfu (known and revered to this day as the "Blue tomb" because so many died there) and returned to win back their country from those who had driven them from it. But, as opposed to the folk song that became Yugoslavia's national anthem, *Tamo Daleko* was not permitted in Yugoslavia, whereas it was very popular in exile. And indeed, the many Serbs abroad view this song as a secret national anthem. Ultimately, the incantation of the song creates a commemorative community, it is the kit that makes the imagined Serbian collective become real through the invocation of feeling and passion. Suddenly, the distance of the homeland intrudes on people's consciousness and bodies, only to make the spirit of Serbia more lively in that the Serbs in the singing crowd in San Francisco's Serbian Orthodox church mirror themselves in the yearning soldiers on Corfu more than 80 years ago. But the heavy homesickness created by the folk song doesn't last long, and then the *kolo* and other dances start again.

Community of Sentiment/ality

What Arjun Appadurai, in relation to the mass media, collective reading, criticism, and pleasure, has called a "community of sentiment" (1990, 1996: 8) seems to be a useful term in this context, too. For Appadurai the community of sentiment describes a collective feeling of commonality that substitutes face-to-face contact and produces locality in new, globalized ways. In the situation of war and crisis in the homeland, the "elsewhere," as Appadurai names it, can be found in a more fervently celebrated feeling of community abroad. But, whereas Appadurai connotes this celebrated feeling of community exclusively in virtual ways, my findings suggest that this practiced sociality can also be understood in a literal sense as the celebration of commonality on the occasion of collective events.

Quite many people mentioned to me that the war had a positive side to it, namely the growth of the active Serbian community due to a revival of Serbianness among immigrants and the arrival of refugees from Bosnia and brain drain Serbs from Serbia. In other words, with the onset of war, the celebrations were visited more frequently, the church hall was not half empty anymore, and parties took place more often, with a bigger crowd of visitors of various *coloeur.* Therefore, as opposed to Appadurai's definition of the community of sentiment as not depending on face-to-face contact, the "real" social relations obviously do play a role here. To speak with Michael Herzfeld, for long-distance nationalism, I suggest, that the "social uses" and "social poetics" of ordinary people figure as prominent as in the context of the nation-state (1997: 8). Both concepts, Appadurai's "community of sentiment" as well as Herzfeld's "cultural intimacy" seem adequate for describing a situation, in which sentimental commonality is produced and displayed joyfully.

Underneath the church building, in the cellar, or "underground", so to speak, the quiet atmosphere from the divine liturgies, the holy icons, and mystical incense are forgotten, not god but melancholia, sentiment, and joy determine the order of the night. The church is literally turned upside down. But the most important part of the evening is the dancing of the *kolo*, the Serbian round dance, to the little wandering *starogradska muzika* orchestra that mingles with the dancers on the dance floor. At around eleven o'clock young tall and sportive second-generation Serbs from Sacramento dressed in suits, who I see at every major celebration, jump to the dance floor and clap their hands, swing their legs up in the air, hold the women around their waists and lead the circle faster and faster, laughing and screaming, sweating and exhausting themselves. Women of all ages, wearing colorful dresses, smile at each other with complicity, inviting people standing outside the *kolo* with their sparkling eyes, and open up their hands to let new dancers into the circle, only to close them around new hands again. Dances such as these seem to offer an arena for the most sentimental and joyous celebrations of community and of Serbdom. Very rarely before did I see older American Serbs born in the U.S., recent refugees from Bosnia-Herzegovina, and brain drain exiles from Belgrade, in short, all the different generations and factions of immigrants, mingle together without engaging in debates. In contrast to the saying: "Where there are ten Serbs there are eleven opinions," this evening resembled a stage where the crowd demonstrated unity in the most celebratory sense. A red-haired middle-aged woman wearing an extravagant red dress, moving along with the musicians playing the accordion, the double-bass and the guitar, drinking *rakija* and feeding the men with the plum brandy throws the words to me: "*See, we are crazy, we are happy, this is the Serbian sentimentality*!" Then she stops dancing, telling me with blinking eyes: "*You know what? In reality I am a Croat, my parents came here from Croatia, my mother was Dalmatian and my father Croat – but I decided to become Serbian. I love the Serbian people, I love their craziness. This is it!*"

In this vein being Serbian is based on ethnic choice in its purest form, since it refers to an imaginary belonging that is not grounded in blood, soil, or heritage – but in sentiment. The sentiment mentioned with regard to spirituality and on the occasion of music, concerts, and dances seems to be the kit for forming a community abroad that helps to bring together migrants that may otherwise be isolated. For the woman declaring herself as a proud Serbian is tied to the imagined communal cohesion and sentimentality experienced, for instance on a party such as this. But what is that sentimentality? Don't other ethnic groups or non-ethnic congregations of people know similar cohesive sentimental situations?

Habits of the heart: Variations on a theme Balkans

Going back to my table where I sit with my husband, my friend Andreja, his girl-friend Lara, and their friend Zoran Martić from Kraijna, the previous joyous atmosphere is halted abruptly when I hear them indulging in a heated discussion, talking loudly, exchanging words mixed with anger and excitement. The topic they deal with is Martić's cousin, former leader of the rebel enclave *Srpska Krajina* who is an indicted war criminal at the International Criminal Tribunal at The Hague, Netherlands (ICTY) for having organized military assaults in Croatia, among them a rocket attack on the Croatian capital Zagreb. Zoran recounts how he called his now wanted cousin in 1992 on the phone, warning him to not continue his fight for a Serbian Krajina, least to expand his military actions to other parts of Croatia – but in vain. Andreja, laughing and giggling, cynically states: "*He should have bombed Zagreb! NATO should have bombed Zagreb right from the start instead of Belgrade!*" I try to object to this bellicose utterance by mentioning that they could hardly wish somebody else what they themselves suffered, but my comment is ignored, interrupted by Lara reinstating resentfully: "*Oh yes, we should have bombed Zagreb to the ground, then we wouldn't have had all those problems.*" Therefore, an attempt to describe a "community of sentiment" would have to go beyond feelings of joy on the occasion of music and dancing and extend to emotions in relation to the wars in the former Yugoslavia.

What is really at stake in this "we" that engages in a verbal military attack during a party, marking the intrusion of war into a festive mood? How is it that the military, the country, the people, and the Self are used in an identical sense? How comes that during a party in the church hall in the U.S., the tongue loosened from drinking *rakija*, Serbian migrants seem to be so quick to throw in a politically incorrect statement concerning the past wars in the homeland? What imaginary process is at work here? Are these – the sentimental joy and the angry verbal attacks – the emotional ups and downs Serbia's famous pop star Amadeus sings of? It is hard to say for me, whether the couple meant its comments serious or just enjoyed to take up the topic of the war in an uncensored, cynical manner. What seems clear, however, is that old wounds, the loss of Serbian settlements in Croatia, and thus of the presence of Serbs in the new, independent Croatia altogether, were still fresh, with the national question of Serbs remaining unresolved. Whether they meant serious what they said or not, Lara and Andreja were seriously at odds with Croatia. Comparing the more or less untouched city of Zagreb with Belgrade, which suffered from air raids and destruction in 1999, they also compared the relatively positive portrayal of Croatia in the media and negative depictions of Serbia. In short, the world was unjust. Croats got what they wanted, Serbs did not.

With regard to the specific events surrounding Martić, the military conflicts in Krajina hint at revealed splits and divisions within Croatian Serbs and Serbs in Serbia during an important phase in the war.[50] After all, Martić embodied the fighter mentality or rebel "spirit" as well as a loser, since he complied with Milošević's "treacherous" command to stop bombing Zagreb and put the defense of Krajina to a halt. Thus he also gave up on the defense of Serbs in Croatia, a move that many Serbs I talked to have been upset about up to the present. At that moment, the Croatian army started expelling some 170, 000 Serbs from their villages in only a few days.[51] The question surrounding the debate between the three young Serbs in the San Francisco church hall thus is, whether Martić was too militant to begin with (his cousin's position), or not militant enough (the couple's opinion). Or, did he fight too much and therefore rightly deserved the ICTY-indictment or too little? In this vein, the argument signified that the role of Serbian military during the Yugoslav wars of disintegration surrounding issues of guilt, accountability, and victimization was and is by and large contested, to perhaps remain the topic of discussion for many years to come. It seemed to have little effect on the opinions of Lara and Andreja that with the ICTY's indictment of Martić the international community had officially condemned Zoran's cousin. Perhaps, that fact provided them with one more manifestation of the West's unjust treatment of "the Serbian side" during the wars of disintegration.

Considering conflictual issues such as the Krajina and Serbian military moves, the display of commonality and cohesion in the festival lasted only for a short moment.

Clearly, the issues of Serbian political and military actions in the recent conflicts do matter to people such as Zoran, Andreja, and Lara. In order to explore the collective self-perceptions of Serbs further I will now turn

50. At this point I need to provide some background information on Milan Martić. Susan Woodward mentions that as early as 1990, "the radical Serbs supporting Milan Babić had political links with the leadership in Serbia and were well armed and organized into multiple militia (the Martićevci of Milan Martić; units trained by the international mercenary Captain Dragan, with aid from paramilitary forces in Serbia and units of the army) to defend their goal of remaining within a rump Yugoslavia if Croatia, which they believed to be a fascist state, actually split" (Woodward 1995a: 170). By 1993/94, the various Krajina militias were in deep conflict with each other, Martić being a loyalist of Milošević. This changed during the 1995 Croat offensive *Oluja* in the course of which most Serbs were expelled from Croatia. According to Judah (2000: 301) "[w]ith a large arsenal of rockets at their disposal the Serbs could have devastated Croatian cities, but when Milan Martić, the *krajina* leader, had fired a rocket at Zagreb city center in May, during the Croatian offensive in western Slavonia, Milošević had been furious. He then pulled out many of the remaining rockets."

51. Judah 2000: 2f.

to discursive statements with reference to "Serbian" fighting mentality and war which have been at issue in the preceding debate.

As Tim Judah points out, many Serbs could identify with Milošević's nationalist attitude towards Croatia (like in the above example) and later Kosovo. The Serbian President, in taking up issues that had been raised by the Memorandum of the Serbian Academy of Science (SANU) in 1987, and with regard to the state of victimization of Serbs in the contested Serbian province stated: "If we don't know how to work well, at least we know how to fight well" (in Judah 2000: 4). In Serbia clichés, jokes, and stereotypes about Serbs are tantamount and appear to be the greatest export product which Serbs in the U.S. consume with a voracious appetite, often closing in on the binary laziness and fighter ethic. Surprisingly similar to Milošević's characterization is a comment from the former opposition leader and Serbian prime minister Zoran Djindjić, who was assassinated in spring 2003: "Serbs are lazy, undisciplined, and without self-criticism. Our greatest mistake is to believe we were stronger than all the others" (in: Seierstad 2001: 7, my translation).

That the stereotype of lazy, militant Serbs was not only prevalent in the political elite of the country, but also among exiles, was made clear to me in various ways, while conversing with Serbs in the Bay Area. One day in the late afternoon after work, drinking coffee and espresso in one of Berkeley's university cafés, Andreja tried to explain to me again what it is that makes Serbs so special. This time, in contrast to the positive allusions to sentiments and emotions, he referred to the absence of an action, or a negativity: "*Did you ever see us work before? [laughs] We sit and talk and drink coffee, but we don't work. See, it's probably from the Turkish empire: for 500 years the Turkish ruled us and the Serbs were rebels. We just didn't work. Do you remember in Andrić's book*[52]*, when the Turks had the Serbs built the bridge and we just destroyed it immediately after! This will happen again, if the West wants us to work for them, we will simply refuse. So far we didn't comply with the West, that's the problem.*"

Instead of simply stating a stereotype, Andreja couches his allusion in a ready-made historical narrative that causally links past phenomena with the present. An absence of work ethic is here explained as a historical relic stemming from forced labor under Ottoman rule met by "rebel laziness." To note here, Andreja employs the term "we," thereby creating a horizontal collective, that means a cohesiveness of people through historical time. In fact, the majority of Serbs employ not the lyrical "I," but the epic "we," which is also the national "we." Ironically, Andreja himself works long hours each day, 12-hour work days being no exceptions, with his daily coffee consumption in the evening figuring as his meager leisure activity. How else can I therefore understand his narrative, but as an imaginative

52. The famous *Bridge on the Drina* 1984.

flight into a nostalgically envisioned past with very little relevance for his own personal present? Not working can be explained by the ideal of bravery and the resistance against hegemonic empires, boycotting power – the Turkish of the past and Western countries of the present here being equaled. Being lazy and being a fighter are thus two sides of the same coin, based on an eternal historical truism.

Curiously, allusions to a fighting ethos and pride seem to belong to a cultural imagery of Serbs that is located in a long-standing scholarly tradition, too. Meštrović, Letica and Goreta in *Habits of the Balkan Heart* (1993), go as far as trying to understand the violent disintegration of Yugoslavia by linking the "national character" of Serbs which, they pose, is delineated by a lack of democratic traditions, to the tragic end of the multinational state. They contend:

> "The Dinaric and Ural social types described by Tomašić (1948b) display a cultural tendency toward insurrection and violence. For example, it is well known in Yugoslavia that Serbs and Montenegrins adhere to a sort of cult of the warrior. They have continually dominated the police and armed forces. They habitually own guns and engage in hunting as part of a machismo set of values. Within Yugoslavia, they are known for being stubborn, irascible, and emotionally unstable." (Meštrović, Letica, Goreta 1993: 36)

The Croatian authors perpetuate not only a simplistic description of Serbs as "bad" and Croats as „good", since the latter are assumedly more democratic than their Eastern neighbors, by ascribing an ideal type, a mental set of character traits and social values. Above all, they claim to understand the underlying dynamic of the Third Balkan Wars by way of analyzing ancient ethnic, social and nationalistic tendencies, "habits of the heart," of the various peoples of the Balkans that, as they claim, have taken precedence over pressures for democracy. Decades after Ruth Benedict's (1934) "national character" studies, which have rightly been critiqued for their drive for homogeneity and simplicity, the authors seem to be oblivious to the inherent dangers of creating ethno-national typologies. That culture and politics do not stand in a causal relationship and that national power play and international factors contributed as much to the fanning of the flames of the dismemberment of Yugoslavia, gets ignored (see Woodward 1995a). Essentialized emotional dispositions of the peoples, strictly speaking "Serbian character traits," are reified once again, this time by academics to explain a war.

The absence of a strong work ethic was also pointed to me, when interviewing Serbs in Germany[53]. Sitting together in the back windowless room of a Balkan shop in the center of Reutlingen, the air thick with cigarette smoke, and lots of naked female breasts and blond hair around us on cheap posters decorating the wall, one of the 'Gastarbeiter' men confessed: "*You know what? In Yugoslavia, the economy did so well that we didn't have to work more than three hours a day. Here, they need at least eight hours for that!*"[54] Andreja told a joke along a similar vein: "*A British, a French, and a Serb meet and compare their incomes. The British says: 'I earn 2000 pounds a month, I spend 1500 and save 500.' The French states: 'I earn 5000 Francs a month, spend 4000 and invest the rest.' When it is the Serb's turn he calculates: 'I earn one hundred Deutschmarks a month, spend a thousand, and don't know where the 900 come from'.*" According to this joke poverty caused by the wars and economic breakdown in the 1990's led to overspending in an attempt at keeping the relatively high living standard of the 1980's at all costs, if only through obscure ways and secret channels. Self-orientalising statements such as these, laziness, primitivism, a 'Mafiosi,' or barbarian way of doing things, are common. A young researcher in a natural science lab in Berkeley told me: "*Serbs are barbarians, didn't you know that? We are barbarian.*" Here, the speaker provocatively made use of orientalizations or Balkanizations (Todorova 1997) from Western audiences, which he appeared to be well aware of. At play in this statement were inverted depictions of Serbs that he, conscious of the fact that Serbs are also known for the very opposite, studiousness and academic success, as he himself epitomizes, employed in an ironic manner.

Allusions to the heroic and fighter characteristics of the Serbian people in conjunction with the negative "nesting orientalisms" (Bakić-Hayden 1995), that are at work in the above mentioned examples loom large. Dragana Gajković, a business woman in her mid-forties who came to the U.S. as a little girl, expresses her view of Serbs as follows: "*They are lovely people but difficult. It's a very male-oriented culture, and very boastful, very proud. It's warriors and intellectual people.*" The gendered nature of Serbs, as expressed by Serbs themselves, can be uncomfortable for women, at least for Dragana who favors America and American men. She continues her portrait by referring to the patriarchal gender culture and the work ethic already discussed earlier in this section: "*Serbs are bad management people. You see how difficult it was for them to find a united opposition candidate? Everybody wants to be the leader, the master, they are bad with team work, esp. when you are a woman.*" Apply-

53. In September and October 2000, I have also conducted fieldwork among so called "*Gastarbeiter*" migrants in Germany. Unfortunately, I did not have the opportunity yet to continue that fieldwork, make a comparison, or an analysis of this work. However, given the complete lack of scholarly work on former Yugoslav immigrants to Germany, this project seems to be worth pursuing in the future. I am using the present example because it fits very well the theme at hand.
54. This joke seems to also refer to the endemic problem of an unemployment rate and underemployment in Yugoslavia beginning at the end of the 1960's and reaching far into the crisis and dissolution of the country, see Woodward 1995b.

ing examples from recent political developments in Serbia, Dragana constructs a more generalizable picture of Serbs, their pride hindering them from unification, the drive to master things inhibiting them to work together. Far from recurring to a static, fixed portrait of a people, the characterization is imbued with an analysis of events and situations that goes much further than the description itself, including a critique of gender inequality and social problems.[55]

That the topic of the warrior belongs to a crucial cultural repertoire that was revitalized in the 1990's, also surfaced in people's reaction to the NATO bombing of Yugoslavia in 1999. Svetlana, a thirty-year-old student at the Academy of Art in San Francisco told me over a coffee in the European flair café "Caffe de la Presse" at the gate of Chinatown: "*During the bombing I got out every night with my friends, we met at the bridges and danced on them, we had parties, we tried to show them [NATO, B.B.-L.] that we are not afraid.*" In the three months of the bombing when the government staged big parties and concerts on Belgrade bridges, it made use of that symbol, in order to not only demonstrate the Serbian stance for Yugoslav integrity, but to try to avert air raids by employing human shields, thereby staging their invincibility.

I heard these stories of bombing nights that were turned into party time more often, the first occasion being in August 1999. Shortly after the bombing was stopped, I traveled to Belgrade where I spent an evening on a boat on the Danube that had been turned into a night club, with a band playing music by Goran Bregović and young women dancing in-between the tables. Sitting on the porch right next to the dark water and watching the thunder and lightening approach until it exploded with hard rain and tremendously loud thunders, the head of the young section of Milošević's socialist party (SPS) recollected proudly how he never went to the cellar and instead spent his nights outside, demonstrating his fearless nature.[56] From this and Svetlana's account, it appears that in a life-threatening situation, where one might expect people to protect themselves safely in the cellars, Serbs still needed to demonstrate their invincibility as well as their pride and lust for life. In a second sense, the stories of fearless nights also reflected the conscious staging of narratives, whereby the self-presentation of the speaker – not the event he was telling, but *how* he told the event –

55. See Simić 1999: 11-29.

56. During a one-week trip to Belgrade shortly following the bombing, a few Tübingen students and I met with various social actors but also this and other government politicians. Our goal was to learn about "the other" Serbia and gain a broad picture of political and social processes in the country, following the years of media representations which had mainly depicted "the Serbs" as the perpetrators. The meeting with SPS members was helpful for getting visas which after years of sanction and diplomatic isolation was not taken for granted.

was central. How could I understand the joyous "Serbian" way of dealing with a state of emergency and suffering?

Budimir Pesić explained to me: "*We are not a cruel people, we are the people of sufferers.*" And Dragan Jovanović, one of the few arrivals in the 1960's and recently retired economist summed up the attitude Serbs have towards suffering and war as follows: "*When Serbs don't have a tragedy they feel bored.*" In this humorous statement Dragan plays with the theme of an endless repetition of war and suffering, a dominant vision of Serbian history as the embodiment of a series of victimizations and fights for the very essence of life, which has to be defended from uncountable attacks from outside. Serbian warriors' struggle, then, is a heroic endeavor to save Serbs from extinction, be it the history of the medieval Serbian kingdom, the 500-year span under Ottoman domination, the liberation wars in the 19th century, the two world wars in the 20th century, or the wars of disintegration in the 1990's. The reading of the past in terms of continuity circles around a cyclical understanding of Serbian history, with Serbs purifying the past of all ambivalent contents and leaving the story of the martyr, the victim, and the "heavenly kingdom" intact. This heroic epic story, Čolović (2002: 55) points out, goes even so far, that "the living Serbs are, as Matija Beckovic formulated it, just the remnants of a slaughtered people."" It appears remarkable that the nationalist imagery Čolović analyzes finds so much resonance in the far away place of exile, California. The narratives I put forth indicate a significant acceptance of the fighter ethic and ideology of victimization, although people live in an entirely different social and political context from the public in the homeland. Nationalist discourses, as this section showed, are very relevant, but they are not uncontested.

Čolović, however, leaves no room for exploring contestation. Being a committed anthropologist who always indirectly implies dissent against politics in Serbia, his work could be critiqued for "essentializing essentialism" (Herzfeld 1997), because he *only* focuses on nationalist discourse and silences the oppositional voices in Serbia. Subsequently, the picture, which he draws is that of nationalist, obsessed Serbs, without distinguishing between the Serbo-centric discourses of writers and "the people," as if taking for "real" the narratives he describes. But in the case of Serbian migrants, essentialism, although playing a crucial role in discourse, is not without alternative. As the latter statements revealed, people are open for debate and for some ethno-national glorifications serve as departure points for bursts of anger and refutation. Taken together, however, the statements on the work-fighter binary form a body of discourse that is prone with stereotypes, essentializations, and drives for homogenization. Based on the feeling of being under attack, Serbs in the diaspora form a "community of sentiment" anchored in a history of victimization, martyrdom and injustice.

Serbs vis-à-vis their 'Others'

Budimir Pesić, an eighty-year-old Serb from Croatian Slavonia who fled Yugoslavia after World War Two laments: "*After the wars [the first World War and the Second World War, B. B.-L.] they praised the Serbs for their bravery and resistance, they were the heroes for Western Europe. And now they are all the demons.*" Again, as in Andreja's example of the laziness that he attributed to foreign rule, outsiders are responsible for how Serbs are. First, Serbs were lazy as an answer to outside repression; later Serbs were made heroes by international powers, because they were "brave" and resisted in the two world wars. In the 1990's those glorious deeds are forgotten and Serbs "are all the demons" -- obviously for no reason. In a similar way, Andreja reinstates: "*We are a peaceful nation, but the problem is that the war always comes from outside, otherwise they would be running. ... The Croats always envied the Serbs for their love of freedom. The Serbs had the Russian influence.*" In this last depiction Serbs are described vis-à-vis their closest 'Others,' the Croats by way of the Serbian "brother," Russia.

As has been pointed out by various authors (Bakić-Hayden and Hayden 1992, Roth 1988, Todorova 1999 et al.), stereotypes in the Balkans about "the Other" loom large. This was reflected in my research setting as well, where Serbs made use of numerous allusions to their 'Others,' be they geographically remote outsiders or ethnic groups living on the same territory. In fact, members of the different former Yugoslav ethnic groups, i.e. Croats and Muslims, who were displaced in the U.S. were closely tied together through memory, biography, and kinship to their homelands. Yet Croat, Serb, and Muslim individuals seemed to have little or nothing to do with each other even when coming from the same country and speaking the same language. Asking her what she felt when she meets a Croat and if they conversed with each other, Dragica Dušić, a young female graduate student responded: "*Nothing. Nothing. The only thing you have in common is the thing that put you in conflict with each other. So what's the point?*" Dragica described to me her strategy of avoidance, since it was not always so easy to go out of each other's way. Upon hearing a stranger talk Serbo-Croatian in a store, in a café or on the street, joy of recognizing a person who came from the same country was immediately halted by caution. If listening to the dialect didn't suffice, because usually one can determine if somebody is from Croatia, Bosnia, or Serbia, she did start a short introduction. But if it turned out that the other was a Croat, the conversation usually ended. With Muslims the case is somewhat different, since many Serbs insist that Muslims are really Serbs who have been forced to convert to Islam during the Ottoman Empire. Therefore, Muslims are incorporated into the Serbian body. Nevertheless, the high number of casualties among Muslims and Serbs during the last war created a huge distance in the diaspora, too. It seemed that it was more common to talk about each other than with each other.

Generally, Croats frequently figure as a boundary marker in order to set Serbs apart, and more specifically they serve as an antidote to Serbian drives for liberation. In the words of Budimir Pesić: "*The Croats are much more German, they don't care if the Germans or Austrians dominate them, they want to be like them. But the Serbs are much prouder and self-reliant, they don't just want to be ruled by the US; they want to do their own project.*" Couched in geopolitics and the historical power play on the Balkans, Serbs are not as radically separated from the world, as it might seem at first glance, but they view themselves largely in relation to their allies or enemies contributing to the presentation of Self. Serbs are identical with themselves, or try to become what they are, whereas Croats are trying to be identical with others, thus losing both pride and identity. To understand the Self then it is necessary to allude to the Other, or various Others, who serve as antipodes or binaries, be it Croats, Muslims, Albanians, or Americans (see Skrbiš 1999: 115-153). My findings correspond to Skrbiš' research among Croat and Slovenian immigrants to Australia, whose statements about the Other were predominantly negative (ibid.: 116).

One can go even further than stating the obvious and conclude, with Liisa Malkki, that narratives about the Other were concerned with an order in a more "cosmological" (Malkki 1995) sense, providing Serbs with a timeless moral world of good and bad, innocent and guilty. Mira Pesić's frequent allusions to the "genocidal nature" of Croats, e.g. serves as a splendid example: "*The Ustaši referred to us, not as a Serb but as a 'Vlach.' Vlach implies the Byzantine heritage, and they had a visceral hatred which was revived in the 20th century to such a degree, that when they were talking about the Orthodox, they would utter only hatred of Byzantine. But so many people cannot understand it in America, it is almost impossible to understand for them, why would anybody do that? It's a pathological thing with Croats, unfortunately.*" Here she is in line with a general discursive pattern of Othering that is predominant among the people I worked with. Of course, this pattern isn't bound to age or generation.

That the images of the Other are based on negative myths of identification, as becomes evident in the narratives, is the main thesis of MacDonald (2002) who argues "that negative myths have formed the nodal point of Serbian and Croatian nationalism, providing a much-needed stock of metaphors and imagery. Such myths enabled nationalists to legitimate many insalubrious and violent acts of statecraft. [...] Without these types of images, a national revival is simply unnecessary" (MacDonald 2002: 27). MacDonald critiques theories of nationalism for downplaying negative aspects in the imagination of the nation, such as persecution, oppression, or victimization. While, in MacDonald's view, Anthony Smith overemphasized the Golden Age as a 'myth of origin' that nationalists resort to,

Ernest Gellner was more dismissive to this positive 'folk concept,' arguing that myths of Fall and Redemption are of utmost importance for reinforcing a sense of tragedy to the vision of the nation. In trying to understand the explosive violent potential of the nation, MacDonald thus carves out a theory of "negative myths of identification," granting priority to those myths that center on victimology and perpetration instead of positive myths of the collective.

We are history!

„The Balkans produce more history than
they can consume locally."
(Munro in Brown 2003: xi)

Luitpold Wolkenstein, Austrian traveler and journalist who wrote about the Ottoman defeat in 1912-13, expected the region to lose its relevance and be consigned to "the cupboard of the yesterdays" (Brown 2003: xi). A century later, 'the yesterdays' have not lost their relevance; rather they seem to be carrying new meanings. In the narratives that I gathered, history, story, and life story are often hard to separate. Indeed everyday life and history were not seen as oppositions, but they were mixed together in sometimes stunning and overtly heated ways and at other times in artistic or poetic form.

If one takes Nada's narrative on obstinate Otherness, the role of the folk song *Tamo daleko* in the production of community, or the many statements on Serbianness: ruminations about the past and the backward view on history are always present. The historical perspective many of my Serbian informants hold was usually communicated to me in a most pervasive manner. What is important about narratives of Serbianness in exile, then, is not only the content but also the form, *how* something is communicated. The talks I had with Serbs represented hours of monologues, with hardly any opportunity for me to ask questions, the interviews entailing masterful narratives of lamentation, legitimization, self-performance, and persuasion. If at a dinner in a Serbian house, at a Slava celebration or during an informal interview, I often found myself in the position of the listener, stories about Serbdom and being Serbian or about somebody's work and everyday activities notwithstanding. Occasionally the long monologues were interrupted by rhetorical questions, such as "you know?," "you see?" or remarks like "I think," etc.. Here I assume that these speech acts reveal a rhetoric of complicity by indirectly asking for my consent to the viewpoints expressed. The participants were using me as a messenger to stake their claims on the United States and Europe, as well as to address the peoples and governments of the International Community.

Talking was not only a praised characteristic, it was also all-intrusive, and sometimes hard to endure, given the rare instances of the possibility to interact or participate on my part. In an extreme case, that of old Budimir Pesić, whose difficulty of hearing enhanced his drive to talk and not to listen, there seemed to be hardly any pause, not even when crossing the street. A few times I had to pull him away from the cars to the safe side of the pedestrian sidewalk, because he didn't seem to be in any hurry when walking from one side to the other and did not even for a minute stop the telling of stories and ruminations of the past that were so center-stage to him. The way that Budimir and others form visions of the world and of Yugoslavia, the role of the Big Powers and History, and how history could have turned to the better if certain events had not happened or if they had been twisted a little, mirrors Wolfgang Libal's (1996: 143, my translation) remark, "[t]hat which they have said often figures as something they have done." Talking and (hi)story telling appears as the most precious activity, if over a cup of coffee, good food, during an interview, or even when crossing the street.

In addition to a need to talk and to communicate Serbs also revealed the need to convince me of the claim: "We are really the victims!" That they are victims for times immemorial was underlined by the temporal specification "always," for instance asking: "*Why do we always have to suffer?*" Many of the conversations I had with people were rhetorically elegant and powerful narratives, prone with historical facts and historical knowledge – bare any trace of insecurity that is often inscribed in the figure of the immigrant. Many Serbs, if willing to be studied at all, insist on their own narrative choices. More often than not they don't want to be investigated in a formal sense and avoid answering straight to questions posed, but rather they dominate the talk and ignore, when possible my questions. Libal states: "Only one should not expect that they always remember what they told you earlier. ... What a Serb says he utters being full-fledgedly convinced, and he loves superlatives... And when it is told that Friedrich Barbarossa who was led to Serbia on his third crusade to the Holy Land learned from King Stefan Nemanjić how to eat with a knife and fork, not a single doubt is appropriate. Since they don't put themselves into question, their statements are not put into question, too" (Libal 1996: 142 f., my translation).

As Budimir pointed to me at the beginning of my fieldwork: "*You first have to read many history books on Serbs, maybe then people want to talk to you.*" Another time he assured me: "*It's nice that you talk to us here – but you have to emphasize our history!*" How Budimir formulates it, history and story telling are set apart from each other, history implying a truth claim and meta-level, while personal experiences are less authoritative, but they can form an intrinsic part of history. Many Serbs present their homeland as the "land of the living past" (Judah 2000: 313), and each of "them" is an embodiment of that past which is communicated with great eloquence. Father Dimitrije, for example, when narrating his life story to me, began by referring to history: "*I grew up in a country that, you could say, was pregnant with history. My playground of childhood times was made up of Greek, Byzantine ruins and the remnants of a Roman aqueduct. Medieval Serbian monasteries had a huge impact on the landscape of my youth. You can say, the ghost of history blew over my life. I lived in history, but we didn't realize it, it was normal for us.*"

Not his birth or his family's origin serves as the introduction to his life story – that means individual circumstances of a life –, but the historical make-up of Serbia, or in poetic style "the ghost of history." Reckoning the country and its history most significant Father Dimitrije does not stand alone. After meticulously transcribing life stories people entrusted to me, I came across narratives where the transcribed pages made up for twenty pages of pre-history before a person's birth that means the history of Serbia or Yugoslavia, only! Thus we can invoke Čolović again, who states: "A Serb exists only as a branch of his tribe, and that means he exists before his birth and even dies before his birth. ... 'It was on Kosovo that I was born, I was on Kosovo before my birth'" (Čolović 2002: 65). But what is most interesting in Father Dimitrije's narrative is the last sentence: "I lived in history, but we didn't realize it, it was normal for us." This statement, I suggest, points to the crucial meaning of the place of exile as a nursery of nationalism and history. At the same time as in the homeland history is not necessarily significant and taken for granted, the perception of the past is sharpened away from "home." For Father Dimitrije, as well as for many others, the spatial and temporal distance of California makes recollections of the past most attractive.

However, the past rarely remains past. Instead of an easily confined history that is hidden in historical monuments or embodied in a ghost, especially in war times, Serbian history intrudes into the everyday public sphere and the private life of a person. The crucial aspect of Serbian history is its presenting at a time of crisis.

A few days after the onset of the NATO bombing against Yugoslavia in 1999, Andreja, my husband Jeremiah, his older sister Dragana, who was just visiting from Budapest, and I were sitting in Andreja's living room in Berkeley, watching the news. Disrupting her plans of emigrating to the U.S. as her younger brother had done eight years before, the war between Serbia and NATO was extremely unsettling to her at a moment when she was not only spending her vacation in California and visiting her brother but also preparing her possible future resettlement in the United States.[57] My husband and I had demonstrated great interest in everything Yugoslavian, Ser-

57. She then quickly canceled this plan in the course of the military conflict, and only returned for a visit in 2003.

bian, Serbian History, and the embattled province of Kosovo. Dragana's anger and frustration became passionate when we watched CNN with the latest news on the first air strikes over Belgrade. After switching off the TV, Jeremiah and Dragana sat on the Persian carpet in the living room, Jeremiah offering his critique of American arrogance, ignorance, and aggression. Dragana, drawing the map of Serbia and Kosovo with her finger on the carpet and explaining the history of the land, indignantly screamed at my husband: "*Jeremiah! Jeremiiiah, History is in us. We are history!*"

Notwithstanding our honest attempts at grasping Serbian History Dragana insisted on the impossibility of separating Serbs from their history. But what was she telling us? What did it mean that history is *in* "them"? Why Dragana's reproach against Jeremiah, after he had spoken according to her attitude? In this certain moment instead of being content with Jeremiah's version of history Dragana's anger at everything American was directed against her American friend, the only American present in the room. How could he dare to explain the violent political turmoils, if to her political liking or not? Serbian history was "in them," it belonged only to Serbs, not to any American; it was something intimate, a possession that nobody non-Serbian could *really* grasp. Perhaps, in peace times Serbian history was another matter, but in the wake of the U.S./NATO bombing of Serbia, an American had nothing to say about "them." What then is the role of history in narratives of Serbs about themselves?

Mark Thompson in *A Paperhouse* (1992), tells of how he met a couple of young Serbian engineers on the train from Bar, trying to explain to him what went on in the war in Croatia. "The Croatian fascists had to be stopped," they said, "the Serbs in Croatia were suffering genocide, as under the Ustaše in the Second World War" (Thompson 1992: 197). When the British correspondent objected by reasoning that during World War Two hundreds of thousands of Serbs had been killed, whereas in Slovenia only a few dozens of Serbs had died before the war started, the engineers frowned and looked unhappy. Beginning to talk about Serbs' sacrifices for the Croats and Slovenes since 1914, and how they were paid back with separatism, the engineers enumerated a series of historical 'facts' about Yugoslav injustice against Serbs.

> "You would think these young engineers had lost at the battle of Kosovo in 1389, rebelled with Karadjordje in 1804, beaten the Austrians in 1914, risen against the Axis in 1941, been terrorised in Kosovo in the 1980's. In Serbs' speech the people are conjured as one person, who is also Serbia; every generation becomes one generation, which is Serbia too. "Serbia has had enough," they warn you, like a lawyer whose client's Jobish patience is finally drained." (Thompson 1992: 198)

So when Dragana cries out that Serbia is in "them," she infers that centuries of battles, fights, war, and occupation is part of her as of every Serb, similar to the speech of the young engineers. What Čolović mentions with regard to the impossibility to transfer to one's self the thoughts, actions and feelings of others seems true here, too. Claiming to possess history bodily and spiritually, Dragana in her verbal attack against Jeremiah conveys: "Those who are outside do not understand anything, they do not participate in anything of ours" (Čolović 2002: 163). Therefore, in congruence with the thesis of obstinate Otherness elaborated above, History was different; it was absolutely impenetrable to intercultural dialogue. But again, as was the case with Nada and many others, the refutation of dialogue was not as absolute as it was posed to be. Serbs' need to communicate, to tell me stories, was paired with the refusal of any outsider's understanding, and this paradoxical relationship to communication with outsiders did not lead to silence but to the paradoxical narratives that I gathered.

Besides claims of absolute uniqueness of being Serbian and the unchangeable quality thereof, I noticed a serious break with these nationalist discourses, which became apparent when the issue of their place of residence came up. This break and its ramifications will be explored in the next section.

Serbian Americans and "Yugoslav" Americans

> „When I came to the U.S. I was rather apolitical and I had nothing against this country. I remember how I received my US passport: I hung up a big American flag at our house! At the beginning of the war I took it down. Today, my sister even calls me a 'radical Serbian nationalist.'" (Dragana Reynolds, 55 years old)

Since the Serbs I worked with do not live in Serbia but in the United States, it is striking how little reference to being American is made. U.S. citizenship is clearly secondary to being Serbian. This is even more striking, if one considers the singular case of the United States with regard to immigration. Nowhere else are immigrants incorporated into the body of the nation-state as quickly as in the United States, and nowhere else do Germans, Indians, Chinese, Mexicans, just to mention a few, become "naturalized" citizens as easily as in America. It needs to be pointed out that as with the meanings of "Serbian identity," the construction of an "American identity" involves creative processes of imagination (Anderson 1991). In the words of Basch, Glick Schiller, and Blanc (1994: 40): "The construction of the 'American people' as white has served to justify and perpetuate the subordination of the African-American population as well as to assimilate certain immigrant populations and exclude others." Due to their skin color and "European" background, Serbs have always been included in the "white" body of Americans, although "assimilation" was not a smooth process for all, especially not for the early immigrants working in the steel mines.[58] Nevertheless, as the authors state, "[b]ecause the United States is a nation of immigrants, the task of imagining an American people has been especially problematic" (ibid.: 41). Therefore, I wish to emphasize that when the participants in my study refer to "being American" the declaration is open to a wide range of meanings instead of referring to a fixed definition.

In order to explore the relationship between "being Serbian" and "being American," it is useful to investigate a major dividing line within the Serbian community along which, I argue, Serbian identity and American identity are negotiated intensely.

One of the most striking oppositions I encountered in my fieldwork is that between descendants of immigrants, second or third generation American-Serbs, who are active in the Serbian Orthodox church, and mostly younger professional exiles who recently arrived from the former Yugoslavia. Not surprisingly, the two groups chosen maintain the greatest social distance possible both in temporal and in spatial terms. Nonetheless, similar disagreements that are at play here can also be found among individuals that are much closer with regard to time of arrival and region of origin. However, for the illustration of disagreements upon Serbian national identity one example shall suffice.

Crucial for the way that members of the two 'groups' perceive each other is often the first meeting in the United States – mostly taking place in the Serbian Orthodox Church, in many areas the only ethnic meeting place. This meeting can be characterized by a good deal of estrangement and suspicion. When being asked what her impression of the Serbian Orthodox church was, twenty-six-year-old Milena from Belgrade who arrived in the United States in 1999 responded: "*I was totally shocked when I first visited the divine liturgy! You should know that in Serbia I didn't go to church often, I was brought up communist, but I did go [to church, B. B.-L.] sometimes. The church there is completely different. So when I saw these people here who don't speak our language, who haven't even been to Yugoslavia, I thought: These are just Americans, and this is an American church!*" Comments such as these are no rarity among the younger recently arrived Serbs I got acquainted with.

It needs to be mentioned that the Serbian Orthodox church plays a singular role in the former Yugoslavia and in the Serbian diaspora which his-

58. See Andrei Simić's and Maria Budisavljević Simić's documentary *The Children of Lazo's Grove* 2004 which focuses on the often devastating experience of Serbian and other Southslav immigrants at the turn of the century who worked in the steelmines of Pittsburgh, Pennsylvania, and Chicago.

torically and up to today is the main religious and social organization for "preserving" Serbian identity[59] (Buchenau 2003, Simić 1996, Vrga 1975 et al.). Keeping this central role of the church in mind, it is no wonder that amazement quickly dwindles when the young immigrants realize that this is the place which is unsurpassed in its value for meeting other young Serbs and practicing Serbian religion (often in this order). Thus, many recent immigrants have actually become members of the parish, visit the Sunday liturgy at least for the main celebrations or even every few weeks, and have thereby brought more diversity to the religious community. Others decide to withdraw for various reasons, one of them being their atheist background they prefer to not give up. As my friend Andreja, who left Sarajevo in 1991 and in some situations calls himself a "Yugoslav," reasoned: "*I was raised communist, I lived all my life in communist Yugoslavia. I never went to church – and now I should go to church in the United States? It doesn't make sense.*" Another informant, thirty-five-year-old Vaso when offering his impressions of the church community to me summed it up as follows: "*They are not Serbs and the church is not really Serbian.*" Nevertheless, Vaso and his wife frequently attend concerts, celebrations, and festivals in the church and sometimes the Divine Liturgy.

Amazement with the first visits to the church was usually mentioned with regard to the parishioners and the procedures in the divine liturgy, for example the use of the English language[60] and the fact that there are benches in the church on which parishioners sit down periodically instead of standing exclusively as is done in Serbia. But in the utterances "they are not Serbs" and "these are just Americans" there lies also a moral judgment of "Americans," who serve as a negative antipode to being Serbian. Ambivalence towards "the American people" and the U.S. government, exemplified best by its foreign policy, are also at play here, pointing at the problematic relationship of Serbian immigrants towards the United States (in times of crisis).

Negative imagery about America

On one hand, Serbs who left for the U.S. often acquired material wealth and a standard of living that they could never have attained in their homeland or as immigrants to Western Europe. On the other hand, that same country that provided them upward mobility and an often satisfying life took an 'anti-Serbian stance' not just in political and media terms but also

59. Or for creating and maintaining a certain vision of a rather static "Serbian identity," since preserving implies that something that does actually exist (which is not the case with identities) is kept in its primordial state.
60. In some churches English is used more than in others. Most often, both languages are spoken, but depending on the priest (if he was born and educated in the U.S. or in Serbia) and the parish, one is the primary language and the other the secondary.

in military ways, when bombing Serbian positions in Eastern Bosnia in 1995 and Yugoslavia in 1999. Thus, strategies of trying to complement the Serbian and the American sides in their lives had to almost necessarily be difficult and schizophrenic.

Moreover, the absolute separateness between being Serbian and belonging to any other nation, which has already been discussed above, takes on special significance with regard to American identity. Čolović (2002: 67) points out that ethnic nations such as Croats, Albanians, Muslims, and Romanians are seen as having *'ersatz identities,'* as having abandoned their true, Serbian identity.

> "Americans have no identity at all, for they are an artificial community, without roots, without tradition, without collective memory, without soul. ... With others, the national identity is in a bad neglected state. Western Europeans, bogged down in materialism, humanism and cosmopolitanism, are left with a kind of sick, limp, rotten identity. They barely remember who they are."

In this sense, the American identity is synonymous with an "anti-identity," a suggestion which was made by several people I got acquainted with.

Milan Gajić put the "problem" of being American as follows: "*Why do you think that Americans are screwed up like this? Because they don't grow roots.*" Americans lack tradition, temporal depth and they have no history. Another participant, my friend Andreja, claimed that memory in the U.S. is so short that Americans forget what happened four or five years ago. As Milan further states, while we drink a glass of wine in a restaurant: "*That's America, it is cheap, it is just facade and entertainment, just look around here [looks at people sitting at tables next to us,* B.B.-L.*], there is nothing in these people, they are just shopping, consuming, they are empty.*"

Mira Connor Pesić laid out the lack of national consciousness among Americans as follows: "*Americans have a very short memory. Indeed, they are not even really a nation. After the war, after the 1990's, they even forgot what was going on. Now they think again that we are from Siberia. So their memory doesn't bring them very far. Like all the Anglo-Saxon colonies, Canada, Australia, the U.S., they are very fast in recruiting their population from everywhere. There is no single country in the world that is not present in the U.S.. In one of my lectures I asked people present how many of their ancestors had been fighting in the independence battles of 1776 and 1864. Nobody raised his arm. But in the old country you can go back 16 generations, people have links to the past. So this here is not really a nation, it's more molecules, not an atom.*"

In all these utterances, the criteria "memory and lack of memory" become the main dividing line. It is assumed that Americans live only in the present and accordingly see the world not in its depth, but only from its surface. With regard to collective identities in Bulgaria, Evgenija Krašteva-Blagoeva (2003) makes a very similar observation:

> "As a foreign anthropologist used to say: "You are living more with the past than with the future." This is an expression of a basic difference between the East and the West of Europe – between "memory and lack of memory." For Westerners, history is more of a curiosity, a subject defined to textbooks. This lack of memory enables them to act with only the present in mind (Longinović 2002: 42). For the small nations of the East history is of particular importance: they are constantly imagining and experiencing it, creating a "victimized history" of their own, and they are always victims in the political games of the great powers."

This manichaeic view of "America" as an "anti-nation" due to its "lack of memory" and the embodiment of American popular culture set apart from ethnic roots and belonging adheres to Simić's (2002) analysis of Southslav nationalism. According to Simić, Serbian nationalism is not opposed to Western democracies but to capitalist American popular culture, which is intruding into every living room on a global scale (Simić 2002: 144). In this vein, Milan's immigration to the U.S., as he now underlines, taught him above all, to speak with Simić, that "[n]ational identity too remains widely attractive and effective and is felt by many people to satisfy their needs for cultural fulfillment, security and fraternity" (ibid.). In other words, in the process of leaving the homeland and taking up a new life in a new country in which the past and ethnic identity are rather underscored, belonging to a "people" or having "roots" is charged with increased meaning exactly because of the disillusionment of American popular culture[61].

Thus, many young émigrés first recognize the "Americans" in the Serbian-Americans who have resided for a long time in the U.S., and de-emphasize the special "Serbian" immigrant past in them. The statements of the "newcomers," as the young immigrants are often called, reveal that the encounter with "old-timers,"[62] or Serbian-Americans who were born in the United States, sets in motion various arguments on difference, boundaries, and the essential 'character' of the nation. As opposed to Čolović's nationalist sources pointing to a spaceless, timeless, and unchangeable Serbdom, in my findings Serbdom is prone to distinctions, changes, contradictions, and "impurities." American-Serbs are referred to by recent immigrants only by way of social distance and in terms of negativity and

61. See Malkki 1992 on "national geography" and the metaphor and meaning of roots.

lack of attributes: "these" people are "just Americans," they don't speak "our" language.

Two collectivities, "Serbian Serbs"/"Yugoslavs" and "American Serbs," are set apart from each other by applying national vocabulary and an exclusionary rhetoric vis-à-vis each other. Serbs raised in the former Yugoslavia refer to their atheism and use of Serbian, "our" language (in terms of it not being used by the "Other") as opposed to the English speaking Serbian Americans, who often haven't visited the homeland. Being Serbian is here defined by language, territory, socialization in Yugoslavia, and in political terms, as having been raised not just in Yugoslavia but in "communist" Yugoslavia. Such territorialized view of national identity precludes all second generation Serbs who are often not proficient in the Serbian language, or who haven't traveled to Yugoslavia. A "pure" Serb is therefore temporally and spatially defined as a Serb who grew up in Yugoslavia and was socialized under Tito's Yugoslav socialism. The diaspora is only seen as American, as having nothing to do with Yugoslavia, and as per se different. If the newcomers render themselves in such stark contrast to the diaspora one needs to ask: How do the recent immigrants see the future of their own national identity in emigration when being Serbian is tied in such a static way to a classic territorialized definition of the nation?

The existence of a diaspora that is different from the population in the homeland creates puzzlement and is not subsumed under the same ethnonational category or Serbian nation (*narod*). The quotes reveal a contradiction, since emigration does not yet fit into the picture of a national identity that the young people who *did* emigrate imagine. In this line of argument no connection is perceived between the diaspora and the homeland, as if the newcomer Serbs were not themselves members of the diaspora, or as if the old-timer Serbs did not in certain ways belong to the homeland or the Serbian peoplehood. Seen from this angle nobody is really Serbian in the U.S. anyway! Transnationalism, so to speak, is erased from the imagination of Serbdom, as if it didn't exist. But what is believed to be really Serbian, if neither he nor the old generation is apt for the term?

---

62. The terms "newcomer" and "old-timer" are problematic concepts, involving temporal 'Othering' as discussed in Fabian 1983. They are being used in the literature on Serbian immigration, without questioning their semiotic content. Since the informants I talked to employ the terms I decided not to omit them, but choose to make clear their relational character. On one hand, to Serbs arriving in the 1940's two persons who immigrated in the 1960's or 1990's are both newcomers, whereas to Serbs who came to the United States in the 1980's everyone arriving in the 1980's is a newcomer. On the other hand, for a Serb arriving in the late 1990's about everyone who lives in the United States for longer than a decade might be called an "old-timer." Finally, "old-timers" is sometimes reserved for those Serbs only who are the descendants of pre-World War Two immigrants. Thus, I employ the notions "newcomer" and "old-timers" only in the relational content that is inferred by the informants.

The more American you are, the more Serbian you are?

If I now turn to the Serbian Americans and investigate their views on the "newcomers" and their national identity in the United States, I find a similar argument of "purity," although the lines of reasoning run differently. First of all let me note, that in the wake of the recent Balkan war there was a general shift from the designation *American*-Serb to *Serbian*-American.

To understand the implications of being American one also needs to take into consideration the makeup of United States society which is based on immigration and is therefore fundamentally different from European notions of membership to a nation-state that are based on blood, kinship, and territory (see e.g. Anderson 1983, Bornemann 1997, Linke 1999). Juxtaposing her insights in national identities in Europe with being an American, Mira Pesić compares migrant identity in both continents as follows: "*In Europe you are a loyal citizen of a nation by birth and you stay one, like Peter Ustinov. Although living in England he was always Russian. You can live in France as a German, but you are a German. In the U.S. it's different. When you come as a German, Serb, Japanese you are not an American yet, but you have to become one.*" In short, that American society with its huge intake of migrants offers and expects an incorporation or acculturation has profound consequences for Serbs and other diasporic people. Whereas in Europe, the national identity of the homeland stays with the first generation and mostly with their offspring for various reasons, migrants in the U.S. can become citizens and Americans within a few years after arrival

Slavica is a sixty-eight-year-old American-born Serb who never visited the former Yugoslavia, but had planned to do so in 1991, when due to the sudden outbreak of the war she canceled the trip. Born and raised in Michigan by Serbian parents who introduced her to the Serbian Orthodox church as a child, she continued to visit the church and sang in the church choir ever since. Although she doesn't speak Serbo-Croatian I met her in a Serbian class in the church where she tried to learn her parents' language, if only for short conversations. "*Many of the newcomers [here in relational terms as all people arriving in the last decades, B. B.-L.] have grown up communist, without religion and lost their Serbdom. In the United States we try to preserve our cultural heritage and be true to Serbian Orthodoxy.*" This statement reveals how Serbian Orthodoxy and the Serbian nation are interconnected. A truth claim is made for being Serbian in the United States as opposed to Serbs who grew up in Yugoslavia.

What she describes with modest words in relation to religion, the "loss of Serbdom" due to "communism," was expressed in more radical terms by Sam Ivkovich, a third generation Serbian American, who is very active in the Serbian Orthodox church and holds key positions in the Serbian

Unity Congress (SUC), one of the most prominent diaspora organizations world-wide:

> "*The later they came the less Serbian they were, and the more Yugoslav they were. I remember being at a friend's home down in the San Jose area, this is maybe five years ago, in the middle of the war, when Yugoslavia was being ripped apart, and it had to be 50, 60 people there... A Serbian gathering, and I would say there were with an exception of my wife and myself one or two other couples they were all young Yugoslavs, meaning from 30 to 55, maybe from 30 to 45, and I asked the host who had come immediately after World War Two, like 47, 48. I said: "How many people are here that identify themselves as Serbs?" He said: "One, they are Yugoslavs." And they were having a hell of a time. These people come here, they benefited from communism all their lives, their parents were communists, and now they feel awkward talking to us Serbs here. It was in the mid nineties, this was the intelligentsia of the Silicon valley, these are very successful, highly educated people, Serbs from Serbia, who were Yugoslavs, and they were having this difficulty of changing to being and acknowledging that they were Serbs. [...] As for myself I have always been Serbian. When my grandparents came at the beginning of the century there wasn't any Yugoslavia yet. They were Serbs, of course. You came to the little church in Moraga, it's the Serbian Orthodox church, and the Serbian churches that were built here from 1894 up in the gold country of Jackson happened to be always the Serbian Orthodox churches, never Yugoslav, although Yugoslavia came into being after World War One. Nothing changed, we were never Yugoslavs. And I will tell you that the people I grew up with as a young boy who were Croatians and Slovenians they were Croatians and Slovenians and never were Yugoslavs.*"

In this statement the regional origin, Belgrade, is viewed as inherently Serbian,[63] so that the *Beogradjanis*' commitment to communism entails an even greater affront against Serbian nationalism. Ivkovich, who has been partly raised by his grandparents in a mining town in the Eastern United States and learned Serbian "on his grandmother's lap," has a family history in the Lika area, before the unification of the South Slavs took place. Thus, the seventy-year history of Yugoslavia was kept at a distance, a distance of "purity" that could only be enabled by exile. In this vein, temporal and spatial distance led to a preservation of Serbdom, while growing up under communism necessarily led to 'betrayal.'

---

63. Belgrade could also be viewed as a very Yugoslavian place, since it was the capital of the socialist state and attracted people from all over the country to live there, with the consequence of many people declaring themselves as "Yugoslavs." However, since Belgrade was firstly the capital of Serbia and never became a place as multinational as Sarajevo, its Serbianness is usually affirmed, especially nowadays.

Or as Michael Djordjevich (see also next chapter), a sixty-two-year old leader in the SUC who came to the United States with his family as a boy shortly after the second World War, put it: "*The more American you are the more Serbian you are.*" In this logic, having been raised and socialized in the United States and taking an actively anti-Communist stance was the only way to remain Serbian, whereas Tito's Yugoslavia suppressed Serbian identity and religion, therefore turning people who stayed into traitors of Serbdom. With Basch, Glick Schiller and Blanc (1994: 42) one can explain this extreme version of hyphenated identity as follows:

> "The political response of the immigrants to this forceful and often forced recruitment into the "American" national polity seems to have been similar to the reaction of subordinated populations to nation building efforts throughout the world. They both "Americanized" and turned to their hyphenated American identities as a base area for political organizing for empowerment."

But the statement reaches further than that, since the absolute "Otherness," posed in so many ways by informants in the previous sections, is at once suspended: being Serbian and being American do not appear as contradictory as they did before. Far from it, the narrative suggests both identity claims to be interchangeable, if not synonymous. As opposed to the classic immigration paradigm of assimilation, acculturation or the "melting pot" (Glazer and Moynihan 1963), becoming American does not imply a departure from the Serbian identity. In fact, at the turn of the millennium ethnic identity seems to be so established, that dual identities do not even pose a paradox. Therefore, Djordjevich's remark appears to foreground how common the concept of hybridity (Bhabha 1994) has become not only for theorists on the subject but for the subjects themselves. In the end, as Djordjevich foregrounds, one can try to benefit from both "identities." Nevertheless, the question of belonging to both Serbia and the United States is an existential issue for many Serbs. In Djordjevich's words:

> *"That [whether to belong to the US or to Serbia, B. B.-L.] we all of us had to face on a really more profound level than you talk everyday – during the war where your allegiances are. I didn't have a difficulty resolving it. Because I said that regardless of circumstances there are some principles that are unchangeable. What's wrong, what's right, what is good, what is bad, what is beautiful, what is ugly. Basically, over our painstaking, historical evolution of humankind, we have come to certain conclusions what these things are. And those principles have no country, they have no borders, they are truly universal, we talk about global, that's truly global. What's right or wrong exists in every situation. As an Amer-*

ican I felt that our country, America after fall of Berlin wall, in November '89 had a world on its palm... It was on the top of the world, it was supreme power. And America should have led the world on a high level. I am practical enough to understand that the foreign policy cannot be moral all the time, but the foreign policy without morality is disaster, particularly for a world power that aspires to be global power like America, which based its power and its appeal on democracy, human rights, free speech and all the principles that are grounded in the constitution of the United States. And that would distress me and annoy me that it didn't. I found America, my country, did a lot of injustices... And as a good American, I fought this in politics. Now, we fought against the big government and intrusion here, domestically, all of a sudden internationally our government became overwhelming, it was trying to tell all the world what to do. And after 9/11 people ask: Why do they not like us? Why do they hate us? Because we are stupid, we didn't do our thing. America was not moral, America was phony. How I resolved this conflict? Very easily. I was trying to go on that straight path. If the Serbia was not there, I would say you are wrong, go and do something different. America was there. I went to Washington and fought and criticized, I had a lot of support in the congress particularly. Within me I try to combine the best of the two cultures. ... Of the Serbian values I regard highest the principle of defending your nation, but in America I think optimism, tolerance, drive are most crucial, a sense of fairness, those are the values that Serbs can stand badly. I think American optimism is basically in the sense: We can do it. We have shown that we can do it. But Serbs can have an optimism, if you want. We have shown, we have survived the Turks, 500 years. We survived all the wars, we survived everything, and we stayed what we are, we can do it."

This narrative sheds light on several issues surrounding the dual identity of being a Serbian and an American. By the way, in the final remark "we stayed what we are," Djordjevich alludes to the same tautological rhetoric already discussed with regard to "obstinate Otherness." Again, it is a nationalist phrase which points to the primordial, unchanged nature of Serbian identity, but bare any content. Stressing foremost his American patriotism, it is well possible that Djordjevich still calls himself an *American*-Serb. In fact, the frequent allusions to "our America," "my America," "to be a good American," and finally the assertion of U.S. hegemonic power reveal an outspoken American nationalism[64].

Grounded in the firm belief in the moral superiority or "goodness" of the democracy and human rights paradigm, which he regards as universal, Djordjevich embodies both a radical liberal ideology as well as a self-righteous American hegemony. His narrative is ripe with binaries, such as

64. I deliberately chose the formulation "nationalism" instead of "patriotism," because I see in this narrative not only the assertion of pride in the homeland, but of a belief in its superiority over other countries (if necessary also by military means).

"good" and "bad," "moral" and "immoral." Interestingly, the apparent contradiction between his country of origin and his country of residence are easily brushed aside, when he states, that "*if the Serbia was not there... America was there.*" Or, if he couldn't go to Belgrade and influence politics there, "*I went to Washington.*" As is the case in Djordjevich's Serbian and American identity claims, Serbia and the U.S. are used interchangeably – and so is nationalism applied to both.

In a way, this logic expresses the basic principle of long-distance nationalist lobbying practices, symptomatic of American ethnic groups successfully copying the very money-intensive model of U.S. political campaigning in order to further their own particular, ethnic politics.[65]

But I still wonder how he can keep an image of the Self and political identity coherent, given the enormous ambiguity that does prevail? Or, how does he combine his anger against some aspects of American foreign policy with his unrevered support of the American nation-state? Here, I am easily reminded of Herbert Marcuse's *One-Dimensional Man* (1964: 19f.), a philosophical analysis of the capitalist American system. Marcuse characterizes this system as "taking in all alternatives or repelling them," in order to avoid change. In Marcusian terms, what he calls the problem of the co-optation of contradiction and dissent, Djordjevich's random critique against the military or foreign policy, which is well apparent in his narrative, is at the same time erased as it is voiced. At the least, it does not impact much on the narrator's unequivocal conservative pro-American stance.[66] Contradiction, in this case, does not disturb a nationalist imagination intended for coherence and unambiguous persuasion.

In contrast to Djordjevich, Mira Connor Pesić does not try to "talk away" ambiguity. Instead, she explains ambiguity by recurring to the existence of a dual identity, pointing to the social position of the immigrant: "*I think, even if we were more people and had invested as much money as Jewish Americans or Arab Americans we wouldn't have been that successful, because we have that principle of 'gostoprimstvo'. We feel, even if we have been here for 50 years or even for five generations, that we are guests and we don't want to smash windows in this country. We are patriotic for Serbia, but so are we for this country.*" Therefore, American patriotism results from the hospitality and, plainly speaking, the economic opportunities offered by the society of residence. In this conceptualization,

65. See also next chapter on the SUC.
66. Curiously, there are more contradictions underlying the relationship between Serbia and the U.S. than the one which is referred to here, the American/NATO offense against Serbia and Serbian positions in the former Yugoslavia in the course of the Third Balkan War. As will be discussed in more detail in part two, many Serbian Americans, including those who were politically conservative and Republican-minded, were always uneasy with the U.S. government's acceptance of Tito's socialist regime.

political dissent, no matter how serious it is, cannot override the fundamental code of thankfulness to the 'hosts.'

Another participant, Saša Gocić, who arrived in the U.S. in the mid 1950's focuses more on the tension developing from the paradoxical relationship between being a Serb and an American:

> *"There's conflict in the church. Like one journalist came to me and asked what I thought of the bombing, if I supported it. I said: 'Who can support that his own sister gets bombed? She is a little older than me, lives in Belgrade, and got bombed already, crouched in a shelter in the Second World War – and now again! How can I support that?' But the priest in Jackson was asked too and he was pro-bombing. He said: 'If you want to be Serbian here you have to be American.' Like, be a big American and you are Serbian. I am a good American, but I am also Serbian!"*

The two utterances reveal slight variations on the same topic: without Americanization or acculturation a Serb in the U.S. cannot be Serbian, or more precisely s/he cannot effectively influence diaspora politics and/or support family and friends in the homeland. While in one (Djordjevich's) statement the complementary relationship between being American and being Serbian is formulated in terms of a success-story, another statement (Saša's) emphasizes the conflict inherent in this logic. As the latter underlines, to be loyal to American foreign policy, even if the bombing of Serbia is concerned, takes the complementary logic too far. And yet, Saša nevertheless feels that he is "a good American" and a Serb. But to take a decisively anti-bombing stance, as Saša exemplified, does not necessarily imply a refusal of American values either.

What are at stake in these narratives are individual interpretative strategies to cope with a paradox that cuts deep through biography, family, and political persuasions. After all, being an American (or a Serb), far from referring to a fixed meaning is open to individual projections and visions: Mira, Djordjevich, and Saša all address what it means to be American and Serbian, and yet they speak about very different things. But what links their narratives is the inherent attempt at achieving a balance between American and Serbian identity in times of deep antagonisms. They have to come to terms with an in-betweenness on an extraordinarily tough terrain. Complex processes of negotiation are at work in order to construct a coherent story of being a Serbian immigrant to the United States at a moment when otherwise established dual loyalties are extremely difficult to maintain. What all three people have in common is an identity politics built on discursive strategies trying to bridge the current gulf between their American national identity (or what people perceive as such) and Serbian national identity (or what people perceive as such) in the wake of political crisis and war.

Symbolic capital of Serbian Americans and 9/11

To understand the connotations of the statement "The more American you are the more Serbian you are" one also needs to take into account the make-up of Serbian diaspora organizations and the Serbian church with regard to questions of power and knowledge. Active "old-timers" or older second generation Serbs, although fewer in numbers, hold key positions and formulate main political agendas. After a life of hard work, professional achievement, cultural assimilation, and financial security, they are acquainted with American society in intricate ways. Many are well to do and have established political networks, as in the case of Djordjevich and Ivkovich who are both instrumental in the SUC. These and other men own big houses in prestigious neighborhoods, drive American SUV cars, Jaguars, or Mercedes, send their children to renown and costly universities, and they invite me to lunch in some of the oldest San Francisco upper-class restaurants, where they use their credit cards and dress in the latest style suits. One of my meetings took place at "Marcus and Neiman," a luxury shopping mall at Union Square in San Francisco.

Proud of being Republicans *and* Serbian nationalists, they lobby in Washington and have connections to politicians in the Republican Party, the congressman of Chicago, Kucinich, even being of Serbian descent himself. Being an American "patriot"[67] and Republican also implies a commitment to the policy of whiteness and assimilation: "At the core of the US concept of nation has been a concept of whiteness" (Basch, Glick Schiller, Blanc 1994: 40). But images of a U.S. identity are also influenced by an American foreign policy that aims at hegemony in the world, and of being incorporated into the powerful political strata of society. Being American, in this sense, thus means "knowing" the American ways to do things and finding oneself in the position to have power for lobbying more successfully for the Serbian cause. This, in short, can be called "symbolic capital" or „social habitus" (Bourdieu 1977).

67. The terms "patriotism" and "nationalism" need to be investigated more closely, as they are used to differentiate between a "positive" pride for the nation or *patria* and a "negative" obsession with the nation to the exclusion of other nations. Nonetheless, this distinction seems arbitrary at the most, since patriotism is usually only referred to with regard to Western democratic nation-states, and nationalism to 19th century Europe or "irrational" and violent ethno-national movements in the present. At the center of this differentiation lies an "Othering" in temporal and spatial ways that takes advantage of a long-standing predicament in Western culture and anthropology, the supremacy of Western "civilization" over Eastern "barbarism" and backwardness, that is in itself ethno-centric and violent. The first is accorded to progressive, non-violent phenomena, while the other is judged negatively, thereby precluding an understanding that lies beyond moral judgment. I argue that it is important to deconstruct the juxtaposition and to analyze the similarities and differences between patriotism and nationalism in Western countries and non-Western countries.

As Aihwa Ong (1999: 88), drawing on Bourdieus *Distinction: The Social Judgments of Taste* (1984), analyzes with regard to Chinese trans-nationals in San Francisco, Chinese-Americans "were intent on learning how to dress, walk, and generally comport themselves in ways that would make them "more acceptable to the Americans." Bourdieu maintains that in modern France, upper-class dispositions and habits (habitus), together with the acquisitions and display of certain credentials, luxury goods and social trappings, are practices that attest to the social distinctions of subjects. Elsewhere, Bourdieu (1977: 181) notes that symbolic capital is not convertible into economic capital. Nevertheless, as Ong points out (1999: 89) "symbolic capital operates according to market logic, something Bourdieu underlines by using terms such as "capital," "acquisition," "credit," "profits," and "balance sheets" to describe the activities surrounding symbolic values that generate high social returns."

That "social taste" attests to the social distinctions of subjects is a more general phenomenon, which I observed among the Serbs I worked with. Younger migrants, wearing baseball caps and dressing in casual sweatpants, by complying to the American social taste visibly violated the style of fashion they were used to in the former Yugoslavia, where elegance, exquisite dress, make-up, and an overall orientation towards Italian trendsetters dominated. The discrepancy between dressing "at home" and in the U.S. was demonstrated in the following statement by Lena Milenković: "*When I go home, I have to buy dressy clothes, so that people don't laugh at me. – My mom, when visiting me was shocked when she saw American women going shopping in sweatpants and not using make-up. At home you don't leave the house without applying lip-stick and rouge.* "Therefore, if wearing modern designer suits or baseball caps, Serbs seemed quite concerned about their visual appearance and compliance to the American social taste. Divergent practices of dressing and visual appearance also created distinctions that cut through the Serbian community.

When asking Mira Pesić what she thought of Ljiljana Dukić, a 36-year-old recent refugee from Bosnia, the old woman remarked contemptfully: "*She has too much make-up and wears mini-skirts. If you work with refugees you shouldn't try to impress them with your body!*" Her description about recent refugees who had lived for years in Germany before arriving to the U.S. ran in a similar vein: "*They stood in front of the IRC (International Refugee Center), homeless people, blacks around them and spoke Serbo-Croatian, not knowing that I understand them. They looked like prostitutes, short skirts, tight shirts, and lamented how great it was in Germany, how much cleaner and prettier.* "For Mira, dress clearly reflects social distinction, or a lack thereof. At play are also generational differences: Not being in touch with contemporary cultural tastes in Bosnia, where short skirts are quite common, the old woman automatically applies her American prudish social taste in order to distinguish herself from other Serbian women.

To conclude, social habit such as dress was a marker of class within and outside the Serbian community. Pointing to the crass misfit of dress in the case of recent refugees Mira demonstrates how she herself adheres to the American ideal of fashion, ignoring the accepted dress codes "back home." Symbolic capital or cultural practices of fashioning the Self according to existing societal ideals entail a crucial domain where "being Serbian" and/or "being American" is negotiated.

"American" values and "Serbian" values, though often rhetorically set apart from each other, sometimes do not differ as much as is intended by the speakers. Instead, they form a complementary nationalist discourse, a double discourse so to speak, that adheres to the ideals of American patriotism, gone nationalist. This can be well illustrated when looking at 9/11 and the repercussions of that event in the Serbian circles. What became a major global scenario, watched by millions of people all over the world, a televised war that simultaneously caught people in New York as anywhere else, symbolized a major tragedy to Serbs, too.

On the very same morning of the destruction of the twin towers, I was first unable to grasp the significance of the event. I called Budimir to set up a meeting as was planned for this morning. Budimir was obviously confused and upset on the phone, lamenting that this was "*a tragedy for mankind*" and that I should better not bother anybody in the next couple of days, that were to become days of mourning. I was quite puzzled about the seriousness in his words, and still not understanding the gravity of 9/11 I called other people, all telling me in a similar way that now was not the time to talk about anything else but the bombing of the WTC. Later on, 9/11 dominated talks with the Serbs that I met. Quite a few people were happy that now "the Islamic threat" that hit "them" in Bosnia and was supported by Western powers, was finally recognized as the enemy. It was hoped that U.S. foreign policy toward the Balkan would change in that Bosnian Muslims' alliance with "terrorist Islam" would lead to a revision of the Serb-American relationship. Finally and much too late, Serbs were to appear as the true allies of civilization against violent Islamism. A few Serbs voiced that they were content that finally the U.S. had to face the wars that waged in the world, paralleling the bombing of Belgrade and especially the Radio Center – which was a small version of a skyscraper and with the upper part burning did pass as a comparison for the gigantic twin towers – with the plane crashes in Manhattan. But most Serbs I met expressed strong feelings of commitment and mourning. In fact, Serbians' reaction to 9/11 even equaled that of the general "nationalist fervor" which took hold in American society and could be observed in the wake of the terrorist attacks on New York in 2001. The next Sunday in the Moraga Serbian Orthodox Church the priest expressed sorrow in his sermon. After the divine liturgy, meeting for lunch and coffee, not only was the latest event the only topic of conversation, but Serbs also participated in the "cult of the flag": many middle aged first and second generation women wore little brooches in the form of stars and stripes, one even wore a handmade sweater with a big American flag woven into the material, covering her breast and belly. Men, too, carried little flags on their shirts, and some remarked: "*This is a great catastrophe for our nation.*"

For me it was hard to believe that only two years after the NATO bombing of Yugoslavia, an event that deeply disturbed Serbians' feeling for the host country, loyalty to the United States would be expressed so unequivocally. In short, 9/11 represented a major "nation-building" event, turning even the most ardent Serbian nationalist into an American, or, bringing to the fore how loyalty to the Serbian nation did not preclude loyalty to the American state.

Chapter 2. The Unmaking of the Yugoslavs

As the preceding chapter has put forth, in order to understand Serbian long-distance nationalism it is important to take into consideration the heterogeneity of "expressive" identity declarations. Ranging from Serbian, Serbian-American, American-Serb, American, to "Yugoslav," identity declarations do not stand for themselves, but are referential terms used by subjects to set themselves apart from each other. Moreover, they change according to circumstances and situational contexts, such as the NATO bombing of Yugoslavia and 9/11. Furthermore, not everybody who declares him/herself a Serb is necessarily a long-distance nationalist. However, a strong feeling of national identity can easily be channeled into nationalist aspirations and political practices. In the following chapter I wish to analyze one set of discourses that has been so far neglected, and that is discourses on Yugoslavia and being "Yugoslav."

In the light of the essentializing narratives on being Serbian in the previous analysis, it is striking how marginalized the declaration "Yugoslav" is, and how it lost appeal to most of the migrants I conversed with. However, it is far from insignificant, and a decade after the war both negative and positive portrayals of Yugoslavia and a Yugoslav identity point to the fact that Yugoslavia still matters. Ochs and Capps (1996: 9) use "dominant stories," a term apt for narratives that emphasize Serbdom. They claim that dominant stories yield a false stability" for "the roar of countervalent stories is ever present, on the edge of recognition." Below I will explore the contested terrain of being a "Yugoslav," and how multiple identities form conflictual perceptions of the Self and the nation.

In the summer of 2002 the shrunk Yugoslavia finally perished from the world map in favor of Serbia-Montenegro, affecting not only people staying in the homeland but also Serbs abroad. Nationalism's victory in the Balkans also meant the demise of the anti-nationalist declaration "Yugoslav." Whereas reflections about homeland events from the distance leave people with ample opportunities to develop strategies of naming, declaring, and identifying themselves, Serbs in the diaspora, too, were under pressure to comply to an ethno-national identity. In the United States, a process of ethnic polarization occurred that was already underway in other diaspora communities all over the world: "[A]s Croatians, Muslims and Serbians in the former Yugoslavia, and the governments that controlled them, were carving up land, possessions and families in the Balkans, roughly along ethnic lines, people from the region living in Australia were breaking away from each other and similarly forming new relationships"(Procter 2000: 55).

Crucial for the nationalistic perspective in the diaspora is the claim that Yugoslavia "never existed" and was wrong to begin with. When I asked Zoran Martić from Croatian Krajina, who grew up in Yugoslavia and left the country as a young man in 1984, when he last visited Yugoslavia, he reacted in a consternated way: "*I have never been to Yugoslavia! Yugoslavia never existed, it was an artificial country, only created by Woodrow Wilson.*" In a similar manner Milan Gajić angrily corrected my use of "Yugoslavia": „*Birgit, how many times do I have to tell you that we are not from Yugoslavia but from Serbia?!*" The fervor with which both men try to distance themselves from the term implies that in order for Serbia to appear primordial and 'natural,' first the "reality" of Yugoslavia and its name have to be discarded altogether. Obviously, the forty-five year period of the socialist country was erased from the memory of many Serbs in the United States as was the case of Serbia under Tito's regime.

In "reality" therefore, the declaration "Yugoslav" fell victim to the war, as did so many civilian inhabitants. Yugoslavia *has* disappeared, as simple as that. According to Sekulić et al. (1994: 89) in 1989 the percentage of people declaring themselves as "Yugoslavs" was at 14.5 % in Bosnia, 4.6 % in Serbia, and 9.0 % in Croatia, or 10.6 % of the total population of the nation-state (Sekulić et al. 1994: 89).[68] In general, caution is necessary when dealing with statistical numbers regarding Yugoslav identity, since many citizens held multiple identities, but could only mention one of them on the occasion of the statistical survey. Furthermore, depending on the regional focus and political inclinations of the scholars themselves, authors dealing with the former Yugoslavia tended to either stress the "myth of tolerance" (Simić 2000: 104) or the "myth of divisions" (as one may add in response to Simić). Simić, who has little enthusiasm for the Yugoslav declaration, points out that "Yugoslav" as nationality was "frequently employed by Croatian and Bosnian Serbs fearing discrimination and thus serving as a means of masking their true ethnic identity" (Simić 2000: 106)[69]. Being more sympathetic with the Yugoslav idea, Andrew B. Wach-

---

68. I suggest that the number of people declaring themselves Yugoslavs politically or in everyday life may have been much higher, since population statistics do not take into account the multiple identifications of people. There were and are many Serbs who ethnically defined themselves Serbian but also declared themselves Yugoslavs. But as Simić points out there were also Serbs, especially in Croatia, who used the declaration „Yugoslav" in order to hide their Serbian background out of fear (according to personal communication with Andrei Simić). See also Simić 2002.
69. Holding that Yugoslavia was an artificial country and led people to hide their "true identity" is problematic, since all nations and ethnicities are artificial. Nations and ethnicities have been "imagined" in the 19th and 20th century, see Anderson 1991. Thus, to pose that a "true identity" exists, ignores the insight into the processes of creation and construction evident in any identity claims.

tel (1998: 1) refers to studies "in the 1960's [which] showed that a majority of the country's citizens held some form of Yugoslav national identity. Beginning in the late 1960's, however, the idea lost popularity precipitously, and at present it is preserved almost exclusively in the consciousness of émigrés scattered thinly all over the world" (Wachtel ibid.). In a more literary way Croatian author and "Yugo-nostalgic" Dubravka Ugrešić (1995: 7) contends:

> "The Yugoslav Gypsies who have scattered all over Europe are the only remaining Yugoslavs today, it seems, and the left-over ex-Yugoslavs have in the meantime become homeless, exiles, refugees, countryless, excommunicated, new nomads, in a word – Gypsies."

But is the Yugoslav idea really so popular among migrants as Ugrešić suggests?

In the following I will explore how people who had not done so previously came to call themselves Serbian, but also how especially young women maintained to call themselves "Yugoslav." I wish to underscore the multiple ways in which immigrants respond to an identity dilemma of global dimensions. As opposed to the rather nationalist connotations of identity I portrayed earlier, the anti-nationalist, "Yugoslav" statements in the present chapter are more personal, showing how political conflict impacted on intimate perceptions of Self.

'Mom, who am I?' – the politics of interpellation

„I don't know who I am, where I am from, to whom I belong ...". (Ugrešić 1994: 18 [transl. from the German, B.B.-L.])

If one meets a person from the former Yugoslavia still declaring him/herself "Yugoslav," to guess that this person is Serbian is in most cases right. Today mostly younger Serbs who grew up in the former Yugoslavia and migrated in the last two decades are faithfully trying to hang on to the country that violently dissolved. But not only generation and date of arrival, also the regional background impacts on identity choices. And to declare oneself as "Yugoslav" can also be a statement against nationalism's frenzy and the ideology of ethnic purity. But not only generation and date of arrival, also the regional and family background impacts on identity choices.

Budimir Pesić, an eighty-year-old retired electrician from Croatian Slavonia who was exiled to the U.S. fifty years ago, is one rare exception to the predominance of the young generation who came of age in the multicultural country and still hangs on to the declaration "Yugoslav." Showing me a map of Yugoslavia depicting the ethnic makeup of the country, he explained: "*The very problem is: Where do you draw the border? See all this patchwork, little spots? Many Serbs don't even know that they are not "pure" Serbs, so they cannot draw the line. That's why Yugoslavia has to grow together again. The people will remember that they once belonged together.*" Having experienced violent expulsion under the Ustaša regime and several years of imprisonment under Tito, Budimir's non-nationalistic pro-Yugoslav outlook is remarkable (see also Part Three). Focusing on the hybridity or mixture of ethnicity in the former Yugoslavia, the return to multinationalism and multiculturalism seems a mere necessity. Budimir's explanation was affirmed by stories Serbs told me about their ethnically mixed family backgrounds.

Whereas most Serbs, especially from Belgrade, sometimes vehemently claimed that they were Serbs, when the question of their ancestors came up, quite a few admitted that a father or a mother, a grandfather or a grandmother was Muslim or Croat. Thus, I came across deeply contradictory and ambivalent uses of identity declarations. For some these 'deviations' were simply not worth mentioning, but for others, especially those who experienced the Bosnian war, they represented a great dilemma that had to be solved somehow, but not always by applying the term "Yugoslav." As Ljiljana Dukić, a middle-aged Serbian teacher from Bosnia married to a Muslim, in California since 1997, who works in the International Refugee Committee (IRC) in Oakland stated: "*The hardest was to determine to which group you belong, to make it fixed. When the war started we were more often asked on which side we are. My children asked me: 'Mom, what am I?' I replied, that they are neither nor, that they were simply in-between. But this position in the middle was impossible, they had to decide for one side, my children are Muslims.*"

From the existential question "what am I" and the (impossible) in-betweenness, Ljiljana's children came up with the ethno-national identity of the father, thereby silencing the mother's Serbian side. This strategy of adapting to the dominant discourse of "taking sides," and trying to fit into the ideal of ethnic "purity," succeeded only by the declaration Yugoslav with which the in-betweenness is sought to be incorporated, instead of suppressed. Svetlana Milenković from Vojvodina, for example, a student of electrical engineering in Los Angeles, who I met at a New Year's Eve party in 2000, had not yet made up her mind "to which side" she belonged: "*I am from Novi Sad and I came here in 1995. But I am not a Serb, at least not like the others here. [looks around, B.B.-L.] My mom is Croatian; her family lived in Vojvodina for four generations. My father is from Montenegro – so what should I be? Yugoslav is the only suitable word.*"

As Robert Hayden (2000: 27) states, the rates of marriages contracted between people of different (Yugoslav) nationalities were highest in Bosnia and Vojvodina, Svetlana's place of origin, where the rates were at 30%. That the multiethnic family background of Svetlana and Ljiljana makes it problematic and painful to identify oneself is understandable, but it is not only people from mixed marriages who have difficulties to come to terms with their ethno-national designation. And, as Ljiljana already implied, "Yugoslav" doesn't need to be the solution to the dilemma. Since being an 'integral' Yugoslav belonged to a past that was highly contested by all former constituent ethnic groups, to many the 'Yugoslav option' did not seem viable either. željko, a musician and tennisplayer from Los Angeles, who had visited the U.S. on a state-sponsored tennis competition in 1991 before the breakup of the country and immediately decided to stay, calls himself "Z," as is written on his baseball cap: "*Yeah, maybe I am Yugoslav, but maybe I am an American? Or a citizen of the world, a cosmopolitan?*" As is clear through making the last letter of the alphabet his nickname, which is as unspecified as it can be, and thereby hiding his obviously Serbian name, željko tried to get as far away from personal and national naming as possible. Such a strategy of radical individualization as a subversion of the national paradigm illustrates how national identity became altogether strange and contested, so that cosmopolitanism proved an exit to the dilemma of "who am I?" Instead of declaring oneself "anything" željko and other people put the question mark center stage – they were putting identity *per se* into question by handling the topic elusively. As Mrs. Alija, a thirty year old Croat married to an Albanian and the mother of four expressed: "*I am a Muslim, I am a Croat, I am a Serb – what about this 'I am'?! I don't need that.*"

Consider the case of two nineteen-year-old Serbian American twin sisters who I met at a private barbecue party or *roštilj*. The twins were born in Yugoslavia but grew up in California. When traveling to Croatia and Serbia to visit their relatives after the war, they realized the agony over declaring themselves, wherever they are: "*What shall I tell them in Belgrade where I come from? After the war [the bombing, B.B.-L.] I didn't want to say that I am American. In Zagreb I didn't want to say that I am Serbian. And in the U.S. I cannot say that I am Serbian!*" The contestations over being American, Serbian, Yugoslav, Croat, Muslim, or of 'mixed marriage' in the diaspora mark a conflictuous, tensed, and painful arena, where the negotiation of identity proves difficult. What is crucial here is the situational contexts of identity declarations: persons may choose to declare themselves "Yugoslav" on one occasion and Serbian on the other. Furthermore, the narratives indicate that identities are also produced by processes of ascription, depending on *where* one is. Useful for the understanding of identity-politics here is Louis Althusser's (1971: 172) insight in "interpellation:"

> "We all have friends who, when they knock on the door and we ask, through the door, the question, "Who's there ?," answer (since "it's obvious") "It's me." And we recognize that "it is him" or "her." You and I are always already subjects, constantly practice the ideo-

> logical ritual of recognition all ideology hails or interpellates concrete individuals as concrete subjects, by the functioning of the category of the subject." (Louis Althusser 1971: 172)

Judith Butler, in her analysis of gendered body politics in *Bodies that Matter* (1993), took up Althusser's notion of "interpellation" by focusing on the constructedness of female and male notions of identity. Obviously, in the case of Serbian immigrants the identity dilemma is not primarily related to gender. However, the Althusser quote also points to the fundamental role of outsiders in the process of subjectivation.

The identity dilemma Serbian migrants find themselves in are especially crucial when introducing oneself to non-Serbs or Americans, whose associations with the word "Serb" are usually prejudiced by the negative media coverage and public discourse on the Yugoslav conflicts. Therefore, any declaration and conversation is always already influenced by the moral judgements and the public stigma against Serbs, in what Althusser calls "the ideological ritual of recognition." It is then no wonder that Serbs often employ moral terms, like "good" or "bad," when vaguely describing where they are from, instead of complying to the "ritual of interpellation." Take for example Svetlana McDonalds, political scientist and lawyer, in the U.S. since 1997: "*Often people ask you: 'Where are you from? – From Yugoslavia. – But where exactly? – From the good part.' Then they stop asking more.*" The fairy tale phrase is here used in order to suppress any political argument about her homeland, which would otherwise almost necessarily ensue. Or take Zoran Martić's statement which, by the way, starts with a sentence very similar to the Althusser quote: "*I do have American friends, and they know, but they don't know much, and I didn't try to convince them or anything. I didn't try to explain what I can't explain to myself, so when people asked me where I am from, I said I was from Serbia, and when they stopped talking to me I kept telling the next time, that I was from Zimbabwe.*" In congruence with the phrase "from the good part," Zoran employs a lie that is so obvious and at the same time puzzling that any discussion can be averted. Here, he indirectly admonishes that it is better to be from "any" country – even some 'backward' African country – than from Serbia. Also noteworthy is Zoran's remark "I didn't try to explain what I can't explain myself," pointing to the inexplicability of the Yugoslav conflicts. Both statements entail strategies of avoidance, aimed at hiding the "real" ethnic identity of the speaker.

All the narratives have one thing in common: to be in exile means to have to identify oneself. Nowhere else is the need to state where one is from, or to name one's national identity, as repugnant as in exile. It is in exile where the "hailing of identity" is unsurpassed in its frequency and intensity. As Svetlana Miroslajević, 34-year-old psychologist and my Serbian tutor in California remarked: "*Back there I was not very focused going around and saying that I am a Serb, I am a Serb on a daily basis. Whereas when you live abroad you have to keep saying that, you know, because even if I say: I am from Yugoslavia. They are like, now, from which part? Because they know, so you kind of have to eventually come to the point if you are a Serb or not. You have to identify yourself.*" The agony over feeling forced to identify oneself again and again couldn't be expressed more concisely.

Introducing oneself to outsiders directly turns into identifying oneself *ethnically*. This process of identification, as the narratives show, is enmeshed in strategies of avoidance, moral play, and subtle political comments. Being Serbian is not really self-evident, and it is not stable either, but it is part of a larger, global discourse about the wars in the former Yugoslavia that are taken into consideration.

Hence, to admit being Serbian in front of outsiders is different from any other ethno-national designation, or in the extreme case to be Serbian is assumed to be identical with being a nationalist. Mira Pesić Connor concludes that the public "demonization" of Serbs is so influential "*that you are already nationalist when you say you are a Serb.*" And Ljiljana Cvetković mentions: "*People tell me that I am nationalist, but they don't understand the difference between national consciousness and nationalism. For them everything is always nationalism.*" Both comments, while complaining about the prejudices people hold against Serbs, implicitly tell of the attraction of the non-nationalist declaration "Yugoslav," which can be inferred to be of use in order to avoid accusations of nationalism.

During an interview in Svetlana Smith's living room, the 44-year-old woman from Belgrade, in the U.S. since 1984, sits underneath a print of the famous black-and-white painting of the bitter Serbian army's retreat over the harsh, snowy Albanian mountains in 1916. When using the personal pronoun "we" for explaining to me the singularity of Serbian suffering in the two World Wars, I inquire closer into what she means:

B: When you are saying "we," do you think it is really "you"?
S: Well, I cannot say "the Serbs," because I am part of that, so that's why. I still think more likely I am ... I am never going to feel I am American myself, because I... there is nothing wrong with Americans, you know, the people are really nice and all that, but the government is a little bit screwed up [laughs], but I will never feel like an American, I will always feel like ... Yugoslav, Serbian from that part of the world.
B: But when you were living there till' 86? Did you feel like a Yugoslav, or more than a Serbian?
S: Oh yeah, oh yeah, I felt like a Yugoslav.
B: And that changed then in '91?
S: Well, yeah, it's ludicrous now saying I am a Yugoslav. I wish I could feel that way still, but when I meet somebody from Croatia, and saying I am a Yugoslav, they are going to laugh at me, you know.

B: But Yugoslavia exists, as a state it does.
S: It does, I met somebody this summer. I was in Yosemite climbing Half Dome with a friend, so I met somebody who said: 'Where are you from?'-'I said: From Yugoslavia.' – 'It doesn't exist,' said this person – 'Yes, it does'. – 'No it doesn't'. – 'So you are going to tell me where I am from? I know where I am from, you know.' So I said: 'Where are you from?' He said: 'I am from Great Britain, good old Great Britain,' you know. I said: 'So, well it's not so good' [laughs].

This narrative illustratively reveals that identity claims are not self-evident, static, or taken for granted constructs; they are embedded in moral, global, political and temporal dimensions. First using a vaguely dual identity, "I feel like Yugoslav, Serbian, that part of the world," as if she could still not decide "what she is," Svetlana expresses ambiguity in a very literal way. As the mother of two makes clear, being Serbian is connected to highly reflexive thinking, it is put into question by encounters with outsiders who set in motion identity claims, and it is constantly evaluated. The majority society, through the "ritual of interpellation" plays a central role in fixing identity claims. In her case, random comments of an Englishman, for example on a hiking trip in the Yosemite national park, clearly influenced her to give up her former declaration "Yugoslav" – if only to avoid such unsettling confrontations with her own past. Instead of just enjoying a nature trip in northern California, she was forced to approach her homeland from yet another angle.

National identity is not only an individual or collective phenomenon, but turns global in so far as the image of the nation vis-à-vis the rest of the world comes into play. By widening the picture and turning a critical eye on "good old Britain," thus forcing the Englishman she speaks with to face the mirroring effect when considering British imperialism and violence, Svetlana opens up a discourse on the moral stakes of Western nations.

In fact, only very few Serbs, when discussing identity with me, discarded the idea of Yugoslavia completely. People could identify with more than one category, be Serbs and Americans, or Serbs and Yugoslavs. As Andreja Marković contended: "*We were always Yugoslavs, my sister and I. We still identify ourselves as Yugoslavs, not Serbs, in our papers and everywhere. Yugoslavia worked well for 70 years. Had we only given it 20 years longer they couldn't have dismembered it, I am sure.*" Since I have heard Andreja's outspokenly Serbian ideas before, this pro-Yugoslav statement, evoked through my direct question about the category "Yugoslav," exemplifies the common insight that identities can be situated and changing. However, taking into consideration his use of the past tense, "we were Yugoslavs," does connote a temporal succession of categories. Other Serbs reflect this idea in utterances, which repeatedly exclaimed: "*How can you be Yugoslav today, if nobody wants to be in your Yugoslavia and it simply doesn't exist anymore? That's the dumbest idea.*"

Curiously, even people identifying themselves strongly and unambiguously with Serbia and refuting Yugoslavia altogether, when asked about Yugoslavia, did agree that Yugoslavia should have existed and should continue to exist – but here they mean the pre-World War Two monarchy, and of course not Tito's "treacherous" communist state. If younger immigrants turned Serbs or older Chetniks and Dobrovoljici who came as DP's after the Second World War, while averting Tito's Yugoslavia, a great many of them remarked: "*I am not against Yugoslavia, Serbs want Yugoslavia, but the Croats and others are against it.*" Danilo Milošević, an old man who could be called 'religious nationalist,' since he maintains his pro-Nedić attitude from World War Two and supports a religiously unified Yugoslavia – under Serbian rule, which he downplays in the conversation – considers Yugoslavia viable, if only "*the others would stop killing Serbs.*" Many of these statements are not to be understood in the sense of a multinational, non-nationalist viewpoints, but sometimes, as in the case of some Chetnik factions, more in terms of a "Greater Serbia" nationalism, as is the case of some Chetnik factions (Banac 1991). In exile the image of Yugoslavia becomes a surface of projections and processes of political negotiation from outsiders as well as insiders, ranging from personal to political, and from regional to global dimensions.

Overall, the statements of Zoran Martić, Andreja Marković, Milan Gajić, and many other men I have quoted so far suggest that the pressure to fix one's national identity and to serbianize is huge among those who arrived in the 1980's and 1990's. While all these "brain drain" migrants shared a Yugoslav past and to a certain degree identified with Yugoslavia, their readiness to comply with constructing essentialism is much more pronounced than in many women's narratives. In fact, one contributing factor for the prevalent "Serbianization" in the diaspora seemed to be the contact with nationalistic or Chetnik circles in the country of destination.

Below I will turn to the women's discourses in order to shed light on attempts at avoiding essentialism.

The Last Yugoslavs and the gendered nature of identity

> „I don't know where my former house is, I don't know where my future house will be, I don't know whether I have a roof over my head, I don't know what to do with my childhood, what to do with my origins, with my languages, I don't know what to do with my Croatian, my Serbian, my Slovene, or my Macedonian, I don't know what to do with my hammer and sickle, my old coat of arms and my new one, or the yellow star, what to do with the dead, with the

> living. I don't know what to do with the past or with the future... I just don't know. I'm walking chaos". (Ugrešić 1995: 37f.)

The author Dubravka Ugrešić is among the few Croatian intellectuals whose writings are a homage to the multinational society and whose horror with the brutal but also subtle changes point to the tremendous confusion and loss the breakup of Yugoslavia meant for many people on an everyday level. Enjoying a similar popularity in the West are Slavenka Drakulić's short stories, which like Ugrešić's works, were partly written in American exile. Ironically, in Croatia the writers have been widely marginalized, for Ugrešić, Drakulić and other Croatian and Serbian women writers[70] experienced an anonymous yet virulent attack on their personal lives and political ideas. The women were called "The Witches of Rio" for "their critical stance towards the dominant nationalist discourse, who at the time had attended a literary conference in Rio de Janeiro" (Jansen 1998: 86). By mentioning the acronym of the Brazilian city, the verbal attack connotes that not only is their gender suspicious, but also their engagement with a global, international conference instead of with the local, national Croatian cause.

From her residence in the United States Ugrešić, inspired by the (Serbian) Yugoslav author Danilo Kiš, expresses the disbelief and pain concerning the rapid dismantling of a state-structure and its ideology, which, in contrast to the small nationalist successor states, had offered its citizens social justice, economic wealth, and peace. Within a few years history, ideology, language, and social relations were abruptly and irreversibly changed, discarding the positive aspects of Tito's Yugoslavia as well as everything hinting at the relative harmony between the main ethnic groups. Ugrešić's writing is meant to investigate the realms of memory on an everyday life level, with the overriding goal to save personal and political stories of the past from state-imposed oblivion.

Curiously, Ugrešić and the other authors who write against nationalism, are women. And many (but not all) of the young women I conversed with shared their anti-nationalistic, pro-Yugoslav attitude with the Croatian exiled authors, whereas many (not all) men rather seemed to put Serbia's past and present center-stage. How can one understand this gendered aspect of writing (and speaking) about Yugoslavia? In his article *Narrations of Post-Yugoslav Identities* (1998), Stef Jansen explained this gendered difference by recurring to Trinh T. Minh-ha's suggestion "that if writers of a diaspora are condemned to write autobiographical work, then it might also be a typical war genre, particularly associated with women" (Jansen 1998: 87). What Jansen puts center-stage here is that women, like the diaspora, are some-

70. Rada Iveković, Vesna Kesić, Svetlana Slapšak, and Jelena Lovrić.

how pushed to write more personal narratives. Although I believe that the relationship between the diaspora and gender is more complex (and cannot be discussed to a satisfying degree at this point), the observation is nevertheless close to my findings: women told me more details about their autobiography, and they laid open more freely their inner conflicts surrounding the breakup of the country and their identity. Women expressed doubts, ambiguity, ambivalence, or pain, as the previous narratives illustrated. While this finding could be attributed to my own gender, perhaps there are more general underpinnings. Hence, to propose from my sample that "Yugoslavia" is rather female and "Serbia" male does seem a proposition that is worth investigating a little closer.

Svetlana Dragojević, forty years old, came to the U.S. in 1997 with her husband and now ten-year-old daughter. The sociologist and lawyer from Belgrade liked living in Yugoslavia and she is still in favor of Tito's socialism and concept of worker's self-management. With these viewpoints she is one of the few who maintained her socialist worldview together with her former non-ethnic identity. Still declaring herself "Yugoslav," although she is from a Serbian family background, she is very active in leftist American politics, works with immigrants, and is writing a book about Yugoslavia during socialism. In a similar style as Ugrešić she ponders:

> *"It seems between 1945 and 1990 we had an empty space, our history was a fiction, there was nothing there. And I am really curious, I asked my friend to do some research in the library, if these books on Yugoslav socialism still exist here. People are now conditioned on not thinking about this period, they spit on all of that."*

For Svetlana, to declare herself "Yugoslav" implies a political, anti-nationalistic statement, which is not only referring to memory politics in the successor states of Yugoslavia, but also to American social movements. Being an activist against racism and the Bush government's imperialist foreign policy, the Yugoslav declaration serves in a broader context of anti-essentialist, anti-hegemonic political practices. By declaring herself Yugoslav she also sets herself apart from a Serbian diaspora she views as too nationalistic and ethno-centric:

> *"The Serbs in the U.S. tend to be really rather racist and closed. I know there is quite a difference between generations of people coming from the former Yugoslavia in the United States. And you can even see, I visited Chicago recently and you can see there, you have many more of these older generations, but so many of them are wealthy and inward-looking, only interested in Serbs, Serbs, Serbs. I never felt that I was privileged in the United States, and I always felt closer*

> *to actually people of color, than to Anglo-Saxon groups. I mean, I am also politically active and support Leonard Peltier, Mumia Abu-Jamal. You can imagine what kind of comments I could get from [Serbian, B.B.-L.] people [laughs]. At this moment I am so much in love with Alice Walker and her work that some of our people including my husband tell me that I went to the other extreme, so whoever is a person of color is good for me [laughs]. I support Iraqi people and even Palestinians and I really believe that you cannot expect other groups to support you, if you don't support them – why would I? And if we [minority people, B.B.-L.] don't make coalitions it's really going to be very hard, esp. for the Serbian people, because they are so small. And if you don't find common bonds and common issues to share with people then it's going to be very hard. [...] Even though they say that they don't like intervention from outside, but in this case or in other cases, when they like it then it's okay. They don't see that there is anything wrong with materialism and all of this consumerism in the United States. And I have problems with that.*"

Svetlana shuns commonality that is only ethnic based and follows a Marxist critique of class, gender, and identity. Her declaration of "Yugoslav" can be understood as trying to overcome this ethnicization of society and politics. In this vein she utters a far-reaching political critique of Serbian community life that I have never heard of anyone else. In Yugoslav fashion, she opposes the recurrence to "ethnic roots," but advocates multiethnic, or multi-cultural cooperation. In practice she is not anti-Serb or anti-nationalistic – and how could she, if, as many participants remarked "*Serbs are the only Yugoslavs left*"? If only Serbs aligned themselves with other minorities, it seems, Svetlana would be more content with the Serbian communities. Of course, Svetlana was a fierce opponent of the NATO bombing, marched in downtown San Francisco, and went to a reading of the local activist, Michael Parenti's pro-Serbian *Killing a Nation* (2000). Apart from the people she knows at her work, she predominantly socializes with other fellow Serbs, visits the Divine Liturgy on Sundays and sends her daughter to „Sunday School"[71]. Nevertheless, her critique of Serbian community life and advocacy for leftism are based on strong antinationalist persuasions. Svetlana's story reveals agency for multiple, hyphenated, non-ethnic based identities, instead of passively internalizing the logic of ethnic "purity'."

Boba Marković is a 37-year-old woman from Belgrade who arrived in Los Angeles in 1991. Growing up in a family comprised of Romanians, Hungarians, Serbs, Croats, and Bosnian Muslims she always declared herself "Yugoslav," without being aware of being Serbian – which she offi-

71. Most Serbian churches in the U.S. offer classes for teaching children and youth the Serbian language, music, folklore, religion, and history. Since these are usually held following the weekly divine liturgy they are called "Sunday Schools."

cially is through her mother and father who originate from Belgrade, her mother being born of Serbian and Montenegrin parents and her father being a mix of a Slovenian woman and a Serbian man. When coming to the U.S. the artist and lawyer was not only confronted with the outbreak of the war in her homeland but also with a diaspora that was clearly separated into the various ethno-national groups, with only one designation lacking, "Yugoslav:"

> *"I don't know, I never met anybody who is declaring themselves as Yugoslavian. [...] I think most people are kind of forced to take sides? It's a force, or they think it's their obligation to take a side, or they should. It's because the national identity is lost and now they are trying to recreate it again and resurrect lots of things that are lost. I don't know. I mean, being here I never met anybody who is like: I am Yugoslavian. It's either Bosnian or it's Macedonian, Serbian, or Croatian or Slovenian. That's it."*

Her experiences with the Serbian community in California are few and unpleasant. And I would have never met her in the church or at a church-related event. Like other participants in my study, I met her by coincidence after the opening of an exhibit of Serbian cartoonist Aleksandar Zograf. As Boba remembers over a glass of beer in a bar in downtown San Francisco, following the visit of the exhibition, a Serbian man who upon declaring himself religious, attacked her for not celebrating the *slava* and for not being religious, shouted and yelled at her and finally offended her as a "spiritual prostitute." This gendered offense against her atheist Yugoslav background, resembling the infamous label "The Witches of Rio," more than attesting to the aforementioned factions in the Serbian community, could hardly be more misogynist. Instead of looking for (such) Serbian company in exile, she tried to make a home with young Yugoslavs like her of the various ethno-national groups, enjoying friendships with Bosnians and Croats. Boba is no exception: many young women that I met narrated that they eagerly looked for the company of people of other ethno-national backgrounds from the former Yugoslavia, and they were proud of knowing persons from other countries and continents that live in California. In this they share a cosmopolitanism that is very close to Svetlana's, they turn the *space* of exile into a *place* of friendship and solidarity with people of multinational background and members of "minorities."

Again, it is not that "Yugo-Nostalgia" was not also shared with other predominantly young Serbian men. Indeed most Serbs, male or female, growing up in Tito's Yugoslavia confessed that "*life was good in Yugoslavia.*" But whereas men tended to turn to Serbdom when Yugoslavia disintegrated and accepted that the country collapsed together with its national idea, women remarkably tried to keep the Yugoslav idea alive. As Boba states:

"*When the war broke out, I suddenly felt this urge to be friends with everybody, and I started like: Oh my god! We have to stick together because of this terrible thing that happened to our country. But it was of course impossible, I don't know, it was pretty much a waste of time. But I kind of felt we got to stick together.*"The women I talked to emphasized the social cohesion with non-Serbian groups from the former Yugoslavia to a degree that could not be found among men. Many of them revealed in the interviews, that they tried to keep relationships with Croats and Muslims, and that they socialized together against the dominant version of ethnic separatism.

How in America Serbs are made – or How in America Yugoslavs are unmade

That women were eager at keeping the Yugoslav idea alive *in a social sense* can be demonstrated by referring to a few more examples of young Serbian women who arrived in the 1990's. But did this attempt succeed? Zorka, a human relations employee who arrived in San Francisco in 1999, confessed to feel like a "Yugoslav." Her Yugoslav identity was reflected by her choice of two friends shortly after arrival, one of them a Croat and the other a Serb, living together in the same apartment. Recollecting the joyous and happy times they had, singing Yugoslav songs and practicing a slow "Yugoslav" life style, she cherishes keeping the multinational idea as a symbolic value. But she is also ambivalent, and more than Boba over time, employed the declaration "Serbian:"

> "*I mean I did in a sense – because I was from Serbia and had that accent – feel Serbian, but I really generally considered myself being a Yugoslav. [...] I usually say I am from former Yugoslavia, and when the next question is: 'Where from?' If am lucky or not, and then I say from Serbia or from Belgrade. I don't know, I still find it hard, I hate saying, it's so tragic, you know, if I say the first thing that I am Serbian I almost feel that I am saying: 'I am very nationalistic by the way and you know?' [laughs] So I am proud of being Serbian, but I don't want that to be the first thing to come out of my mouth, and it's just so confusing to explain what my language is.*"

Both Boba and Zorka told me how their friendships with non-Serbian Yugoslavs loosened after a while and contact ceased. By 1999, during the NATO bombing of Yugoslavia, after a decade of war and the foundation of small states in the former Yugoslavia, declaring themselves "Yugoslav" became increasingly futile. As Zorka suggests, the declaration Yugoslav did become a quest for neutrality and disguise, a way to hide the Serbian origin that immediately associated one with the "bad side" and thereby externally fixed the speaker to a negative stereotype. Therefore, moral value judgments, political opinion, and the external ascriptions by the American public loom large when negotiating one's national identity.

My tutor Svetlana, after living in Hungary for eight years, came to the U.S. in 2001. Although she knows that she is from a mixed marriage, Serbian and Croatian, and claims to be a Yugoslav, she feels that she rather belongs to Serbs. Svetlana states:

> *"But still I have like this idea, that that country was my country... Growing up there you go through that, and you learn that those are your borders. And at the time that you are learning all of this, that was all Yugoslavia. At the time that I learned the language that I speak it was called Serbo-Croatian, so obviously I think that I can keep saying, because that is the country that I came from, the fact is that it dissolved afterwards."*

She adds that outside her homeland her national designation "varies from situation to situation," especially in Hungary where she was often considered to be an Italian or Spanish woman, and where people upon hearing that she was from Serbia and anti-Milošević, felt compassion and reacted friendly. Obviously the need to explain which is usually mentioned with regard to talks in the U.S. was absent in Hungary, where people were more familiar with the neighboring country. For Svetlana, to declare herself "Yugoslav," and being wary of (nationalist) expressions of Serbdom, also implies a critique against the recycling of old stories and the state-media's manipulation of the present through a violent past. Throughout the first half of the 1990's she was in disbelief when watching Serbian TV's display of "Serb" victims and "Croat" massacres against Serbs, which to her served to produce fear and paranoia. This cautious relationship to stories of violence also extends to her family history:

> *"My parents never told me anything about the Second World War which was different from the official history. But then my uncle told me that my grandfather, my father's father, had been killed by Ustaše. He was thrown into a pit and as many others got tied to somebody else with barbed-wire. Shortly before the war they excavated that grave and took the bodies out. I know that they could recognize my grandfather because of that barbed-wire. They made a big memorial at that place, like in the media everybody was just a victim. Then they took the barbed-wire and knocked at that door, where the Ustaša had lived. A man opened and they handed him the barbed-wire, saying: 'This belongs to you.' But he was a little boy when the massacres happened, you know? What did that little boy, now an adult, have to do with what his parents did to my grandfather? It was just saying: The Croats are bad. It was stirring up the old hatreds."*

Defending the Yugoslav idea was a statement against binary oppositions, which could and did lead to hatred and violence. Svetlana's narrative is significant in demonstrating how media propaganda in Serbia was used to create an enemy and stir up fear. Moreover, her family's story reveals that the memory of World War Two played a central role in the course of the Third Balkan Wars, both in the homeland and abroad (see also Part Two). Interestingly, the story of her grandfather, moving as it is, does not extend to the present, remarkable as it is. Thus she proves that she didn't comply with the creation of ethnic antagonisms. Furthermore, her recourse to the declaration "Yugoslav" entailed a certain historical statement as well.

However, in 1999 during the NATO bombing the young woman experienced a phase of ambivalence, now that Serbia was being victimized. Although positioning herself against Serbian policies and Milošević's nationalism, she admits to having been influenced by the international as well as the Serbian media campaigns, the latter claiming that the Serbian president is, as she ironically worded it, *"for poor Serbs,"* and the former reinstating that "*everything is happening just because the rest of the world is against poor Serbs.*" While finding it hard to believe any of this manichaeic world-view, and thinking that it is regime propaganda, something nevertheless dawned on her "*like I started thinking that we do have bad press, and you know, when I am outside I am still identified with that policy and the politics and everything that is happening, and there are people who believe that they know about us, so I had to position myself.*" Svetlana, like many others, succumbed to the need to develop a clear political and personal position. For that stance to develop, the "Yugoslav" declaration had to be necessarily sacrificed.

In all these narratives, we notice the ambivalences of exile women who are torn apart not just between national designations, Yugoslav or Serb, but also between memories of a country where they spent most of their lives and political events in the recent past. All the women are either from ethnically mixed areas, Bosnia and Vojvodina, or from Belgrade, where the Yugoslav ideology due to being the capital of the SFRY, was relatively strong. Interestingly, these memories are predominantly positive, with a striking absence of references to the Second World War and the Ustaša perpetration of Serbs. Whereas in pro-Yugoslav discourses of identity the Second World War is silenced, in pro-Serbian discourses narratives about the Ustaša, genocide against Serbs are tantamount.

The mere one-sentence long information where one is from always already implies the intrusion of politics into one's personal story and the external judgment of the listener in the country of residence.

Thus, what Althusser (1971) calls "interpellation" is very well applicable to the case of Serbian exiles. Svetlana, Boba, Zorka, and others "are always already subjects," but in exile they "constantly practice the ideological ritual of recognition all ideology hails or interpellates concrete individuals as concrete subjects." In the former Yugoslavia their names, places of residence, and language's dialect always already demarcate that they are Serbian. In the U.S., where these regional intimacies are not known, where it is not obvious "what they are," they constantly have to state "who they are," meaning, to which ethno-national group they belong. But whereas the gendered subjectivation, or interpellation in Althusser's sense, refers to a more or less fixed category, the Serbian women's subjectivation is in flux and in the making. It appears that through their indecisiveness, the outside pressure to conform to "ideology," which means "to take side," to "identify" with one group or the other, one country or the other increases, thus making the interpellation of national identity even more forceful. They need to be interpellated again and again, until their subject position is fixed as is the norm. Until in the end, following a major political event such as the NATO bombing, even a persistent "Yugoslav" like Boba comes to the conclusion of declaring herself Serbian – if only sometimes.

The examples of Serbian women make it clear that their "Serbian-ness," in addition to being influenced by the events in the homeland, receives new impetus by external ascriptions and constant interpellation made by Americans. More poignantly said, we can conclude that the young women's declaration as Serbian, ambivalent as it is, is a product of the unmaking of Yugoslavia both seen from the tragedy in the country itself as well as of the terms of "purity" and clear-cut boundaries which were established in the Western media public. Furthermore, a process of Serbianization appears to have been fostered within Chetnik-dominated and nationalistic circles, such as the Serbian church. I argue, that exploring the stories of these women and other Serbs in the U.S., one does not find out "how Americans are made" as Perec and Bober (1997) undertitle their work on immigrants on Ellis Island, but how in America Serbs are made.

Chapter 3. Creating one Voice: the *Serbian Unity Congress*

> "Not only does conflict accentuate the cohesion of an existing unit; it also mobilizes its members, bringing together persons who have otherwise nothing to do with each other".
> (Skrbiš 1999: 20, drawing on Simmel)

"*Dobro veče, dobro došli ...*," Michael (Miroslav) Djordjevich, leading spokesperson and former President of the Serbian Unity Congress (SUC) welcomes the visitors to the annual *Djurdjevan* ball in the hall of St. John's Serbian Orthodox Church in San Francisco in a few Serbian words. The rather small man with short-cropped gray hair, broad shoulders, and a ruddy face, wearing an Armani type suit looks very much like the self-made California businessman that indeed he is. Immediately switching to his impeccable English, Djordjevich continues his talk in a self-congratulatory manner that seems to be the ingredient of lobby events: "*I am happy to see that all of you, members, friends, and strangers came to our first ball. This is a great honor to us. We try as hard as we can to improve the fate of Serbia and to establish connections between the homeland and us.*" Djordjevich dedicates his time and money to Serbia, as he briefly outlines in his talk this Friday evening on the 11th of May, 2002:

> "*I had the great opportunity to visit Serbia and Republika Srpska four times in the past twelve months. The situation there is very bad, one out of four lives is in poverty. Now it is on us, as we are the only people who can with competence help and order the chaos the country is in. After so many years of bad treatment by the Tito regime and then Milošević, this is now the first time that we can establish cooperation between the homeland and the fatherland. And I have to say, who if not us with our professionalism here and the ways we learned that the economy works, could change anything over there? In Belgrade I talked to businessmen and they didn't even know what the stock market means. So there is a lot of work to do and we can't expect anything much to happen soon, as it will take years and years to come to make a modern society out of Serbia. But this year we got the unprecedented chance to make come true our dream of a close cooperation.*"

This evening in spring 2002 Djordjevich comes up with yet another attempt at bridging the divide between the Serbs in the homeland and Serbian-Americans in the host country, when informing the small crowd in the dance hall underneath the church that the Serbian government established a diaspora committee consisting of twelve members, two of them from the U.S., one from Canada, and one from Australia. In fact, two American members are prominent middle-aged Serbs from the Bay Area.

In this chapter, I am concerned with the story of one, if not *the* most influential Serbian diaspora organization in the 1990's, the *Serbian Unity Congress.* With the foundation of the SUC in San Francisco right at the onset of Yugoslavia's breakup, Serbian diaspora politics were nourished by the increased awareness of the "Serbian question" in a time of crisis, demonstrating how political activism among migrants can be seen as the product as well as part of war. My underlying questions are the following: In which ways did Serbs in the diaspora influence the politics in the homeland as well as the discourse about the war in the United States? And, were they successful in gaining recognition among their kinsmen and officials in the homeland and abroad?

First, I will analyze the personal story and political history of one of the SUC-founders and current president. Crucial for understanding the SUC is the history of Serbian political activism in the U.S., mainly the events leading to the church split in the 1960's. I will look in detail at official long-distance nationalist practices, lobby-events, the publication of pamphlets, articles, and movies which helped to shape the viewpoints of many Serbs regarding the recent wars in the former Yugoslavia. Finally, I will discuss why Serbian long-distance politics, as represented by the SUC, were foremost ineffective. Ultimately, the SUC provides a key to understanding Serbian long-distance nationalism in the wake of the recent Balkan Wars.

The Serbian Unity Congress and the Serbian Lobby

David Bruce MacDonald (2002: 68) states that "the rise of numerous academic institutions," among them the SUC, "dedicated to the promotion of nationalist views proved to be of immense importance" for forging a "Serbian propaganda war" that was needed to consolidate Milošević's power. For anyone interested in the study of Serbian long-distance nationalism the SUC must be paid attention to, for it is a mouthpiece of the politically active Serb diaspora and forms a crucial element of Serbian long-distance nationalism on a global scale. What Basch, Glick Schiller, and Blanc (1994: 143) stated with regard to Vincentian and Grenadian immigrants is equally true for Serbian immigrants: "It is through organizations that constructions of deterritorialized nations, [...] have gained force."

Throughout the war and beyond the SUC played an active role in events taking place in the homeland, by way of distributing material about the conflicts, collecting money, sending remittances, and supporting political parties, projects, and instrumental political figures in Serbia and Bosnia, among them former President of Republika Srpska and now wanted war criminal, Radovan Karadžić. However, one of the most significant aspects of diaspora lobbying entailed the attempt to impact U.S. foreign policy by sponsoring senators and congressmen in Washington in their political agendas towards Bosnia.

Among the sparse literature dealing with Serbian diaspora politics is the study *The Serbian Unity Congress and the Serbian Lobby. A Study in Contemporary Revisionism and Denial* (1994) by Brad Blitz, former Ph.D. student at Stanford University, affiliate of "the American Committee to Save Bosnia," and head of the "Students Against Genocide" (SAGE). Meant as an explicit warning against the danger of the largest Serb-nationalist organization in the United States, his work is based on 18 months of monitoring Serbian activists in the San Francisco Bay Area. In fact, some of my interlocutors have been among those 'monitored' by the Stanford student, and for the context of the text it is important to know that their outrage about Blitz's "anti-Serbian propaganda" they call the article, still comes up in talks we had.[72] Blitz' article aims at shedding light on what he calls the "disinformation campaign which targets the media, university campuses and research centers" (ibid.: 2). At the core of the study lies the description of the methods used by the SUC to influence public opinion about the nature of the war in the former Yugoslavia. Leading assumption of the author is the perception that the Bosnian war is a genocide which he furthers by attacking the Serbian lobby for declaring it a civil war.

As Blitz points out, the organizational structure of the SUC consists of a few one person offices, the central one of them being located in the Kolarevich vineyards in Napa Valley, another one in San Francisco run by Dragana Gajković[73], and another one, the Washington office with Danielle Sremać. Sremać has received public attention as a result of a series of

72. Some of my main interlocutors, Mira Pesić Connor and Dragana Gajković, had personally met Blitz when he asked them for a meeting, but their contact ended in a confrontation. At a conference about the war in Bosnia, Blitz did not invite the representatives of the Serbian Woman's Caucus, but Mira and Svetlana nevertheless came, as they told me. When wanting to contribute their viewpoints to the discussion, which was dominated by Croatian and Bosnian Muslim activists, they were asked to be quiet. Still, Mira is excited when she recalls how she stepped up in the front of the room, accused Blitz of undemocratic behavior, and told the audience about her experience in Jasenovać and the unjust demonization of Serbs in the American public. In short, Blitz's treatment of the Serbian diaspora reveals how charged the debate about the Yugoslav wars was and with which intensity scholars, journalists, and diaspora activists confronted each other at public meetings and in public writings.
73. Blitz does not use pseudonyms in order to protect the personalities of his subjects, most of whom he did not talk to. In order to protect some of the persons he denounces, at least the ones I conducted research with, I will therefore refrain from using the real names. Other names of people I have not personally met and who are also prominent in the public are not changed.

interviews on CNN and NPR's "Talk of the Nation" in June and July, 1994. According to Blitz, the SUC worked very closely with two information centers, Serbnet (which includes the Serbian American Media Center) located in Chicago and Los Angeles-based SAVA (the Serbian American Voters Alliance). Both of these organizations produced materials that were distributed by the SUC as part of their speaker tour programs and press kits.

Headed by William Dorich, SAVA published "The Suppressed Serbian Voice and the Free Press in America" (1994), a voluminous 300-page-collection of pamphlets, letters to state officials and newspaper articles mainly documenting the Serbian victims in Bosnia, the 'misinformation' about the wars in the American public, and distortions of facts throughout the disintegration of Yugoslavia. The book has been produced in honor of the burning of the relics of St. Sava in 1594 that has "taught the Serbs that you can destroy the body, but not the spirit of the Serbian people. ... in his memory we cry out for our freedom, for democracy and for equal justice under the law in the United States of America, in Bosnia, in Croatia, and in former Yugoslavia" (Dorich 1994: 3). Linking the suffering of Serbs four hundred years ago directly with perceived present-day injustice against Serbs in the U.S., the authors inscribe a classical nationalist agenda of continuity on their material. Among SAVA's news campaigns are a series of cartoons, one of them depicting a native American Indian and the "Trail of Tears" which is compared to the persecution of Serbs by Albanians in Kosovo (ibid.: 78). These and other examples suggest that the paralleling of world-historical events of persecution forms a main strategy of SAVA. The publication is symbolically loaded and epitomizes the Serbian "victim-centered propaganda" (MacDonald 2002) during the Yugoslav wars. Throughout the book a number of photos of mutilated *Serbian* bodies are presented which are directly paralleled with the image of massacred Serbs under the Ustaša regime. In fact, the work is framed by a documentation of killed Serbs during World War Two, starting with a list of 550 children victims, and ending with the names of 1030 adults, each with surname, family name, age, and the information of the village they inhabited. Obviously, the strategy of naming and therefore personalizing one's ethnic group's victims is here employed, in order to appeal to the *collective* suffering and at the same time to enable the identification with killed *individuals*, thus targeting the emotional involvement of diaspora Serbs with 'their' massacred ancestors.

Blitz distinguishes between direct and indirect lobbying campaigns, the first implying financial contributions to public officials, such as House members and candidates running for office, and the latter regarding SUC-financed public relations firms. Here, the author documents ample evidence and provides details about the money flows as a strategy to impact on the American media and U.S. foreign policy. Among the recipients of donations from the SUC Political Action Committee (SUC PAC) are Rep. Helen Delich Bentley and Rep. Dan Burton. Bentley, former President of Serbnet has been the most vocal pro-Serbian voice in the House. In 1993-94 the SUC-financed public relations firm “Manatos and Manatos, Inc.“ conducted an indirect lobbying campaign in order to unite Serbian and Greek interests. Prominent figures and sponsors of the SUC, like Michael Djordjevich, George Bogdanich, Director of Serbnet, Milan Panić, the former challenger to Milošević, and members of the Greek-American community made noticeable contributions.[74] During my fieldwork the pan-Orthodox alliance was frequently mentioned to me, whether regarding the huge majority (99%) of Greek citizens who were against the NATO bombing of Yugoslavia, or mutual visits of each other’s churches in San Francisco, including the holding of joint concerts of Orthodox music[75].

According to Blitz, together with leading figures of Serbnet and the SUC prominent individuals in the Hellenic community have made repeated donations to influential political officials at critical periods in the Bosnian War: “For example a flurry of contributions were made at the time of the Serbian assault of Goražde (April 1994) when NATO re-issued a threat of air strikes and when the divergent agendas of NATO and the United Nations were made public“ (Blitz ibid: 6). This case is especially noteworthy since it shows how contributions were used to directly influence events taking place on the ground during the Bosnian war. Following Blitz, the most popular recipient of these multiple contributions is the Chairman of the House of Foreign Affairs Committee, Representative Lee Hamilton, who received over $30,000 in multiple contributions from leaders of the Serbian and Greek-American communities. The aim of this campaign was first, to lend support to potentially sympathetic congressional representatives by bolstering their campaign funds and second, to create an image of a powerful lobby. “The impression given is that of a community of individuals who can unite quickly to raise large sums of money when necessary and may therefore carry some influence“ (ibid.).

74. As Blitz contends, in the 1990’s the Serbian lobby was dependent on the Greek-American alliance. The San Francisco based “Manatos and Manatos“ which presents a number of Hellenic institutions as well as the City of San Francisco, was well suited for the task of promoting Serbian interests, since it included outstanding clients such as the embassy of Greece, the United Hellenic American Congress and the Pan Cyprian Association of America.

75. There has also been going on a serious debate about the creation of an American Orthodox church in order to unify the nationally separate Orthodox churches in the U.S. This religiously based Pan-Orthodox idea stands in line with a general trend towards Pan-Orthodoxy which implies the political as well, see Roudometof 2000, 2001.

Turning on the media

The SUC operated on several levels, most important being the targeting of politicians, diplomats, and the media in order to turn public opinion around in favor of the Serbs. 1994 was a year of central importance, not just in the Balkans with the siege of Sarajevo, the breadline massacre, and the increasing effort of international peace negotiations to end the killing in the former Yugoslavia, but also with regard to the SUC's political activism. In the same year the SUC and Serbnet distributed the 26 minute video "Truth is the victim in Bosnia" to members of Congress, national and regional newspapers, television and radio stations. This video, in BBC format, contains three interviews with former U.N. General Lewis MacKenzie. MacKenzie states that the Western media favors the Croats and makes the most notable claim that the breadline massacre in Sarajevo was staged by the Bosnians to gain sympathy from the West (Blitz 1994: 7).[76] Interestingly, according to the Croatian American Association, MacKenzie was on the Serbian lobby's payroll, receiving $15.000 by Serbnet (Serbian American National Information Network) to make two organized media tours which included, first, a testimony before the U.S. House Armed Services Committee, second, meetings with influential congressmen, third, a speech at the Conservative Heritage Foundation, and forth, numerous newspaper interviews and television appearances (ibid.: 30).

Another important documentary that appeared long after Blitz' study was completed is "Yugoslavia – the avoidable war" (2002) by Martin Lettmayer and George Bogdanich, director of Serbnet. The documentary portrays the roots of the dismemberment of Yugoslavia with original footage from Ustaša cruelties in the Second World War and analyzes the different stages of Croat nationalism that, in the filmmaker's view, led to the renewed fighting in 1991. Including interviews with scholars such as Susan Woodward, British diplomat Lord Carrington, and former New York Times journalist David Kenny the movie, which was partly financed by the SUC[77], is a powerful account of "the other side of the story." As the documentary tells, not Serbian nationalists or Milošević started the war, but radical right-wing Croat émigrés were ready to destroy Yugoslavia since at least 1987, arming themselves with the support of the CIA and the German government.[78]

The above mentioned films and documentaries are widely known in the Serbian diaspora and often referred to as a source of "truth." What Fu-

76. See also footnote 3.
77. According to personal communication with Michael Djordjevich.
78. Apart from the allusion to the CIA and the German government, Paul Hockenos' 2003 analysis of Croatian émigrés mainly supports the view offered in the movie, namely that radical right wing Croatian émigrés had been supplying the Tudjman regime with arms and money since the late 1980's.

glerud (1999: 8) mentions with regard to long-distance nationalism among Tamils in Norway seems to be equally true for the Serbian lobby in the United States: "If you wish to locate the driving force behind Sikh separatism in Punjab it might be necessary to go to Canada. The Tamil diaspora's most important source of cultural authenticity is the video."

Blitz notes that in the meantime the SUC managed to co-opt Marxist/ Socialist organizations as well as respectable members of the academic community in support of their position. For example, the briefing produced by the London-based Campaign against Militarism (CAM) entitled "20 things you Know About the Serbs that aren't true" maintains that Serbia is simply the victim of Western imperialism – the West's latest „whipping-boy." "The CAM briefing even argues that the encirclement of Sarajevo by Serb forces is defensive concluding that Sarajevo is not really besieged" (Blitz ibid.: 9).

The SUC worked together with a number of non-Serbian journalists in order to produce a more credible version of the "truth." In January 1994 Peter Brock of El Paso published an article in Foreign Policy accusing the press of being partisan and anti-Serb. Following Blitz, Brock maintained regular communication with Dragana Gajković, SUC executive director and in the eyes of Blitz "chief propagandist in the San Francisco Bay Area." Heading the "News Analysis Network" and being a member of the "Serbian Woman's Caucus" among Gajković's main agendas was to challenge the allegation of systematic rape, which to her mind was grossly exaggerated in order to satisfy a sensationalist, 'simple-minded' press. Instead she furthered the claim that rape was committed on all sides.

Curiously, today Gajković, who I met a few times in the European flair cafe "Caffe de la Press" in downtown San Francisco speaks in quite moderate words about the Balkan wars: "*The Serbs were definitely not the lambs in the conflict. Indeed, I would agree that the atrocities committed by Serbian soldiers and paramilitaries were the worst.*" One decade after the war in the former Yugoslavia started, the activist fervor which had spread in the San Francisco Bay Area has left little traces, not even in the talks of some of the main activists themselves.

In the following, I will turn to one major representative of the SUC and explore his long-distance nationalist story in the context of the history of Serbian émigré political activism.

The story of Michael Djordjevich[79] and the church split

As is the case for many exiles, Djordjevich is convinced that only the diaspora knows how to turn Serbia's fate around, if not exclusively him. Djordjevich's self-confidence is not unparalleled, if one looks at the example of Milan Panić, a Serbian American from Los Angeles who became the President of Serbia in 1991. Following a short electoral campaign against Milošević, Panić successfully demonstrated that an outsider from the diaspora can win the sympathy of the people, if only for a short period of time. After only six months in office, Panić increasingly lost political and public support and returned to Southern California. In the end, the manager's political career revealed that the expertise in running a Californian pharmaceutical company does not help much when dealing with political and economic matters in Serbia.

The story of the SUC is also the story of Djordjevich, a business and finance manager in the United States since 1956 when he was eighteen years old. His father came from a wealthy family in Serbia and was a royal officer during the Second World War, when he was captured by Tito's partisans and interned in a prison camp. "*When my father came here, he was a big anti-Communist obviously, and he remained anti-Communist to the very day today. And a patriot, a Serbian patriot, really a patriot.*" Djordjevich recalls his childhood memories of the Wehrmacht's 1941 bombing of Belgrade, his family's flight out of the city to the countryside, and the many dead that lay on the road to Belgrade upon his family's return. Following the war he decided to leave the country, because a young ambitious man with aristocratic background he didn't expect to succeed in communist Yugoslavia. He first went to Paris, then moved to the United States, Milwaukee and Chicago. Djordjevich finally settled in San Francisco, where he lives today with his family, one of the diaspora's most influential persons.

Djordjevich told me his life story while meeting in the upper-class restaurant "Big Four" in the downtown hotel district overlooking the Powell Street station valley with the shopping area, cable cars, limos, Grace Cathedral and San Francisco's notable star hotels with butlers in uniforms standing in front of the entrances. Actually, he left politics a long time ago, following the turbulent events of the end-1950's and early 1960's, before he together with his father founded the SUC in 1991. Inside the dark, classic-style restaurant with heavy oil paintings of men in uniforms, apparently 19th century American politicians, golden lamps, green leather sofas and chairs it is easy to imagine his high time in Serbian diaspora politics so many decades ago. "*I was very active against Tito's visit in 1963. We actually had*

79. Here I do not use a pseudnym, since Djordjevich is a public figure who personally allowed me to use his real name.

bigger demonstrations here than in Chicago. Tito had to cancel his visit to San Francisco because of us. And for my activism I was put on the black list of the secret police, and I was told by my friends in Washington at that time that if I would ever come to Yugoslavia I would be arrested for anti-government activities abroad and be in big trouble."

Paul Hockenos (2003) in his brilliant study *Homeland Calling* describes how President John F. Kennedy's invitation to Marshal Tito to visit the United States initiated a series of salient events in the Serb diaspora. According to Hockenos, the aging Yugoslav President was delighted to have the chance of demonstrating "recognition as a world figure" (ibid.: 120ff.). Having been on the victor's side in the Second World War, Tito then headed the growing "non-aligned movement" of mostly Third World countries that challenged the rigid Cold War dichotomy. The dawning of a closer relationship with the United States would be a showcase for Yugoslavia's independence from the Soviet Union and prove his liberal-minded conception of socialism. For the first and last time during the Cold War the patchwork of Serbian American groups started a series of rallies, protests, and pamphlets to chastise Tito's ten-day visit in October. Tito's trip was marked by trouble from the start, when Serbian Americans tried to stop him at the airways from entering the country. "Thousands of signatures were collected and sent to the U.S. Congress, where hard-line anti-Communist Republicans were particularly receptive to the émigrés ire. The House and Senate passed resolutions against the visit. [...] Rumors circulated about a possible assassination attempt. With a non-stop barrage of phone calls, organized groups of older Serbian American women harangued San Francisco's Fairmont hotel, where Tito was scheduled to stay" (Hockenos 2003: 120). On October 20 two Serbs managed to enter the hotel and almost reached his door, where they were wrestled down by security guards. Tito then canceled his visit of the West Coast, leaving the diaspora excited about its proclaimed victory.

But the feeling of triumph on the side of Serbian Americans didn't last long. Tensions between the Serbian Orthodox church in the United States and Yugoslavia grew to unbearable proportions, when Bishop Dionisije in Chicago openly opposed the "communist" regime in Belgrade, accusing it of boycotting the American churches and disturbing worshipping Serbian Americans by sending disguised communist spies to the diaspora. In exchange prominent laymen and some clergymen raised charges against Bishop Dionisije's "most improper personal life and the misuse of church property" (Vrga 1975: 29), among those accusations loomed an affair with a young Serbian American student (Hockenos 2003: 122). In 1962, the self-centered and ambitious bishop made a public statement to the effect that the Serbian Diocese in America – by the way the only diocese outside Yugoslavia – should become independent. During these years of conflict, church officials and members already separated along ideological lines, the "unity" faction representing mostly pre-World War Two immigrants and their offspring, which remained loyal to the mother church, while the „autonomy" faction consisting mainly of post-World War Two political exiles succeeded in forming their own church by cutting all administrational and political ties to the homeland (see Vrga 1975). According to Djordjevich and many other commentators Tito had indeed sent his secret agents to provoke the church schism in order to seriously weaken the Serb diaspora (see Buchenau 2003, Hockenos 2003, Vrga 1975). But what really happened and what was exaggerated never came out. Up to today older Serbs engage in lively discussions about the topic, testifying to the significance of the schism in the diaspora.

Djordjevich is still outraged when he talks about the *raskol* or church schism which spread from the U.S. to all Serbian Orthodox churches in North America, Europe, and Australia. Soon after the tumultuous events, Djordjevich turned his back on his kinsmen in exile, since the split left him bitterly disappointed: "*The Serbian diaspora essentially spent a lot of its energy and money: the church split probably cost 50 million dollar in those times in a legal phase. Totally stupid! It was all going to Tito's cap.*" The church split is indeed a crucial historical moment in the Serbian diaspora, pointing to the immense cultural and ideological differences that would persist into the 1990's and the new millennium.

If Serbs didn't fight communism effectively, then Djordjevich would set on another horse trying to engage in American party and government politics in the shadow of the Cold War. In 1964, Djordjevich became chairman of the "California Young Republicans" where he was responsible for organizing ethnic minorities for the Goldwater campaign in the presidential election. Two years later he was on the state-wide campaign committee helping Murphy and Reagan win the governor post. "*When Reagan became governor I was asked to go with him to Sacramento, because we all knew that this was a stepping stone, a station towards Washington. That Reagan was going for President. So all of the friends and others were saying: come along with us to Sacramento, Michael, we got to go to Washington.*" Despite the promising career that the young Serbian immigrant's rapid political ascension offered, Djordjevich refused to climb the political ladder, as he now claims, for financial and familial reasons, since political campaigning demanded the investment of a lot of money out of one's own pockets. Instead of a political career, from then on he channeled his manifold talents to business where he made use of his university degree he had acquired at UC Berkeley. Until 1994 he sat in the executive branches of several successful multinational corporations, participated in the stock exchange and made a millions of dollar fortune.

Today Djordjevich claims that he is somewhat tired of politics and dedicates much of his retirement time to another, as he coins it, 'personal' matter: banking. In 1996, following the Dayton accords he founded an

American option bank "*with the sole purpose to help finance small businesses and private enterprises in Serbia.*" But while Djordjevich is convinced of the necessity to develop Serbia by acquiring banks, he angrily recalls how Milošević obstructed his business plans, so that he had to leave Serbia and now invests in Republika Srpska. The agile man from San Rafael seems to be in his element again, attempting at managing Bosnia's fiscal system, as if it were an American company. If one looks at the first half of the 1990's, however, Djordjevich's political aspirations are tantamount. He even admits that he thought of running for the Serbian presidency.

With the fall of the Berlin Wall, Djordjevich jumped on the Eastern European train, immediately raising to the opportunity at the right moment, when he sensed, as he formulates it, that "*the bells have called for communism.*" At the historical turning point, Djordjevich immediately realized that the old organizations with their roots in pre-World War Two émigré groups and post-World War Two Chetnik circles would not suffice to carve out a diaspora activism that kept up to the challenges of the present.[80] A new organization was needed, so he founded the SUC:

> "*We met with Andrei Karadjordjevich, the nephew of the present crown prince who was very active. We met here in San Francisco, in fact not far from here, a block away. My father and he were talking about reviving some of the existing Serbian organizations. And I thought, no: They have too much of a burden of the past. I said: Let's create a brand-new organization, with the purpose of getting professional people, because this country will need know-how. We'll need investments and in particular we need know-how to set up new standards of doing things. And they agreed and that's how the SUC came into being, conceptually at least. And then in 1990 we held a founding congress in Cleveland.*"

Upon Djordjevich's initiative, Serbian immigrants who had never met before would come together for the first time, starting to form a diaspora that played an active role in the conflict and up to the present.

Djordjevich presents himself as a self-confident "ethnic entrepreneur"[81] in the sense that he instrumentalizes his national identity at the right point in order to acquire personal benefits. Being used to giving interviews and telling his viewpoints to the wider public, his story is strikingly factual, bare any emotions, and lacking personal revelations. Djordjevich

80. One could certainly say that the SUC is the first transnational Serbian organization, since the earlier 20th century organizations had mainly zeroed in on the Serbian communities in the diaspora and their Royalist, Chetnik ideology, instead of focusing on the homeland-diaspora relationship.
81. This concept has been inspired by Prof. Werner Schiffauer. As opposed to the common use of "ethnic entrepreneur" as an ethnic business man, I use the term for connoting the self-conscious use of ethnic identity and collective sentiment in order to follow personal and economic goals.

does not speak about his life story and innermost feelings, or underlying motivations, but how he can launch big projects, such as a Republican campaign, the SUC, or banking, that are based on his ethnic identity. In a way, compared to the plethora of discourses on being Serbian I have presented in the preceding chapters – statements that could be categorized as "expressive identity" –, Djordjevich does not deal with his personal story at all. Following Safran (1999) his identity is merely "instrumental," in that he strategically employs his ethnic identity in order to make profits in a specific situation. In doing so he proves great skills in political maneuvering, knowing when it is the right time to start a project and when to depart from it in order to undertake something more profitable.

What the Serbs want

Djordjevich's reemergence to politics started with an essay in pamphlet form entitled "What the Serbs Want," a little booklet he doesn't miss to bring me this day, together with "One hundred irrefutable facts" about the war. In his 1989 booklet Djordjevich is confident to speak on behalf of "the Serbs," claiming that under Tito "the Serbian people were forced into a state which has ever since suppressed and denied their national identity, heritage and strivings," although "the Serbs" had under "superhuman" sacrifices during World War One and World War Two proven their heroism to fight for the allies (Djordjevich 1989: 4). As a consequence, Serbs needed to be unified under one state, in concordance with the movements of "national liberation and anti-colonialism" (ibid.: 5).

There is no mentioning of other ethno-national groups and their rights, nor of population movements or "ethnic cleansing". What is at stake are only Serbia's "vital interests." That this "Greater Serbia" (a phrase Djordjevich never employs) nationalism, based on the fact that Serbs form substantial minorities in Croatia, Montenegro, and Kosovo, as well as a near majority in Bosnia would necessarily lead to a violent breakup, must have been clear to the pamphlet's author. According to the introductory issue of the SUC, "[t]he goals of the Serbian Unity Congress can be summarized as follows. The S.U.C. short-term goal as adopted at the New York Convention is to get the sanctions [against Serbia] lifted. The long term goal is to contribute to the *reconstruction of the territories on which the Serbian people find themselves* [italics mine]"[82]. That this is a very dangerous idea bearing resemblance to Serbian expansionism in the face of the large non-Serbian populations on the territories where Serbs live is obvious. In fact, throughout the war Djordjevich and the SUC didn't give up on the idea of a "unified Yugoslavia" with Serbian self-determination.

82. "Introductory Issue," Serbian Unity Congress, No. 42, 12/26/93.

1989 marked not only the revival of Serbian nationalism with Milošević's famous speech on the 600-year-celebration of the battle of "Field of Blackbirds" in Kosovo. 1989 is also an important date in the history of diaspora-homeland relations. Djordjevich recalls the reemergence of diaspora activism as follows:

> "*After Tito, from 1980 to '89, the whole thing was in flux in Yugoslavia; now, a number of people in 1989 went back to the commemoration of the Kosovo Battle, including my father's younger sister and cousin, and a number of people from our community, Sacramento, Los Angeles, all across the country. They were over a million people in Kosovo for the commemoration. That was the fist real effort on, if you will, the American Serbian diaspora going in any significant. But they did that as individuals, not as organizations. But I think the thinking coming out of that was achieved, finally there is someone who is recognizing what the Albanians have been doing to the Serbs in Kosovo for 50 years.*"

This passage is insofar interesting, as it manifests the importance that the 600-year-celebration of the Kosovo battle played not only in national or local terms but also on a global, transnational level, linking Serbs in the homeland with those in the diaspora – and that for the first time after decades of silence.[83]

In the same year the main heads of the SUC launched an ambitious economic program, called the "Loan for the Reconstruction of Serbia," aimed at borrowing money to promising applicants in industry, agriculture, tourism, and trade to revive the economy. Members of the Djordjevich family, chemical tycoon Milan Panić, and former university professor Radmila Milentijević from New York, another important diaspora figure, paid huge sums of money. As Hockenos (2003: 126) states much of the $151 million fund was used to bring Milošević in power and revealed widespread fraud and misuse of capital. Curiously, nobody among my interlocutors ever mentioned this information to me, obviously in the attempt to hide unpleasant impressions. And while the diaspora supported Milošević, he himself did not offer the diaspora much in exchange, except for granting Milentijević a ministerial post.

Unlike Croatia's president Tudjman no diaspora figure ever reached power in the homeland as did Šušak under Tudjman, and the request for voting rights, which had been granted to Croatian exiles to garner commitment for the HDZ (*Hrvatska Democracija Zajednica*) right from the start, have been left unanswered by the Serbian government and remain on the Serb diaspora's agenda up to today.[84] From 1990 on, Tudjman initiated national reconciliation with Croatian exiles of World War Two, developing

83. See also Hockenos (2003: 109-113).

the "*Iseljena Hrvatska*" program, roughly translated as "exiled Croatia," emphasizing the *involuntary* aspect of resettlement, successfully embraced the Croat diaspora (Hockenos 2003: 47). The latter implies that he didn't regard Croats in the Canadians as Croatian Canadians but generations of "Croats in Canada." As for Serbs such a close, effective relationship to the homeland is only wishful thinking. Indeed the dividing line separating politicians in Serbia, educated in a Titoist style, from diaspora figures who in the homeland have been for decades tabooed and were declared "enemies of Yugoslavia," remains huge. On both sides suspicion, mistrust, and a deep feeling of alienation dominate each other's attitudes.

Serbian politics "made in Washington"

After eating lunch with Djordjevich, he handed me an assortment of pamphlets, among them the "Hearing before the Committee on Foreign Affairs" in the House of Representatives, which his headed by chairman Lee Hamilton. This congregation on May 11th, 1994 was one of the most successful events in Djordjevich's long-distance nationalist career. In his opening remarks Djordjevich contends that

> "[T]he principal blame for the Yugoslav tragedy must go to the Yugoslavs in general and to their political leaders in particular. It was these leaders who abused the latent nationalist forces in their respective republics in order the legitimize their monopoly of power. The leaders in the secessionist republics also succumbed to influences coming from the newly unified and resurgent Germany and certain Islamic states."[85]

Instead of admitting Serbian blame, Djordjevich mainly accuses Germany and Islamic states for pursuing expansionist policies. That the then president of the SUC achieved to be invited as a witness to a special hearing on U.S. foreign policy toward Bosnia and the Balkans is quite remarkable and rightfully deserves Djordjevich's lasting pride. However, his appearing at the Committee of Foreign Affairs, following a two-day-visit of the then Bosnian Serb President Radovan Karadžić in Pale in March of the same year, stirred up anger from the Croatian American lobby.

To the spokespersons of the Croatian American Association (CAA) not all sides were to blame for the tragic war in the former Yugoslavia as the

---

84. At the time of my writing, émigré Serbs received the right to vote. For the first time in the history of Serbian immigration they could participate in the presidential elections in the summer of 2004.
85. Hearing before the Committee on Foreign Affairs, 103rd congress, 05/11/1994: 33.

SUC tried to bring forth, but only Serbian nationalist and hegemonic policies. The CAA suspected that the Committee provided Mr. Djordjevich "with a platform from which to legitimize Serb occupation of neighboring countries."[86] In fact, the summary report of the "conversations with the Bosnian Serb leadership" which is attached to the hearing's protocol supports the impression given by the Croatian American representatives. Downplaying Serbian violence that was waging in Bosnia at the same time, Djordjevich underlines that it is "our strongest overall impression that the Serbs in Bosnia desire peace but without surrender."[87] Throughout the report the SUC president expresses his trust in the "good intentions" of the rebel republic's leadership as well as of Milošević's will to cooperate with UN peace keeping troops. "Apparently, the wounds of war are deep, and President Karadžić and his associates strongly stated that „we cannot live together with the Muslims: we want to live in our own state." These statements are but elegant formulations for the legitimization of armed struggle against Bosnian Muslims in Bosnia. That Djordjevich has achieved to be granted such an important podium for expressing his political views, with the prospect of actually influencing American foreign policy, and the Bosnian war directly, is of salient importance, underlining the political power that the SUC did hold at certain crossroads during the war.

Four years later, in May 1998, the Serb diaspora welcomed the then Bosnian Serb President, Biljana Plavšić, at St. Archangel Michael Serbian Eastern Orthodox Church in Saratoga. Three years after signing the Dayton Peace agreement that officially ended the war, in the sunny Silicon Valley she distances herself from her former boss and ally, Radovan Karadžić. This day Plavšić presented herself as a proponent of a 'moderate' Serbian nationalism. According to Dolinsky from "The San Francisco Chronicle" Plavšić stated that "[E]xcesses were committed on all sides, but at least in the case of the Serbs, ..., outside the command structure. Even Ratko Mladić, known to the world as the 'Butcher of Srebrenica,' is no more guilty, she said than Croats and Muslims who are not indicted" (Dolinsky 1998b: A 10). Downplaying atrocities committed by Serbian military and paramilitary, this quote at least puts into doubt the adjective 'moderate' in the characterization of the Bosnian President. Almost a year before the war in Kosovo, her insistence on the province's status must have rung a bell among Serbian Americans: "On Kosovo, where the Albanian majority demands independence, Plavšić said Serbia should no more give it up than the United States would give up Texas if Texas had a Mexican majority" (Dolinsky ibid.: A 10). Not mentioning the excess of violence committed by the Serbian police in Serbia's autonomous province since the 1980's,

86. Hearing before the Committee on Foreign Affairs, 103rd congress, 05/11/1994: 52.
87. Hearing before the Committee on Foreign Affairs, 103rd congress, 05/11/1994: 58.

the metaphor doesn't work. What the comparison does achieve is to shake the audience's hearts. Supposedly, Plavšić's reception in the church was overwhelming and warm. Her aide in the U.S., political scientist and journalist Srdja Trifković worded her stance on Serbdom as follows:

> "It is all so confusing. Throughout history, you have been Serbs and Croats, then you became Muslims, then you were Turks, then you were indeterminate, then you were Yugoslavs, then Muslims again, and now you say you have decided to become Bosniaks. Good, at least we know what to call you from now on ... We have never been anything but Serbs." (Dolinsky ibid.: A 10)

Ridiculing the identity politics in the former Yugoslavia which indeed did effect Bosnia's Muslims but also Croats and Serbs most dramatically during the country's disintegration, Plavšić produces the image of a fixed, "rooted" Serbdom, the ingredient out of which nationalism is made. Here she draws on established binarisms hinting at the 500-year span of Ottoman domination of Bosnia and Serbia. Juxtaposing the "Muslim traitors" with the "Serbian warriors" has been a current element of propaganda during the Balkan wars of the 1990's. What is interesting about Plavšić's visit to California is that it took place in the Serbian Orthodox Church in the Silicon Valley, providing a show case for how religion and politics are interconnected with Serbian diaspora activism. In fact, the churches in the Bay Area have so far been quite receptive to the SUC, ranging from priests having signed in as members to holding monthly meetings in the church halls. To note, in 2001 Plavšić, an indicted war criminal, has surrendered herself voluntarily to the International Criminal Tribunal at the Hague (ICTY).

Usually, at parties and celebrations I visited in the church hall, there were visitors from all the different groups and factions within the 'Serbian community,' but at this SUC dinner I didn't meet a single refugee. And in fact, Bosnian Serb families struggling to survive in the expensive San Francisco area told me with frustration that they did not experience the solidarity Djordjevich praised so much. Perhaps, the community solidarity had thinned out over time, and the refugees arriving around 2000 came after the high-time of diaspora activism had already ceased. Certainly, the Serbian unity as proclaimed by the SUC talk heads conceals the fact, that attempts at closing the socio-cultural gap between the mostly atheistic, non-professional recent refugees from rural Bosnia, who love to play soccer instead of attending the divine liturgy,[88] and the religiously organized Serbian American 'old-timers' have failed.

Djordjevich is convinced that due to the church split, the diaspora's possibilities to influence the homeland are still close to non-existent. The ideological ramifications underlying the schism have still not been overcome since the fall of communism, with Milošević heading a socialist party and government in Serbia. For Croats it was much easier to establish intimate diaspora-homeland ties, since Tudjman built his nationalist campaign on the right-wing, partly Ustaša émigré circles in North America who rallied support for a Croatian political movement they saw in line with their own cause.[89] Hardly anybody admits this, least Djordjevich who rejects any statements regarding the diaspora's support for the "communist" Milošević, but in fact the SUC did initially stand behind the Serbian President's agenda, if only for its nationalist aspirations. According to Hockenos (2003: 108) "the diaspora belonged to Milošević, as long as Milošević pursued a nationalist agenda – in the political arena and on the battlefield. [...] in diaspora churches and Serb cultural clubs worldwide, Milošević was heralded as a bold nationalist reformer (a reincarnation of the nineteenth-century Serb hero Karadjordje!) who might restore Serbia to its proper place as first among nations in Yugoslavia." But when my interlocutors addressed this touchy issue, I received very different evaluations about the diaspora's relationship to Milošević.

Far from admitting the SUC's prior sympathies for Milošević to me, Djordjevich nevertheless makes the point crystal-clear: Milošević was not nationalistic enough. He became a traitor, not because he (together with Tudjman and Izetbegović) was waging a war, but precisely because his military operations weren't reaching far enough. His withdrawal from Croatian Krajina and Republika Srpska left many nationalist-minded diaspora Serbs bitterly frustrated. While the diaspora's support for Milošević had from the beginning not been univocal, by 1995 Milošević had lost appeal to most Serbs in the U.S. But at the turn of the millennium the embarrassing issue of diaspora support of Milošević has been carefully hidden and silenced.

> Djordjevich grudgingly sums up the state of homeland-diaspora relations as follows: "*They [Serbs in Serbia] don't want us, they are afraid of*

88. Here I am referring to a situation I observed at the annual Serbian Orthodox Western Diocese meeting in Jackson. In the evening, before a big communal dinner, mostly older first-generation and second generation Serbs gathered in a tent and attended the divine liturgy, which was held in English. Outside the tent, not far away, young men and boys, mostly recent refugees, continued playing soccer in the evening sun, conversing in Serbian. While I stood inside the tent listening to the small church choir singing songs in church Slavonic, an older first-generation man whispered to me how "lost these people" outside were and what an affront against the church and Serbdom their behavior was. To my mind, the divide between the various immigrant groups could be hardly grasped better than in this example.
89. See also Hockenos 2003: 42-59.

> *us. Why? There is a simple reason for their mindset, I told you how they think: here we come from America, we are independent, we come in there to help, not asking for anything, we know some rules and codes of behavior. In contrast to that their parliament is a joke they don't even know how to apply basic parliamentary procedures. We were arguing that maybe 20 % of deputy seats should be reserved for people from diaspora, so that they can bring knowledge of the Western democracy. What Tocqueville said about America, habits of the heart, the democratic, the freedom oriented, and open-minded mindset. To respect individuals, no matter what religion. They don't know how to do that, on top of that, they have no sense of organization. They are illogical, they have no ability to logically create a process of things, it is all improvisation in the given moment. They don't think, they think in terms of day to day.*" After a short pause Djordjevich continues his speech: „*You cannot rebuild the country that way. They need diaspora badly, but as Dobrica Ćosić, the former President of Yugoslavia told me, in' 98 he told me. He said: You people from diaspora see that we are very sick. We are very sick. We are like a very sick person who doesn't want to take medicine. And you are bringing us medicine and a cure that we don't want to take.*"

Given such a determinedly negative view of his kinsmen in the homeland, by making use of the metaphor of 'disease,' which reveals the asymmetrical relationship between 'healthy' Serbs in the diaspora and 'sick' Serbs in Serbia, it is no wonder that cooperation is prone with failures. After all, a general respect in each other's virtues seems to be absent, at least from Djordjevich's side. Djordjevich's talk reveals another issue, that is the question of democracy and the nation-state: who is inside it, and who is outside? In *Marketing the American creed abroad* (1999) Yossi Shain explores how diasporas in the U.S. and in their homelands take part in political transitions at home. His results are outright positive: Eastern European diasporas, he suggests, are especially instrumental in bolstering transitional homeland democracies. With regard to the Serbian case as well as the Croatian case such optimistic outlook is hardly adequate, given the significance that a few persons can acquire in homeland-diaspora relationships. What kind of democracy does Shain mean?

Ultimately, the problem of diasporas concerns the question of representation, since the diaspora is not represented democratically – they don't vote (as a diaspora or in the homeland), and a majority of Serbs living outside of the former Yugoslavia do not participate in diaspora politics. And to provide 'the diaspora' (which in his conception consists of only a few 'professional' people) with twenty percent of deputy seats, throws a shadow on the 'democracy talk' Djordjevich gives.

Having in mind that most diaspora Serbs are not active in diaspora life, those who are could hardly be given the huge responsibility to determine which policies the citizens who stay in the homeland deserve. So far, the ones with the most money and the loudest voices have been able to participate in the 'transnational democracy' Djordjevich envisions, and there seems to be little effort at changing the situation.

In any way, the lobbying event on Turk street was only sparsely visited, possibly due to the relatively high entrance fee and the dress code, making the evening more costly than the usual casual festivals and celebrations. Perhaps, the low number of visitors, who didn't miss the chance to meet and dance on St. George's Day – *Djurdjevan* being a family saint and a spring festival – reveals something else about the relationship between the diaspora organization and the Serbian community. Whereas Djordjevich is widely known through publications on the Internet, letter writing to Congress people and other persons of power in American society, many Serbs I talked to, especially young ones, did not know of him, lest recognize his name! Strikingly, most of the younger migrants were absent this day – the SUC simply didn't mean much to those who came during the last ten years. And most "old-timers" who had been active in Chetnik organizations for the last fifty years probably didn't feel the need to plan for a Serbian future in a new organization.

The SUC reflects the typical mode of immigration politics in America, "client-politics." According to Christian Joppke (1998: 18) client politics is

> "a form of bilaterial influence in which small and well-organized groups intensely interested in a policy develop close working relations with officials responsible for it. Their interactions take place largely out of public view and with little outside interference. Client politics is strongly orientied toward expansive immigration policies."

It is widely known that Hispanics play a role in American electoral campaigns, Hispanic lobby groups being able to have an impact on immigration policies and other issues. Small ethnic groups such as the Serbs, making up far fewer clients, received very little sympathy in American government circles and apart from the speech delivered by Djordjevich at the Foreign Affair's Committee, have had relatively little impact on officials whatsoever. Another problem arises out of the fact that the clients Djordjevich tries to represent are so divided, unlike other ethnic groups.

In fact, twelve years after its foundation in San Francisco and three years after the bombing of Yugoslavia, with the wars of disintegration ending in a 'grand finale,' the SUC had obviously lost its political appeal and didn't reach out to the many. Whereas Djordjevich prided himself with the high degree of professionalism of the organization's key figures, its touch of exclusivity appeared to alienate a great bulk of younger, university enrolled immigrants as well as older, not so highly educated ones. However, a lobbying event such as this didn't only serve to replenish the organization's budget and advertise its present activities, it also attempted at reinstituting itself as a site of cultural festivities, entertainment, and community-building. Into its 13th year of existence the SUC opened up to embrace the "Serbian community" as a whole, seeking to create the image of unity once again in the history of the Serbian diaspora.

Conclusion

In this first part of the book I have opened up a variety of issues and theoretical ideas in order to shed light on the politics of identity and long-distance nationalism among displaced Serbs in the San Francisco Bay Area. Inspired by recent thinking about the prevalence of ethnic identity stretching across national borders (Anderson 1994, Appadurai 1996, Procter 2000, Skrbiš 1999 et al.) I have sought to explore how people perceive of their personal and national identity vis-à-vis their homeland and the host-society. The conversations and observations reveal that the recent Balkan war was a central event and marker of identity abroad, setting in motion manifold processes of identity change or affirmation of identity.

At first glimpse, the material may offer a striking prevalence of essentialism in the narratives and statements I put forth. In fact, the attraction of collective labels and a desire for national belonging seems to be remarkable at a time, when terms like tolerance, multiculturalism, pluralism, and hybridity come along as catchphrases in the age of globalization. The Yugoslav case seems to provide us with manifold questions regarding both ethnic identity and hybrid forms of belonging, not only in the homeland. As Pamela Ballinger (2003: 261) states:

> "The striking absence of discussion about former Yugoslavia in the hybridity and borderlands literature points up the limitations of much of the Anglo-American analysis of these phenomena. ... Rarely, however, are postsocialist areas such as the Balkans or former Yugoslavia discussed in this anthropological literature on borderlands, despite the fact that the region has been profoundly shaped by its interstitial position between competing empires, states, religions, and political ideologies."

I suggest, that my material revealed highly contradictory voices with regard to hybridity and essentialism. On one hand, many seemed to share the belief in a multicultural homeland and regarded him/herself as a "Yugoslav" and a "Serb," thus manifesting the power that non-ethnic based identities had in the former Yugoslavia at various historical times. In the United

States such hybrid declarations survived, added by the hyphenated category "Serbian-American," or when meeting somebody from the same hometown or region, that regional identity became center-stage. Therefore, it needs to be underlined that identity is an imagined, fluid, situational, and context-based phenomenon that resists easy processes of fixing. Nevertheless, on the other hand, there was hardly anyone who did not succumb to the force to define oneself ethnically and discard any hybrid declaration as "Yugoslav." A great many also fervently indulged in the celebration of Serbdom. In an age of increasing deterritorialization we can witness a drive to the resurgence of national belonging and static categories of identity. The national order of the world, dividing people into clear-cut national entities, such as Germans, French, and Indonesians or ethnic identities, e.g. Hutu, Tutsi, Latino, Serb, and Croat is still the only valid point of orientation for many people all over the globe, those in the homeland and those abroad. Obviously, many of my informants were self-conscious about the inherent contradiction between ethno-national 'absolutism' and hybridity, but at the same time remained helpless as to how to solve this specific categorical "in-betweenness."

In *Essentializing Essentialism, Essentialising Silence* (1997) Pnina Werbner attacks the academic drive for political correctness and the rejection of label after label. According to Werbner (ibid.: 229)

> "at issue are problems of both representation and self-presentation. ... Increasingly, the tendendy has been to label all collective representations – whether of ethnic and religious groups, or classes or nations – as misplaced essentialisms (so that as anthropologists we can no longer study a 'society', a 'community', a 'culture' or a 'people'). Yet, this indiscriminate accusation of essentialism, applied uncritically to all objectifications of collective agents, has tended, I shall argue here, to obscure processes of collective representations and self-representations which are *not* essentialist."

At issue are the very questions of belonging, as opposed to the hard-core ideology of individualism, where everybody stands alone in an increasingly complex world. In this vein, too, Glick Schiller and Fouron (2001: 271) have emphasized the important aspect of community, solidarity, empowerment, and social and political activism that exiles who ascribe to being Haitian derive from their ethnic bonds.

The identity discourses of a relatively large number of Serbs who participated in my research do not stand in isolation. Identity discourses are a prerequisite for long-distance nationalism at the same time that long-distance nationalism, as exemplified by the *Serbian Unity Congress*, may be influenced by and may influence these discourses. Clearly, the SUC operates with essentialist images of Serbdom and the conviction to know "what the Serbs want" that are based on simplistic and exaggerated visions of the collective. Claiming to democratically represent "Serbs as such" the SUC obscures the fact that although working in a democratic country, they are not representative of the Serb immigrant population at all. And, interestingly, while using homogenized, nationalist versions of being Serbian, the transnational practices of lobbying are deeply imbued with American ways of political maneuvering. Thus, hybridity can be practiced, while essentialism is evoked in words.

Overall, the statements and narratives I have presented so far reveal not only people who are suffering from the Yugoslav wars of disintegration (see Procter 2000), but many of the participants in this study are also self-consciously participating in the same debates of victimology, 'Otherness', and history that have fueled the conflicts in the homeland. With regard to these issues, which I understand as key issues among my interlocutors at the time of my fieldwork, some have been more ambivalent, aware of the inherent contradictions and dangers, like Lena, than others, for example Michael Djordjevich, have univocally celebrated the renewed sense of community.

Having outlined discourses on identity or identity-politics among Serbs in the Bay Area, I wish to have made clear how personal and national identity are imbued with multiple meanings, e.g. history, that can change over time and depending on the situation. In the following part of this book I will look in more detail at life stories of a few individuals I got acquainted with. Due to the central role of history in the previous chapter, the next chapters shall analyze versions of the past and the connection between memory and long-distance nationalist activism.

Part II. Living in the Past: The Role of the Second World War

Chapter 4. Remembering War and Displacement

> "You wish to see the house where I was born, gentlemen? But my mother gave birth to me in a hospital in Fiume, which has been knocked down. You won't be able either to put a memorial plate on my house, because it has been knocked down as well. If you wanted to you could put up three to four plates with my name written on different houses in various cities and countries. Even then I wouldn't be able to help you as I don't know which was my father's house, I don't remember where I lived in my childhood, and I rarely know in which language I conversed. What I did keep in my mind are images: a bent palmtree and an oleander somewhere at the shore of a sea. The Danube streaming along in a misty green, a children's rhyme: Ene mene mu... (Kiš *Der Heimatlose* [*The Homeless*] in: Ugrešić1994, transl. mine)"

Memory takes on extremely poignant forms and contents, when a person or a group of people has suffered violence and exile. Whereas the worst possible scenario may be the case and the memory of places and houses could be vague or even forgotten, the images of them remain powerful and pervasive. This is the message delivered in the quote by the great Serbian writer and storyteller Danilo Kiš whose story is ripe with traces of displacement, in the course of which remembering and forgetting stand in fierce competition. Since his life trajectory has repeatedly and all of a sudden been disrupted – leaving a house, a village, a story of his ancestors without being prepared – memory has undergone serious cuts and erasures. Perhaps the greatest fear is that, without having the time to materially or systematically store it, memory may have been as much the victim of displacement as the victim him/herself. Thus, to be a survivor of a 'lost world' and the witness of horrible times creates a heightened self-consciousness, an awareness of the Self. People try to remember the outlook of the house they lived in and the village where they were born, names of former neighbors, names of the dead as well as of the living – and if they forget a name they may feel deeply disturbed. Some persons almost obsessively "re-member" (calling attention to the reaggregation of members[90]) minute details of their flight, dialogues that took place while escaping, encounters with strangers, and stories told by others. Even if what is left are (only) images and forgetting has taken its toll, as Kiš in the above quoted passage implies, vague and random as these memories may be, they are deeply inscribed into the displaced person's mind. Barbara Myerhoff in *Remembered Lives* (1992) contends: "Sometimes the image is the only part of their lives subject to control. But this is not a small thing to control" (Myerhoff 1992: 232). In other words: "What remains are our images" (Žbanić 2003).

Synopsis

In this part of the book I am concerned with a particular aspect of diaspora politics, anthropological perspectives on life histories and the interaction of latency and transposition within the memory of violence. More precisely I am interested in how a few selected individuals who are active participants in long-distance nationalism and some of whom are even leaders narrate their past stories of violence and victimization in conjunction with transnational practices in the present. Focusing on three case studies of individuals who were driven from their homes during the Second World War one necessarily needs to confront the issue of the generational make-up of diaspora politics and the role that past expulsions and war play in the world of Serbian émigré life today. Meandering through the realms of memory, violence, and long-distance nationalism, my guiding questions address the significance of the past in traversing both time and space in the wake of the latest Yugoslav wars of disintegration. How are past experiences accommodated to the present, or made to fit actual and changing circumstances? With regard to Kiš's quote: What is the role of trauma, the fragmentary character of remembering a past that has not been worked through? Which rhetorical strategies do my interlocutors use for presenting their life stories?

First I will look at "worlds made" in the narratives and investigate the ways that people "make themselves up" when telling their lives and how they link individual stories with the collective history of the nation. Drawing from theoretical ideas on memory and narrative, i.e. Maurice Halbwachs (1992), Paul Connerton (1989), and John Gillis (1994), my central hypothesis is that in the diaspora the Third Balkan Wars serve as a mirror for reliving the Second World War due to the lack of reconciliation and remorse in the Tito era and after communism's demise. Unsettled accounts

90. Myerhoff paid attention to this quality of remembering as "re-membering," emphasizing the recalling of "figures that belong to one's life story, one's own prior selves, as well as significant others who are of the story. Re-membering, then, is a purposive, significant unification, quite different from the passive, continuous fragmentary flickering of images and feelings that accompany other activities in the normal flow of consciousness" (Myerhoff 1992: 240).

made way to yet new unsettled accounts. Or, the experience of violence forms the core of the specific Serbian case of long-distance nationalism. Second, I turn to the material side of memory by analyzing the salient importance of houses, landscapes, and architectural artifacts that displaced Serbs keep in their exilic places to transform them into spaces. More than just a memory practice, I argue that the remembrance of lost houses is also a central marker for staking claims to a "lost world,“ claims which have been especially dangerous in the wake of the bloody conflicts in the 1990's.

The Case Studies

Why do I focus on old people and the Second World War instead of on the recent violent disintegration of Yugoslavia? With the outbreak of the Third Balkan Wars, notwithstanding the misleadingly simplistic character of the statements of "ancient-old ethnic hatreds“[91] or the "repetition of history,“ frequently made in the media and in political discourse to explain the wars, many of the old did indeed pass through their innermost private reviving of "the past“ which to them, in a fundamental sense represented a repetition of (their) history. For old Serbs who had been political exiles after the Second World War the ten years of war in their homeland set in motion an intense process of retrospection into their personal and collective memories[92]. But these stories reached further than the storyteller could envision. I argue, that the status of old people in Serbian culture as "bearers of tradition“ (Simić 1978) which cultivates the role of the aged to transmit history, enhanced historical revisionism in the diaspora. Many of the old men and women who told me their life stories are prominent in diaspora circles throughout the generational groupings. They are not just storytellers: what is interesting about them is their diaspora activism or how they put their memory into practice. It is precisely this linkage between memory, violence, and long-distance nationalist practices, which I want to investigate in this chapter.

My choice of focusing on three persons is grounded in the belief, that only by looking closely at the case studies can one understand the cultural embeddedness of certain memories and practices. That the choice fell on these and not other individuals is as arbitrary as it has to do with a certain intimacy I established with these persons and the significance their person-

---

91. The impression that the violent conflicts in the former Yugoslavia have been caused by deeply rooted old antagonisms and have been hopelessly inscrutable to the outsider has been presented first by Robert Kaplan in his travelogue "Balkan Ghosts“ (1993: 22-23).
92. Maurice Halbwachs in *On Collective Memory* 1992 underlines that individual memory is unthinkable without the social interaction with other people, and "it is individuals as group members who remember“ (ibid.: 22). Hence his statement "We are never alone“ (ibid.: 23) to express the dependence of individual and collective memory.

al stories and diaspora activism have in the San Francisco Bay Area. Again, most Serbs abroad are not political activists, and the majority is not at all involved in Serbian community life as these and other people I worked with are. But as Paul Hockenos (2003) has demonstrated, for diaspora research, it is quite important to analyze the identity politics and transnational political strategies of key figures. This then is the characteristic which all three narrators share: they are politically prominent proponents of Serbian exile nationalism, and they are driven by stories of victimization during the Second World War.

First, I will present the three life stories in a successive manner. Each life story will be followed by a short interpretative comment. Second comes a lengthy analysis of the narratives that stretches into chapter five.

Saša Gocić: The humanitarian person of the year

Saša Gocić is a sixty-five-year-old mechanic and owner of a car workshop in Stockton, California. In the U.S. since 1957 he wasn't involved in Serbian diaspora politics before the breakup of Yugoslavia in 1991, when the erupting violence urged him to act on behalf of *Save Serbian Children* (SSC). Founded and run solely by himself, SSC is a humanitarian non-profit organization lobbying for the medical treatment and cosmetic surgeries of badly wounded Serbian war victims from Croatia and Bosnia in Californian hospitals. Over the last ten years Saša collected about ten million dollars – this is the figure he states – to finance the travels, medical costs, and living expenses for 135 Serbian children. He himself hosted 33 children and their parents in his own house. As he proudly confesses, for his dedication to the recovering of the war victims he received the price of "the humanitarian person of the year" in Fresno in 1998. On the wall hangs a local newspaper article with a photo of Saša holding the award in his hand. The small man with dark dyed hair and a mustache wears a T-shirt with the "Target" sign, a symbol for state-sponsored Serbian resistance and resilience against the NATO powers in Belgrade of 1999. He speaks with enthusiasm, anger, and pride into my recording machine. These days he is occupied with loading and sending a container with 'humanitarian' goods for 'persecuted' Serbs in Kosovo.

Upon entering his air-conditioned living room in the hot inland town in California the interior decoration of his house strike me immediately. The paraphernalia provides a rich insight into the life story and long-distance nationalism of its owner: A huge Serbian flag fills the left corner of the room, next to it are a couple of certificates and awards for SSC, complete with the original signatures, one from Radovan Karadžić, President of Republika Srpska during the Bosnian war and now a wanted war criminal, another one from Biljana Plavšić who followed him in office and after turning herself in has been sentenced at the International Criminal Tribunal at The Hague (ICTY) in 2003, and a third one from the *Serbian Unity Congress* in San Francisco – all uttering praise for Saša's outstanding help on behalf of the "Serbian cause." On the opposite side of the room one can see the portraits of his son, with Bachelors hat after graduation at UC Davis, and daughter. Next to the door to the terrace hangs a photo with a newspaper article from the "Sacramento News," depicting a girl with a missing arm and large burning wounds on face and body. A few old black-and-white shots of ancestors and homes in Lika, Croatia, where he comes from, decorate the wall, and finally one sees a small dark enamel sign with the house number "35 Jezero" written on it in white letters. As Saša contends, he took the house number as the only object from his burnt down house when he visited his childhood place in 2000. What is interesting is how he connects the telling of his own past with the suffering of a Serbian woman in today's Bosnia from whom he receives letters telling him of how her Croatian husband maltreats her:

> *"I would really like to help her, to be honest. The biggest problem is that the Muslims and Croats are mistreating the children because she is a Serb. But I don't know why they don't look like father is Croatian. Don't they feel? And then regardless who cares what nationality is? Maybe that's, maybe we Serbs need to be punished like this, we always say: But let them go. But I still say if I go and step in their shoes, I would be the same as they are. I says, the kids, this is not their fault, this is not their fault! I remember when they were beating us during World War Two, when my neighbor, I remember him, when they took him by hands and legs, it was winter, and I was probably five or six, but I remember that better than what I ate yesterday. They were throwing him into the snow and kicking him and he was crying. They were beating him, he was a boy, and I was scared to death. And I know, I can't remember his last name or anything, but they call him like "Sukrila," means candy, "Zucker," the word is "Zucker"*[93] *[...] And I remember they called him that, that boy, and they were beating him, and I was scared to death, and they asked me, I remember, if there was guns and stuff like that in the basement of our house. They asked: 'Partisan?' I said: 'No, no Partisan.' [...] Everything was burned, entire village was burned! My father was blind and he was upstairs, I was hiding down in the basement, they got me and one of them grabbed me by the hand, I cried: 'Bring me upstairs!' One of the guys from Ustaša was holding a gun under my father's nose. He was telling him: 'Pipni stari, pipni stari!' You know, feel this, old man,*

93. Using German terms and phrases as Saša is doing here for the word "sugar" has not been exceptional in the interviews I had with older people. Like many DP's who left Yugoslavia after the Second World War in the mid-fifties Saša spent a few years in Austria and Germany where he applied for an American visa. He still enjoys practicing some German with me, which has been his first foreign language before he learned English.

feel this. So my father held his hands down, he knew that if he just tried to grab the gun they would kill him. And I remember one thing: that a guy walked in, and I was there, I was crying, and he spoke foreign, I am sure German, and he starts yelling something in German. He was some kind of higher officer or something, and then that guy left my father. My father spoke German, he was living in Berlin and spoke two or three languages, so I think that saved him. All the village people ran, but my father stayed home, because he was already old and blind. "Jezero" is the name of our town, our village is called Jezero, which means lake. It was like three lakes up there and my house was not even 100 m from the lake. And we were standing above the lake, and I remember like some kind of popping noise. I remember asking somebody: 'What is that what makes so much noise?' And they tell me the tiles are getting hot when the houses were burning, all of our houses are covered with Spanish tile, and from the heat they were popping. I remember asking that particular question, I don't know why that stuck in my mind, because I hear that popping, popp, popp, popp! That stuck in my mind, I remember like today, standing and looking, the second house from my house, when it was burning, I remember that house particularly, big, fallen, it burst up and I looked at it. I remember just like now. Most people don't realize how much that affects kids, and they say the children should forget! The faster you forget, the faster the enemy will hit you again. I don't believe in nothing anymore, because they killed my three brothers, and my mother and my relatives. They took my brother, not that day, they took my brother to a prison in Zagreb. He was in concentration camp and when he came back Partisans attacked in Zagreb at the railway station and he escaped from there. When he came back we couldn't recognize him, he was nothing but a bone. What you see in Dachau. And my neighbor, he too escaped the day when they took my brothers and another brother. He was going on a hill and jumped on a wagon, it was a horse wagon full with potatoes, with the horses, and he jumped and rolled, they shot at him. He escaped, but they took my neighbor next door, he was an older man, he walked maybe 25 km and then they shot him. He couldn't walk anymore and told the Ustaša, my brother was behind him, but they said: 'Walk, old man, stari'. My brother said, he took a handgun and shot him three times in the chest like this and they kept on walking. There was like a bigger town where I was born, he says, we walk, but that day they burned all our villages, everything, everything. I grew up in that house, my house was probably the only one that survived, only 20% of it was burned. My father, when he came back from the United States[94] he built a good house, it was stone, thick, and the beams were about two feet big. They put a fire in there but didn't wait till it burned, and kids and some women, we stayed, they took men, all men, and only women and kids and old men stayed. My mother got killed in 1944, she was visiting her uncle and they got her on the road and took her in the woods and shot her three times. We found her after three weeks, my oldest brother, three brothers got killed next to me, right next to me. We went to the snow, it was winter and we turned

> *the fire out, and that day only two houses survived. One was my father's house. That house survived because it was all the way near the lake and they didn't want to walk one km, only to burn one house. And villagers finally rebuilt their homes; the third house from mine was just rebuilt before the war. I remember how my neighbor, Ilija, always lived in this little shack that he built, not bigger than an American garage. They finally built a house, it wasn't, I bet you, ten years before now, this war, and then boom! They burned it; everything was burned again! So it's every generation that's got to go over and over burning, goddam, and rebuilding, but finally they cleansed all the Serbs. Name me one nation that was totally cleansed, except the Serbs in Europe! You cannot name it, only Serbs in Krajina.*"

This narrative begins and ends right in the middle of violence and suffering. When asking Saša about his past, the perpetration of Serbs in Croatia is center-stage, suffice to tell the listener any episodes in his life that preceded his victimizing experiences. If there is one interlocutor in my overall sample whose speech is dominated by images, fragments, and moving depictions of violence – elements pointing to the persistence of trauma – it would be Saša, whose narrative, consisting of the repetitive mentioning of "*I remember*" and "*that stuck in my mind,*" is a homage to memory. In retelling his childhood memories Saša gets as close as he can to Danilo Kiš's fragmentary style of remembering. One horrible image follows the next: the beating of a neighbor's son, the threatening of his blind, old father with the tip of a gun, and above all the burning of the house with the intense popping noise caused by exploding tiles.

What Ochs and Capps (1996: 7) state with regard to trauma and narrative adheres to Saša's narrative as well: "[W]hen an experience is too devastating to incorporate into one's life story such experiences invade present lives in the form of somatic sensations or fragmented memories, i.e. flashbacks, but are not narrativized into a coherent sequence [...]." Saša's account exemplifies the presenting of a past that has not been worked through. Linear time and chronology are abolished as the narrator moves from his experiences as a five-year-old boy to events in the 1990's, presenting the violence in a cyclical manner. Interestingly, except for the ideolog-

94. Saša's father was already an old man when his youngest son out of ten, Saša, was born. At the turn of the century he had temporarily worked in the steel mines on the East Coast of the United States. Many Serbs of the early migrations (until the 1920's) had returned to Yugoslavia like Saša's father. It was only after 1924 with the introduction of the immigration quotas that entering the country got more difficult and such returns ceased, since an acceptance to the U.S. meant permanent settlement and a return to the homecountry would cause a loss of status and ban on a repeated entry. In a way then, transnationalism was a common phenomenon before the introduction of the immigration quotas, whereas in the Yugoslav case the assumedly classic state of being an immigrant and having cut the ties to the homeland, a more modern and contemporary principle.

ical designation "partisan" used by the perpetrators to find out whether the Gocić family is on the enemy side, the narrative is emptied off any ethnic or political categories. When describing the actions of the intruding Ustaši, impersonal pronouns such as "he" and "they" are applied except once, so that the attackers appear strikingly empty, bare of any ethnic trace. Only the framing comments in the narrative's beginning and end directly hint at the ethnicization of the violence, which is characterized by 'Croat hatred' against Serbs. Ideological oppositions which go beyond ethnic categorizations, such as Chetnik-Partisan, Ustaša-Partisan, or Communist-Royalist, which during World War Two crisscrossed ethnic designations and granted the civil war its highly complex, bloody outlook, are absent. The recollection of the suffering of Saša, the child, is dominated by family losses, personal and material destruction that reach deep into the present, mirroring the immediacy of violence on a child's mind that has not been filtered through official historical accounts or political analyses. He can be called a "dormant transnational," because before the advent of war he for decades engaged in his professional and private life in the U.S., without turning to his immigrant past. I selected the above passage out of a five-hour-interview, because it is in this narrative that Saša speaks most about himself and this in a very excited, emotional, loud, and intense manner, marking his childhood experiences as some of the most salient events in his life. Abstracting from the trauma of the "innocent," Saša develops a manichaeic worldview based on now increasingly ethnicized categories, Croats against Serbs, to explain the renewed conflict in the former Yugoslavia in the 1990's. What is crucial in Saša's life story is how after a fifty-year break between his war trauma and the disintegration of the homeland, his transnational activism appears to automatically latch on to the figure of the innocent child, as if the recent wars meant a continuation of suffering, this time to therapeutically help both the wounded children and Saša, the still suffering preschooler.

Mira Pesić Connor: The metamorphosis from a businesswoman to an activist for the Čelebiči Trial

A cultural anthropologist, successful businesswoman, and active member of the Serbian community in the Bay Area, Mira Pesić Connor is a person that everybody knows. The seventy-nine-year-old petite, energetic and always busy pensioner is one of the founding members of the *Serbian Unity Congress*. Furthermore, she is the eldest out of three women that constitute the *Serbian Women's Caucus*, a subsection of the SUC devoted to gathering witness accounts of former Serbian camp prisoners during the Bosnian war (1992-1995) to formulate indictments at the International Criminal Tribunal for the former Yugoslavia at The Hague (ICTY). A result of her work with witness accounts testifies to the 1998 held Čelebići trial, the first trial against non-Serbs at court in the Netherlands. Mira also volunteers for Muslim, Croatian, and Serbian refugees in the area who need legal, bureaucratic or language assistance. I have not met one Serb during my whole fieldwork, who does not know Mira and has not heard of one of her projects, has not been helped by, or worked together with her at some point. Living in the prestigious Berkeley Hills in a big early 20th-century stone-house, which she shares with her younger sister, overlooking the green valley with the San Francisco Bay, and the city skyline at the horizon, the location and outlook of her home reflect the socio-economic success she achieved in the country she came to more than 50 years ago. The interior of the house is decorated with heavy wooden antique furniture, distinguished modern oil paintings, and numerous bookshelves filled predominantly with history books on ancient civilizations in the Balkans and Asia, Serbian History, and Croatian death camps in Jasenovać during World War Two. In 1941 Mira was a girl, when she and her family were expelled from their home and interned in this biggest Croatian concentration camp, before they got transported to Serbia. Next to the bookshelf by the fireplace hang a woven picture with four "S," the Serbian national slogan *Samo Sloga Srbina Spasova* (Only Unity Saves Serbs) and a seemingly modern icon, an abstract oil painting with a blurry martyred Christ. While conducting one of our numerous conversations, some of which we recorded, the telephone rings repeatedly. There hardly passes an hour in which no refugee calls her and asks for assistance, tells her about family conflicts where she could negotiate, or arranges meetings with her to go to court or to the social welfare agency. Downplaying her quite remarkable career as an outstanding San Francisco businesswoman, she mostly presents herself in very simple clothes, declares herself to me as an anthropologist, is proud of her studies at the Chicago School of Anthropology with Robert Redfield and Ruth Benedict as one of the first European Holocaust victims after World War Two, and loves to talk about American foreign policy, international political issues, and Serbian History. Like many of the older migrants, preceding her retirement in 1990 she was hardly aware of the Serbian community and visited the church only for the major annual celebrations. However, with the outbreak of war in the former Yugoslavia, Mira suddenly felt a strong determination to undertake everything possible to help refugees from *all* national groups, not just Serbs, who started arriving in the Bay Area. *"We know how it is to come to this country with empty hands. We ourselves have experienced victimization and exile, so we know exactly what these people are going through.*" She also takes a political stance on the events in the homeland by participating in public debates, holding speeches, and writing letters to local and national newspapers. Underlying her impressive engagement for "the

Serbian cause" is her knowledgeable, well-read, and intellectual outlook on Serbian history, which she connects to her own life story.

> *"I was born in Croatia, the region of Slavonia, in the center of the Serbian settlements in Croatia, namely in the area of Kapuk mountain and Vilogora. My town was basically like any other Austro-Hungarian town, except it had the most magnificent setting, because it was in the mountains, there were rivers, there was a little lake, truly very, very progressive town with about 4,000 to 5,000 inhabitants. In that region Serbs were situated for at least 400 years, there were about 180 Serbian villages and, of course, the question is: How did the Serbs come to live there? My family and hundreds and thousands of others came there as a result of the Turkish penetration in the Balkan Peninsula. After the siege of Vienna in 1529, most of the Serbs who already were under the Ottomans started moving northwards. After the fall of Serbia in 1459, most of the Serbian nobilities of Smederevo and northern parts started fleeing across the Sava and Danube rivers. At that time the Turks were actually in the middle of the Pannonian valley after conquering Hungary in 1527, they were continuously making inroads into the Habsburg Empire, when it was not yet an empire. It was simply Austro-Holy Roman Empire; the joining of the Austro-Hungarian parts occurred only much later. The Turks stayed in Budapest for over a hundred years and they made the second assault on Vienna in 1683, I think. In this interim period of about 150 years the Turks stabilized their position in Central Europe, and the Habsburg court realized, the Turks are going to stay there, unless the "limes imperii," or the border of the empire was secured. For that reason they realized that the Serbs had no other way but to flee northwards into the territories of Austro-Hungary and then they allowed them to come there in rows. They came from the Southern part of Serbia, from present day Kosovo etc. The military records in the archives of Austria already recorded our last name in the second half of the 16th century, maybe some time after the 1550's. [...] What is interesting about our people moving: They usually moved as an extended family, so usually it was more than one family that moved in, therefore the place in which my father was born was composed only of people of our last name, and secondly they also come from a village that was called "Sekulinci" ... [...] I remember very well in 1936, I was coming home from school and I heard a horrendous voice almost inhuman, and that was Hitler's voice. It was an afternoon, I think it might have been in March, that I remember, the windows were open and there were not too many radios, but we did have a radio, and it was just something I will never forget. It was like an announcement of horrible times to come. The Ustaša had a plan, which was established by Zagreb that one third of the Serbs are going to be deported and one third is going to be slaughtered and one third is going to be expelled. Well, we did not know this plan completely, but realized that something is going to happen. So after the proclamation of the Independent State of Croatia on April 9th, everything changed overnight. Serbs had to wear*

the blue ribbons and the Jewish families had to wear the yellow band. They needed the properties of the Serbs and they started picking up the Serbs immediately. They would be coming up with a Roman Catholic priest and offered you to accept Catholicism, and we could not do that for various reasons. So anyway, they did offer us to convert to Catholicism. That very afternoon, when they came to offer us to convert, we experienced something very extraordinary, and that's why I always try to remember this. A Croatian lady, Mrs. Latsan, heard from her husband who was working in the city hall not as an Ustaša, he was doing some work there in the building, and he heard in a telephone conversation whereby they will come at about five or six o'clock that day to pick up all the prominent Serbian families, and that they will come and pick us up, and pick up the Mirković's, pick up Redo, pick up all the prominent Serbs. And she ran to my mother and said: 'Mrs. Pesić, I have to tell you something, but, please, don't tell anybody, because they will kill me. They will come and pick you up.' The woman was hysterical, she cried. This happened in the afternoon about two o'clock. Well, it was almost incredible, you were born there for centuries and somebody is going to do this. And that is why I would simply say, when people ask why did the German Jews wait so late. Because they could not believe it, exactly as we could not believe it. So my mother was so stunned and first actually couldn't compose herself to believe that and she tried to actually pacify Mrs. Latsan. I heard that and I said I am not going to take a chance, I am going to take "ruksak" [Slavicized Germanic word for backpack, B.B.-L.], which we had in the store, and I prepared for each of us a ruksak with the most important things, socks, a towel, toothpaste, toothbrush, soap, and most important parts of the wardrobe. And everybody had a "ćebe" [blanket, B.B.-L.], I don't know how to call it anyway, something to cover himself, in case we would be going to sleep. And I also picked up all our birth certificates and all our pictures, family pictures, so that we would have something, and since I was a fragile tiny person I put all of these things into a towel and rolled the towel around myself and took "siharice" – do you know what siharice is? Safety pins, and put these around myself and basically was ready. And the Ustaši did pick us up. It was maybe about six o'clock. They also picked up our Mirković's, the neighboring family, then the Gretel family, Lusanović family, and Vidanović family which was a local priest. They picked us all up on a big truck and put us into a huge building, I think they probably put us into a school or something and by about ten o'clock and midnight there came a woman whom we later recognized as a professor, she was a professor of French, and she came and asked us to open up all of our purses to see what we had and picked up everything. Of course, we did have some jewelry and things like that, that was typical for the middle classes in Europe to have, she picked up that and came to my grandmother. And saw that my grandmother had a very beautiful set of earrings and in those days everything was very original, original gold, original stone and so on, and she looked at that, and my grandmother looked at her. My grandmother was young, she was about fifty or something,

> *and she looked at this professor, who was a great Ustašica, and said to her something [laughs heartily] which could have cost us our lives. She said: 'If you need these for the good luck and prosperity of your shitty Croatia, take it!' We were stunned and of course Baka [grandma, B.B-L.] unlocked the jewelry, pulled it out and gave it to them. So they put us into the wagons, railroad cars and took us to Sisak and unloaded us there, and Sisak is a town not very far from Zagreb, still on the other side of Sava, very close to Jasenovać, and they had the military barracks and that is why they used these as a camp. Before us they apparently had there by the things that we have seen the first collection of the Serbian Orthodox priests ... and the name of any of these Orthodox Priests were available in certain publications of which I have a copy. Anyway, they killed these people and they buried them, but since it was summer they did not apparently bury them deeply enough so the soil started boiling, so to speak, and we realized what it was. And anyway, so they would march us all out, they would surround the Serbs with all the bayonets and then they would start talking to us. And I do remember very well the little boy, little son of a friend of ours from our town who was about five years old and the Ustašis were really brutalizing us, and one of them, I remember, said: 'Who among you is a Serb? Let him raise his hand.' And we realized that this was a provocation and everybody was silent. And the little Bata pulls his father and he said: 'Daddy, aren't we Serbs?' Shortly after we were deported with all the people from Banja Luka and all of those from where I don't know, hundreds and hundreds of us. This was apparently the last transport of alive Serbs to Belgrade."*

Like Saša, the fascist Ustaša in Croatia victimized Mira as a youth, together with her family. Like Saša, Mira's homeland ties had loosened during the almost fifty year period of Yugoslav socialism, and like Saša the outbreak of war in 1991 set in motion a remarkably energetic diaspora activism. Unlike Saša, Mira was interned in a concentration camp and then expelled to Serbia. Unlike Saša, Mira's narrative is not ripe with fragmented images which reveal trauma, but it is a very elaborate story with a concise structural development. Reconstructing life before the foundation of the Ustaša state and depicting minute details of her family's captivity, Mira focuses less on the immediacy of images than on the precise explanation of historical events. Instead of still being overwhelmed with what she went through as a sixteen-year-old, Mira's narrative aims at mastering the experiences that once deeply hurt and humiliated her. The way that Mira remembers is highly rational, chronological, and aiming at completeness, while she meanders through personal recollection, historical reasoning, and background information she acquired after these tragic years in her early life. As in Saša's narrative, her use of direct speech contributes to the lively, 'authentic' character of her remembrances. The ideological master narratives of the 20th century, socialism, capitalism, and fascism which had explosive ramifications in the former Yugoslavia, are pushed into the background. But, in another passage of my lengthy interviews with Mira, she insists that though she left Belgrade in 1948 due to the rigorous version of communism under which she with her aristocratic upbringing didn't see a future for herself, she never rejected socialism. Even under the McCarthy era she strongly opined that she would rather choose communism and not capitalism. What is most salient in Mira's account is not political ideology but a search for justice, to achieve official recognition of the Jasenovać concentration camp and the Croatian attempt at eliminating the Serbian population in Croatia. Mira's childhood memories from World War Two, her activism for the Čelebići trial, and her commitment to help refugees from the former Yugoslavia, no matter what ethnic background they have, suggest that survivors of mass destruction often become "seekers after justice," as Myerhoff following Lifton pointed out (Myerhoff 1992: 236).

Righting past wrongs at the International Criminal Tribunal for the former Yugoslavia at the Hague (ICTY)

In 1995 Mira was already connected to a diaspora she didn't have much in common with before, when she first met Serb refugees who told her of Bosnian Muslim detention camps in the Tarčin area. At that time the International Criminal Tribunal (ICTY) in The Hague, Netherlands had been implemented for two years and Mira was outraged about the degree to which only Serbs were indicted. At the same time "*the media was selling the story of rape*" in Bosnia. In her mind this was all exaggerated, not mass rape committed by Serbian soldiers was the problem, but on all sides men 'occasionally' raped women 'as in every war,' just that politicians and journalists exploited this to ruin the image of Serbs. Here she is in line with the "North American News Analysis Group," an off-shoot of the Yorkville Station, N.Y.-based Belgrade Club, which countered in a publication:

> "This is preposterous and shameless propaganda. Rape in war is one of the most tragic but common forms of brutalization. Anyone who asserts that one side is guilty of it and other sides are not is either lacking all common sense or is an astute propagandist. The only way to stop rape in Bosnia-Herzegovina is to stop the war. The brutalization of Muslim and Croat women has been frequently reported. *The untold story is about the rape of Serbian women by Muslim and Croat forces.*" (quoted in Hockenos 2003: 143, Italics mine)

In general her arguments follow the same pattern, whether with regard to rape, concentration camps, or massacres against civilians: Yes, she admits, all these things have been committed by Serbs, but they have also been committed against them – just, and that is the scandal, that crimes against Serbs are neither being reported nor punished. She based her insights on writings by the French journalist Jacques Merlino whose publication *Les Vérités Yougoslaves ne sont pas toutes bonnes a dire* (The Truth from Yugoslavia is not being reported honestly) (1993) includes an interview with James Harff, director of the public relations company Ruder Finn Global Public Affairs. In the interview, Harff explains how his company received hundreds of thousands of dollars, mainly by Croat émigrés, to influence public opinion about the "genocide" in Bosnia. Harff admits that he didn't care if the death camps he reported about really existed or not, to him the dissemination of unverified information didn't pose a problem. More important was to "accelerate the circulation of information" and to succeed in the difficult task to convince the influential Jewish public in the United States that a "Holocaust" was taking place in Bosnia (Merlino 1993: 129). In fact, many authors recognize that Ruder Finn was a powerful tool of Croatian Americans to represent the Yugoslav wars in a way that would paint their fellow countrymen in a favorable light (see Hockenos 2003: 57). Like other émigrés, Mira was well read in about everything concerning the wars in her homeland, and West European or Northamerican based authors such as Jacques Merlino, Danielle Sremać, Michael Parenti, Edmond Paris, and Emil Vlajki had done their due to set the record straight.[95] In short, Mira was deeply convinced of the "shared responsibility" of all ethnic groups in the Balkan Wars. Certainly the moving accounts of newly arriving refugees opened up old wounds that she wished to heal, pointing to the pervasiveness of a "wound culture" (Ballinger 2003: 11, 39) in the former Yugoslavia.

In 1993, she and two other women, the SUC's executive director, Dragana Gajković, and Dragana Gakić set up a woman's organization, "The Serbian Woman's Caucus" dedicated to form a case against Croat and Bosnian Muslim war criminals. "*We knew that we could gain more credibility if we founded a woman's organization, since women were regarded as victims and innocent in the Balkan Wars,*" Mira admitted in one of our conversations. The women pressed the tribunal, asking why the court had not indicted a single Bosnian Muslim commander. Showing me the rich correspondence with

95. Sremać, author of *War with Words* 2000, is a second generation Serbian-American with Greek ancestors and the official representative of Karadžić's Bosnian Serb mini-state, who headed the Serbian American Affairs Council (Hockenos 2003: 144). Michael Parenti's *Killing a Nation* 2000 was a thoroughly pro-Serbian media analysis covering the 1999 NATO bombing and the preceding ten years that to his mind, were nothing but a systematic attempt by the International Community, Kosovo Albanians, and Croats to defeat the 'stubborn' Serbs (see also part three). Vlajki's *Demonization of Serbs. Western Imperialism and Media War Criminals* 2001 follows a similar line of argument, whereby *Paris' Genocide in Satellite Croatia* 1961 offers the historical perspective to the problems in the Balkans.

the then chief prosecutor Richard Goldstone from South Africa and later Spanish Carla del Ponte, she demonstrated that she was in regular contact with the juridical leaders of the tribunal and in some of her letters she had personally confronted them with her own story of Jasenovać and the "unfair, inhuman" treatment of Serbs by the International Community of which the ICTY was considered to be a tool. The investigators responded that they lacked evidence as well as the resources to go after every alleged human rights violation in Bosnia and Herzegovina. Thus, the "Serbian Woman's Caucus" from its base in California went after them herself. Up to 1996, Mira and her colleagues were busy at compiling a list of a dozen alleged camps run by Bosnian Muslims and Bosnian Croats. Mira's role was mainly to work directly with witnesses in the United States, recording their stories, transcribing, translating and documenting them, as she had learned in her anthropology classes, while the thirty years younger Gajković and Gakić traveled to the Hague and the former Yugoslavia on various occasions.

The SUC appointed their own war crimes investigations, meeting with former detainées in Bosnia, scouring the refugee centers in Serbia and Montenegro for witnesses. Finally the ICTY zeroed in on the Čelebići camp in central Bosnia where Serbs had been interned in 1992-93. The outcome of the SUC-initiated investigations was the indictment of four Bosnian Muslims for grave breaches of the Geneva Conventions. In November 1998, the court sentenced one of the camp guards and two of its commanders to sentences of seven to twenty years for war crimes, including murder (see also Hockenos 2003: 151f.). Lewis Dolinsky from "The San Francisco Chronicle" notes, that the women's „regret is that although Zdravko Mučić, Hazim Delić and Esad Landzo were convicted, the Bosnian regional wartime commander, walked. Delalić's conviction could have suggested a pattern of misbehavior by Bosnian government forces" (Dolinsky 1998a: A 10). Indeed, Mira is convinced that Izetbegović was as guilty in war crimes committed in Bosnia, as were Tudjman and Milošević. For Mira and her two colleagues as well as for the SUC Serb lobby the Čelebići sentence meant a small deserved victory which changed history.

However, in 2000, with the sentences having been reduced, and with no other trial to follow, "*although we had even better documented prison camps,*" Mira is bitter. She opines, that not only that Delalić could walk out unpunished demonstrated a lack of will to prosecute Bosnian Muslim war crimes. The women had heard "terrible stories about a Bosnian camp, Tarčin, that had operated starting in spring 1992. Tarčin held Serbs, not Muslims, and they were kept there even after the Dayton agreement treaty was signed in October 1995. The women informed Representative Ron Dellums, who wrote a strong letter to President Clinton. Clinton told the Bosnian government that everyone had to be freed – no ifs, ands, or buts. In January

1996, Tarčin was shut down" (Dolinsky ibid.). Thus, the Serbian Women's Caucus achieved another small victory. Still, Mira states that she regrets that she ever cooperated with the tribunal, since through her cooperation they granted it more credibility and acknowledged the ICTY as such. Gakić's and Gajković's comments run along the same line: "*If we had known that the tribunal doesn't indict any other Bosnian Muslims and Croats we wouldn't have undertaken all those efforts, only to legitimize a wrong cause.*" According to Hockenos the SUC project "War Crimes Perpetrated against Serbs" was also regarded as a political strategy to "authenticate the historical view that Serbs were victims of equal magnitude in the war in Bosnia" (Hockenos 2003: 129).

In 2002, ten years after the ICTY's implementation all women resentfully admit that this strategy had clearly failed. For Mira who had searched for justice in her own painful course, the juridical project had always been a historical project as well, but to mix up the wrongs of the two wars, the Second World War and the Third Balkan Wars, was a lost undertaking.

Father Dimitrije Aleksandrović: The Chetnik diaspora and the reburial of the dead

Father Dimitrije Aleksandrović, the seventy-six-year-old retired priest of San Francisco's Serbian Orthodox church is a prominent diaspora figure who, as he himself states, maintained his Second World War ideology unchanged for fifty years and saw his exile as the continuation of the political struggles in his youth. A member of the *Serbian National Defense* (SND), the *Serbian Benevolent Society* (SBS) and the *Serbian Unity Congress* (SUC) Father Dimitrije has engaged in the exiled Chetnik movement ever since he set foot on the 'new' continent. The gray bearded priest who still opposes "communist Yugoslavia," or what he sees as the likewise communist successor state thereof, admits that he has lost touch with the society in his homeland. Laughingly he remembers: "*Once a man from Serbia told me: 'Father Dimitrije, your ideas about the old country are under a glass cover, well preserved.*'"

Upon entering his house in the wealthy neighborhood Diamond Heights at Twin Peaks, my first sight meets the stone bust of Father Dimitrije's bearded head, which decorates the hallway. Several icons and smaller oil paintings of monasteries and churches in the living room send a clear message about the profession and belief of its owner. The classic Victorian sofa points to the huge window remarkably overlooking the Bay. Like a bird's eye pretty much all of San Francisco's neighborhoods and vicinities are set out in a chessboard fashion. The son to a wealthy merchant in Southern Serbia, Father Dimitrije took part in the Royalist nationalist movement during the Second World War as a 17-year-old. Under Tito's regime his father and he were imprisoned and physically maltreated. After the war, upon facing harsh disadvantages as a dissident at school and college, the young man left Yugoslavia in the mid-1950's and joined the growing number of political exiles. After receiving his priesthood in the Saint Sava monastery in Chicago, Father Dimitrije was sent as the first priest to San Francisco's Serbian Orthodox parish, which at that time didn't have a proper church yet. Participating in building the church "at his own hands" in the late 1950's, the priest later took a pronounced stance in the 1963 church schism which had dramatic effects on the Serbian diaspora. Representing the "autonomy" faction of the "Chetnik" church Father Dimitrije vehemently claimed that the church was being undermined by Tito's spies and therefore needed to break free. This position finally won over the "unity" faction, resulting in a thirty year long *raskol* or split of the church in two churches, parishes, and administrations which would seriously weaken the Serb diaspora in the long run.

With the disintegration of the homeland Father Dimitrije rose to the opportunity, went back for a visit for the first time since his emigration on a SUC "Mission of Friendship and Goodwill" in 1991 and networked globally with politicians "on the ground." Among his meetings were talks with Šešelj, Drašković, Karadžić, and Milošević who he refused to shake hands with, because, as he retells, "*I told him that first he should take off that red star on his hat. You can't be a communist first and then a nationalist.*" On this trip to Serbia, Kosovo and Bosnia he participated in the reburial of the bones of hundreds of dead Serbs who were thrown into pits at Jadovno during the Second World War. While he recounts this part of the travels, his wife Ljiljana brings a photo album, showing me the pictures of countless bones and crying old women around them. Agitated, the *Protinica* (retired priest's wife) utters: "*See, they never had a proper burial, so we had a big ceremony, a march, and built a church on that spot. Only a couple of years later the Croats destroyed the church. That's what happens: they hit the Serbs again and again.*" Father Dimitrije proudly states how at a dinner in the Bosnian town, before opening the meal Karadžić would ask Father Dimitrije, the only priest present, to be the first religious man to read a prayer since 1945.

Sitting comfortably in a Victorian chair by the window overlooking the city and nipping at his "Turkish" – or better "Serbian" – coffee Father Dimitrije recounts:

> "*I was born in 1928 and I remember the Kingdom of Yugoslavia. It was a healthy situation and it developed very well. In the 1930's and 1940's I lived in Dubrovnik, in Mostar, I lived in Sarajevo, and I traveled to Dalmatia. But the latent struggle already started, specifically for some Croatian leaders. The Muslim leadership was very anti-Yugoslav at the time. During the war my father, who was a wealthy man from Belgrade, was active in politics. He had an organization, called "Savas nacije Jugoslavije," the Allies of the Nation of Yugoslavia, which was a big organization with my father as the leader. They put*

him in prison for two years for interrogation, he was in court and had a trial. He was sent to the camp, while my mother and I stayed in prison. He supported Mihailović and spoke German, so they accused him of supporting Germans, but he was released after a month and didn't suffer too much. He was more patriotic than political, he was a civil engineer, and after he was released they sent him to the front in Srem against Germany, when the communists sent the young, best Serbs to the front. They mobilized kids basically and they were massacred. After the war we always complained about communism and they chased me out from the Gymnasium. I could not study, because I was an 'enemy of the people.' We weren't reactionary, we were against communists, so I stood at that position all my life and as a young man. I didn't have any direct war experiences, I had just helped Chetniks with some logistics in Belgrade, but didn't fight in the war. But the affair with my dad came out, and they imprisoned us and took us out, and when they released us in 1951 we went out on the street, we were homeless, my mother and I. For two years I had been in an interrogation prison. They treated us very badly, very badly. They broke my nose and my chin; they insisted that I have to tell them what foreign people come to our home. Never, nobody come, so I couldn't tell them. I am walking in with 90 Kilo, when I walked out I was 40 Kilo. It was really bad. So, we lived somehow, I enrolled, I finished Gymnasium, privately, in three months, and then after that I enrolled in a new University of Theology at Belgrade. I came here and met my beautiful wife and then life turned to better. I have lots of memories; the strange thing is that not too many memories are bad. The prison, I never want to go to prison on Alcatraz, I never want to go to Alcatraz, I don't want to go to Alcatraz. As a priest I should go, but I can't."

Father Dimitrije's narrative hardly deals with the violence experienced during the Second World War, but with the Communist regime's violence against its former antagonists, in this case the Royalist Chetniks (Croat Ustaši were hit brutally by Tito, too). Not inter-ethnic hostilities are center-stage, but the inner-ethnic fragmentation between Partisans/Communists and Serbian Royalists looms large. Up to today Father Dimitrije's world-view is characterized by this antagonism between the big ideologies of the 20th century, Communism and capitalism, which influenced not only his own life trajectory in such a fundamental manner but caused a major division among Serbs in the homeland and abroad.

Unlike Saša and Mira, Father Dimitrije never had a break from his struggles, rather, the end of the Second World War meant to him the beginning of a long period of activism against Communism which he continued in exile. Father Dimitrije does not focus on the violent events during the Second World War, because he hasn't experienced them. His bodily pain was inflicted on him much later, in one of Tito's prisons in the early 1950's. What is most salient is the ideological orientation of the narrator, which frames the story from his father's economic political categorization at the beginning, to his anti-Communist persuasion in the middle of the passage. In Father Dimitrije's story there is no development. It is rather a statement of fixed principles which the priest follows with remarkable continuity. This then, I suggest, is the core message delivered in his account: the humiliation he experienced in post-World War Two Yugoslavia resulted in a determination to take an active role against Titoism and Communism, the ideologies he not only despises most, but which also serve as a reading of the recent events in the former Yugoslavia. Father Dimitrije's first visit to his homeland after several decades resembles a "trip through memory" (Ballinger 2003: 72), putting the "genocide" against Serbs in World War Two center-stage. To take part in the reburials of the dead and to bless the meal following the funeral of skeletons and bones fifty years after their death occurred is, of course, grounded in the outrage against Croat massacres of Serbs. Furthermore, it is a statement that "our history is in the cemetery" (Ballinger 2003: 179). The example of Jadovno points to the crucial importance of the rediscoveries and reburials of victims of the 1941-44 wartime massacres during the 1990's (Denich 1994, Hayden 1994, Verdery 1998). Finally, his anger is directed against Tito's refusal to reckon with the terrible past, which to him is also communism's main failure. Instead of ethnic explanations to the country's conflicts, Father Dimitrije regards the Cold War legacy with its ideological struggles most significant.

Narrating persecution and violence

The accounts Mira Connor and Father Dimitrije present are not spontaneous narratives of their lives, which have never been told before. A prominent businesswoman and lay lecturer on Balkan history, and a priest and diaspora activist, they are used to giving interviews and telling people about themselves. Holding a second degree in History and just having finished his Master's Thesis about Draža Mihailović and the Chetnik movement, Father Dimitrije speaks with confidence, knowing that he is not just an actor in history but also a witness thereof and an expert in historical matters.

Talk about history in the Bay Area took the form of narratives of a specific type. One of the most obvious characteristics of the migrants' telling of their lives was its didacticism, for which Mira's narrative is an excellent example. Mira's life story had the form of an educational lecture and read like a history book on the socio-cultural development of the "Military Frontier" or Croatian Krajina. My transcribed version of the interview covers more than six typed pages on the origin of Serbs in Croatia alone, before it turns to the story of her ancestors and own life. Rooting her story firmly in the landscape of her birth town and the historical makeup of the area, she eloquently lays out not only her past, but the collective past of her nation and the knowledge she acquired about the geographical place she comes from.

Many of the accounts and conversations recorded were characterized by the skilled use of such formal devices as rhetorical questions, repetition, repetition with variation, and tonal emphasis. Paul Connerton (1989) underlined the special rhythm and form of life stories, which often have "no silence and no chronology" (ibid.: 15). Moreover, Connerton alludes to the cyclical time and the significance of series of cycles in life histories. Saša's narrative reveals in minute detail the destruction of his village, the killing and expulsion of its inhabitants, the burning of houses as if they were animated objects and how the five-year-old experienced all these terrible events. While he tells me this story Saša gets loud, almost screams, and changes the speed of narrating, talking very slowly and intensely when it comes to the burning of the house. Using the word "remembering" thirteen times this passage is a homage to memory, the necessity of remembering the trauma of Saša, the child, who is also "all the Serbs." Repeatedly stating: "*I remember that better than what I ate yesterday,*" "*that stuck in my mind,*" or "*I remember just like now,*" the narrative emphasizes how wartime memories of his childhood are conflated with the present almost sixty years later. Uttering the statement "*I never want to go to Alcatraz*" three times and "*they treated us very badly*" twice, Father Dimitrije, too, employs the rhetorical strategy of repetition as a marker to key events in his life.

In the process of narrating, numbers and statistics were used for both documentary and performative ends. Moreover maps were of salience, whenever it came to 'verify' facts and provide chronologies of historical events.[96] In the words of one participant in this study: "*Serbs have a lot of materials. They keep everything.*" Mira is an excellent example for this statement, since she has dozens of boxes filled with witness accounts for the Čelebići case, but also newspaper articles, letters, and other documents. The 'storage of the past' appears of crucial importance for exiles and extends from the life story to about everything in relation to the history of the nation.

As Mira's narrative demonstrates, numbers and the citation of historical records were likewise deployed as rhetorical devices for persuasion and 'proof."[97] Her style of narrating the origins of Serbian settlements in Croatian Krajina is authoritative and persuasive. Weaving together personal memories, the landscape of the area and the outlook of the town with historical data, she provides the listener with the crafted "evidence" of a lost world. The old woman narrates the history and life in her hometown "ex-

96. On the importance of maps in Serbian nationalist imagination, see Procter 2000: 54-81.

actly as it was" by documenting, verifying and applying the bird's eye's view of someone who has authority precisely because "she was there." Mira's remarkably elaborate speech encompasses a holistic description of the land where she grew up in: depictions of the ethnic composition of the town, names and characters of neighbors, greeting forms among the different confessional groups, the design of school books and their Yugoslav ideology.

Especially noteworthy are the names the old woman (and also Saša) remembers. What Maurice Halbwachs (1992) stated with regard to names may be true for the narratives, too: names are "the anchor of memory" (ibid.: 71). The metaphor of the anchor also illustrates that remembering is based on the recalling of names, and shapes the way that memory works. Because Mira remembers names so well, the presenting of little details of her captivity is enhanced. Mentioning small items, i.e. safety pins, blankets, and backpacks, notably in the Serbian language, provides her narrative with authenticity and presenting which make it coherent. Thus she strives not only for the integrity of her account, but for integrity as a person who has control over her past (Meyerhoff 1992: 232).

Central are the harmony and peacefulness prevailing in her descriptions of town life, underlined by her statement: "*we never had any conflicts in our town.*" The outcome is a romantic image of the town she grew up in, similar to Pamela Ballinger's (2003) observations among the *esuli*, World War Two refugees from Istria in Trieste: one can speak of the evocation of a "lost paradise" (ibid.: 183) and "pervasive idealizations of prewar life" (ibid.: 186) which omit any problems that did result from the specific socio-economic order of life in inter-war Croatian Krajina, especially for the Croatian population. The idyllic picture she draws serves to present "the Serbs" as distinguished, wealthy, educated, or to put it in a nutshell: innocent.

Like Mira, I met many other old Serbs who made use of similar devices of narrating the past. I suggest that the representation of harmony and 'objective' historical detail serves as a prelude to the horrible events to follow, so that the contrast between "good times" and "bad times" appears tremendous. She represents herself, her family and "the Serbs" as the pure victims whose violent perpetration cannot be explained, since any disharmony preceding the Second World War which did indeed prevail[98], is carefully left out.

97. Interestingly these main elements in the narration of the past correspond closely to Liisa Malkki's (1995: 53) analysis of the memory of violence among Hutu refugees from Burundi in Tanzania. It seems worth speculating about the impact of a certain Western epistemological way of knowing on exiles' accounts. In Mira's case the link between objective, scientific knowledge and her own past is more than obvious given her university education in the United States.
98. For a very thorough historical discussion of political and ethnic conflicts in the Kingdom of the Serbs, Croats, and Slovenes (SHS), see Ivo Banac [1984]1991.

And yet, despite the self-confident styling of her account, it seems that the urge to legitimize her own story reveals a latent insecurity. In the context of war in Bosnia with Serbs figuring as brutal aggressors in the eyes of the Western public, people like Mira were eager at fighting the stereotype of the "butcher of the Balkan" and at great pains constructed a counter-image, based on their own victimizing experiences. Obviously, her story was not enough in itself, with reference to her own individual life trajectory alone. What was crucial was to render a whole understanding of what went on in Yugoslavia's past, and by linking the Second World War with the Third Balkan Wars to produce a "mythico history." Liisa Malkki (1995) in her study *Purity and Exile* about displaced Hutu refugees from Burundi staying in Tanzania, explains the notion of "mythico-history" as follows:

> "[T]the mythico-history is misread if it is seen simply as a series of factual claims. For the "facts" it deployed, true and false alike, were only building blocks for the construction of a grand moral-historical vision. [...] The "worlds made" through narrations of the past are always historically situated and culturally constructed, and it is these that people act upon and riddle with meaning." (Malkki 1995: 104)

What is crucial in Serbian versions of a "mythico-history" is the prevalence of a memory of violence that is used to form political claims in the present. Linking personal stories of persecution with a grand-historical narrative, the memory of Serbian suffering in World War Two represents a core dimension of Serbian long-distance nationalism. Thereby, the narrators also foreground a very strict sense of diaspora, that is based on persecution and violence. In a way then, the life stories told by Serbs resemble "worlds made", based on complex renderings of the nation's historical past through the prism of the present, as seen from the angle of one's own biography.

Below I shall look closer at how the narrators "make themselves up" and form mythico-historical versions of a Serbian past.

The long shadow of the past and long-distance nationalist practices

> "History is reduced to "memory," oppression to "victimhood" [...] (Comaroff and Comaroff 2003: 297)"

During my fieldwork I encountered several people like Mira, Saša, and Father Dimitrije, who had experienced expulsion and violence in the Second World War. These interlocutors, old by now, although holding quite diverse views of their life's past, shared one characteristic: they were eager to tell their story especially to young people, or to me, the anthropologist who was expected to have a large impact on the public sphere, what they went through, so that their stories would not be lost through death. According to Anthony Kerby (1992: 45) "we are 'story-telling animals' precisely because we are already caught up in a story, and already committed to meaning." Thus, experience and narrative, history[99] and story are not separate, rather interpretation has always already started. Of course, the three individuals whose dramatic lives are told above did experience the events they talk about, but more than that their storytelling is a mode of comprehension that necessarily takes second place in relation to the experiences comprehended (Kerby 1992: 41). Through their storytelling, younger people who did not experience expulsion themselves identified with this past, sometimes as if they themselves had lived through these stories.[100] Hence, stories of perpetration acquire a powerful life of their own, influencing how tellers and listeners view their homeland's history and their group's past, transforming individual stories into collective memory.

The strength of historical consciousness among Serbs seems to lie in the way that even people who did not experience victimization nevertheless identify with the stories told by survivors. This can be illustrated by the example of Milan Gajić, electrical engineer who emigrated in the mid-80's. On the occasion of one of our conversations, during which he didn't seem to get tired of correcting my 'wrong' use of the term "Yugoslav" instead of "Serbian," he implored me: "*Listen, Birgit, how many times somebody has to shoot your grandfather and your father and your brothers and your great-grandfathers and – mothers, and so on, to teach you, that we do not want to be with you, okay?*" Curiously, as one of the recent brain drain migrants Milan's rejection of anything Yugoslav is quite striking, since Yugoslavia shaped his childhood, youth and even adult life. I imagine, that like many others Milan experienced a Serbianization in the wake of the Third Balkan War due to his exposure to nationalist church circles. It suffices to say that Milan's male relatives have not been killed in World War Two; rather he is referring to similar stories heard from others. It is exactly this enlargement of personal stories to historical "truths" that resembles Malkki's concept of "mythico-history." People like Milan construct and *Ur*-scene of the killing of the male line that is based on the Second World War, thereby imbuing the binarism between Croats and Serbs with mythic proportions. In a similar vein as Milan, former Croatian President Tudjman legitimated his Croat-

99. In contrast to this, Halbwachs 1992 draws a stark distinction between history and memory, the first denoting the historian's realm of official documents, archives and the like, while the latter solely focuses on personal, direct remembrances which are independent of historical accounts.

100. See chapter one, section "We are history!" which deals with the salient importance of history and suffering even for younger individuals who have not experienced war.

ian-ness by alluding to his family's past. Tudjman dedicated his book *Horrors of War* (1996) to his ancestors who were killed in the Second World War: "In memory of my father, my brother, and my stepmother, who fell victims in the wastelands of history." To many Serbs, the "age-old" tragedy of the Balkans is a family saga, starting with the clubbing of the grandfather in the Second World War and ending with the shooting of the grandchild fifty years later, similar to Vuk Drašković's (1984) novel *Nož* (knife).

Tamara Hareven calls these memories which are believed to be a precious, unique cargo not only of the old, but also of the collective, "generational memories" (Hareven 1978). They provide collective definitions taking up the questions of who 'we are' and why 'we are here,' which as humans 'we' cannot do without. In contrast to this, Connerton (1989: 3) suggests that "generational memories" are not necessarily a connecting element across generations, but they can point to the impediment of communication by different sets of memories. Referring to a scene in Proust, Connerton retells how Marcel upon returning to fashionable society after a long absence, engages for the first time in conversation with a young American woman who had heard a lot about him. What happens between the two is what Connerton calls "alienation-effect:" "Their conversation was unintelligible because the two of them had lived in the same social world but with an interval of twenty-five years." They didn't have recourse to the same memories, the same names, in short: "their vocabularies had nothing in common" (ibid.). The stories of Saša, Mira, and Father Dimitrije have to be seen in this light, they are very specific for their generation who experienced the Second World War, and their memories also set them apart from people who hold very different sets of memories, especially the younger brain drain immigrants who came of age in socialist Yugoslavia and know very little about these past conflicts. Nevertheless, since in the 1990's the Serbian experience of suffering in World War Two has been put on the agenda in a grand style both in Serbia and in the diaspora, one should not underestimate their collectivizing effect and impact on several generations. Therefore, as the Serbian material suggests "generational memories" can comprise both dividing and connecting elements.

Memory and identity, Gillis (1994: 2) denotes, are dependent on each other: "identity and memory are social and political constructs that need to be decoded" (ibid.: 5). The stories often took on a poetic and artistically crafted form, striving for integration and coherence of shattered communities, lives, and landscapes. In their telling, the old people appeared to aim at perfecting a disturbing past in the context of a present that was as unsettling as the past. What is striking in all the narratives is an omission of the violence in Bosnia during the 1990's, whereas the Second World War figures as *the* war. Equally unsettling is the absence of the relatively peaceful forty-year period of Yugoslavia.

Moving back and forth between present events, as in the account's beginning, and past times such as the Second World War Saša's narrative omits the nearly fifty years of relatively peaceful coexistence between the main Yugoslav ethnic groups. He also silences the Croatian and Bosnian Muslim deaths both during the Second World War and in the 1990's. *Only* Serbs are the victims, not one of the other constituent nations living in the former Yugoslavia. The statement: "*But I still say, if I go and step in their shoes, I would be the same as they are*" reveals how time and space are crossed, leaving only complete identification between Saša, a car mechanic residing in the U.S. for more than forty years, and Serbian villagers in Bosnia. Had the Balkan Wars of the 1990's not happened Saša and other Serbs may not have ever felt the urge to delve so intensely into past trauma – least to develop a long-distance nationalist activism.

The violence he experienced throws a shadow onto the present: 1941 and 1991 are made to conflate. Insisting on the repeated and complete 'cleansing' of Serbs, which turns them into the singular nation of suffering, he makes use of an event in 2001 – the victimization of a mother living in a mixed marriage in today's Bosnia – which perfectly matches the narrative of the Second World War, thus linking the two traumatic events and enlarging them to epic proportions.

Notwithstanding the geographic distance to the homeland the memory of wartime massacres and the renewal of interethnic violence diminish any temporal and spatial distance. In suffering all Serbs, the victims of the Second World War, the exiled ones and the ones who stayed, are alike and unified in a common national cause, the struggle for survival, if necessary by force. Saša even claims that Serbia needs the atomic bomb, since not the big nations that have one would need it, but "*small and totally defenseless nations which get attacked for no reasons, such as Serbia.*" Here he is in line with the "Memorandum" of the Serbian Academy of Science and Arts of 1986, signed by twenty-two members of the Academy, thirty-one prominent intellectuals and four Serbian Orthodox bishops, which is a manifesto of Serbian nationalism. In the "Declaration against Genocide of the Serbian people" the memorandum runs as follows:

> "The history of Serbian lands ... is full of instances of genocide against the Serbs and of exoduses to which they were exposed. Processes of annihilation of Serbs in the most diverse and brutal ways have been continuous. Throughout their history they have faced the fiercest forms of genocide and exoduses that have jeopardized their existence, yet they have always been self-defenders of their own existence, spirituality, culture, and democratic convictions." (SANU Academy of Arts and Science 1986)[101]

In Fresno, a white middle-class town in the fashion of suburbia and a two hour ride away from the Bay Area where he has acquired some popularity, Saša seemed to have been successful with his tale of the defenseless Serbs. The case of Saša is a prime example for how crucial the memory of violence is for the specific case of Serbian long-distance nationalism.

Displaced Serbs in the United States had long lobbied for re-exporting the "Jasenovać-debate" to the homeland and opening "old wounds" that had still not healed, best exemplified in Mira's story of expulsion and internment in Jasenovać and Father Dimitrije's attendance of the reburial of the dead in Bosnia. But Jasenovać is certainly the focus of attention when dealing with massacres of Croats against Serbs.

The Jasenovać debate

To many Serbs, Jasenovać and other camps run by the Ustaša epitomized the degree to which Nazi-backed Croat fascists perpetrated Serbs, Jews and Gypsies in Yugoslavia, similar to the Holocaust against Jews. By the early 1990's their stories about Ustaša cruelties in the course of which an estimated 500, 000 to one million Serbs were killed,[102] helped mobilize young and old to envision a more radicalized version of Serbian nationalism. In *Balkan Holocausts?* (2002) MacDonald states: "The Serbian Unity Congress, for example claimed Jasenovać as 'the third largest concentration camp of the WW II occupied Europe,' a common theme in Serbian writing, which advanced a clear case for a Serbian 'holocaust.' The Serbian Ministry of Information also saw Jasenovać as a Serbian 'holocaust' – a holocaust that acted as a precursor to Croatian and Bosnian Moslem aggression fifty years later" (ibid.: 162). In a similar manner, Patriarch Paul asserted at the beginning of the war:

> "Nothing can be worse than Jasenovać, where during four years of war, 700, 000 people were killed ... Jasenovać is the scene of the most

101. See Anzulović 1999: 124.
102. The numbers of the dead vary greatly and are itself at the core of the debate about the Second World War. Whereas some authors argue that between 800,000 and one million Serbs died at the hands of the Croat Ustaše and its Muslim allies (Simić 2000: 105), others estimate a total of 487,000 murdered Serbs (Despalatović 2000: 89). On the other hand Franjo Tudjman defends the number of only 50,000 (MacDonald 2002: 167). Clearly, the „number game" was of major significance during the wars in the 1990's, because Serbs could perform as the victims in Croatia who needed to defend themselves on the basis of unsettled accounts of the past, while Croats undermined their claims for national independence based on their historical victimization by Serbs.

> important horrors committed against the Serbs, the place of ... their annihilation, their extermination, their execution, their torture, where they suffered under a blood lust, the like of which could not be paralleled by the antichrist himself ... This is the new crucifixion of Christ. This is the sin of sins.“ (MacDonald 2002: 163)

Jasenovać is decontextualized: the suffering of the other during World War Two, for example, Croats who claimed the massacre of Partisans against Croats in Bleiburg[103] at the end of the war, as their 'Croatian Golgatha,' is silenced. The highly complex factions in the civil war, with high casualties on all sides, are played down in favor of a simplistic ethnic reading of the violence.

Internet sites, propaganda material, and exile magazines greatly exploited their version of the thesis of the repetition of history and a timeless Croatian hatred against Serbs, so that paired together life stories and political lobbying achieved a powerful moral congruence, helping to convince Serbs in the U.S. by both private and public stories that Serbian violence in Bosnia was defensive and therefore legitimized. However, recurring to Croat fascist massacres in World War Two was not a new phenomenon in the Serbian American diaspora[104], but the outbreak of war in 1991 became emblematic for a self-fulfilling prophecy, intensifying the enmity against Croats and Bosnian Muslims and creating an opportunity to undermine the claims for Serbian rights to territory in the former Yugoslavia.

What is tragic about this dynamic is that many of the older migrants, such as Mira and Saša, had in the preceding decades indeed put their stories to rest and to a certain degree come to accept the reality of a socialist multicultural Yugoslavia. But the fervor with which their homeland was lit up in flames mirrored the intensity with which they delved into old antagonisms and old suffering again, thereby imbuing it with an acute presence. As Gillis (1994: 8) remarks, "temporal unity sites“ emerge at those times

103. In May 1945, the remnants of the NDH army fled towards the Austrian frontier from the winning Partisan troops. About 50,000 Ustaši soldiers, among them Pavelić, Maček, the Croatian government and a huge number of criminals, but also citizens and some Chetniks were caught at the border by British troops. Trusting the anti-Communist sentiments of the allies, they believed their promise to be put in Austrian prison camps and not be sent back to Croatia. The British, however, broke their promise and followed Tito's orders of sending the captives back to Yugoslavia. Upon their return near the Slovenian Bleiburg, the Partisans executed most of them and threw the bodies into pits. See Tanner 2001: 169-170. How many Croat really died at the hands of the revenging Partisans, has never been proven. As Tanner contends, "[t]he question of how many Croats were killed at Bleiburg is difficult to estimate. Like the question of how many Serbs were killed in Jasenovać, it is hedged around with propaganda. Some Croat nationalists insisted that up to 200,000 were killed. Others have put the final death toll from Bleiburg at 30,000 (ibid.: 170).

104. See Bennett 1978, Hockenos 2003, Padgett 1979, Procter 2000 et al.

of a break in the past. While new refugees trickled into California, bringing with them tragic stories from the frontlines themselves, safely hidden in remote corners of their memory, those who had stayed in exile for decades already, were ready to talk about their past trauma.

Past wars and silenced wars

Why are stories about the Second World War so salient, although equally dramatic experiences could be told about the recent Third Balkan War? Why are old and young people, even refugees who experienced war and displacement in the 1990's so silent about it, and don't hesitate to take part in lively discussions and stories about the Second World War?

In *How Societies Remember* (1989) Paul Connerton retells a story of Carlo Levi about a strange encounter with history's entailments in Southern Italy. Upon visiting a village, Gagliano, he noticed the town hall with a marble stone inscribed with the names of all the villagers who had died in the Great War (World War One).

> "And yet, in all his talks with the peasants of Gagliano, nobody ever mentioned the war, to speak of deeds accomplished or places seen or sufferings endured... They neither remembered the war as a remarkable event nor spoke of its dead. But of one war they spoke constantly. This was the war of the brigands. Brigandage had come to an end in 1865, seventy years before; very few of the peasants were old enough to remember it, as participants or eyewitnesses. Yet, everyone, young as well as old, women as well as men, spoke of it as if it were yesterday." (ibid.: 20f)

Connerton neither explains this remarkable phenomenon of remembering and forgetting, nor does he inquire further into the world of memory of the people in Gagliano. However, in the present case of Serbian exiles in the U.S. I wish to investigate this aspect of memory a little further, since the similarity with which people of all ages more or less silence the recent wars of disintegration and instead delve into the Second World War, which occurred almost sixty years before, is striking.

Øivind Fuglerud (1999: 73) in his work on long-distance nationalism among Tamil refugees in Norway, emphasizes that refugees focus on the present to the relative exclusion of past and sometimes also future. Quoting Beiser (1987) he contends that the first exile years can be understood as a 'psychological moratorium,' "where an active effort is made not to let traumatic experiences of the past intrude the projections of tomorrow" (Fuglerud ibid.). The concept of 'psychological moratorium' would also help to understand why the displaced people (DP) after the Second World

War, i.e. Saša and Mira, were first busy at establishing themselves in their new country, thereby avoiding an active memory work about their horrible past experiences. Perhaps, the same is the case for today's refugees: Boro[105], a forty-two-year-old Serbian refugee from Bosnia who had experienced incarceration and starvation in a prison camp, not entirely different from Father Dimitrije's story, upon hestitatingly telling me his war experience contended: "*I work and work and work. This way I don't have the chance to think too much about the past. I work six says a week, sometimes seven, thirteen hours a day. I have to earn a living for my family.*" Perhaps, this way Boro is protecting himself from the pain he experienced with as much distance as possible, whereas dealing with his past now would overwhelm him. After all, delving into the world of work can be an existential strategy of distracting oneself. It may well be that as an old man Boro, too, will delve into the traumatic experience he had as a young man.

Maurice Halbwachs (1992: 48) explains this linkage between age and memory with the need to progress, since the present and past are not as important as the future. Whereas older people are more interested in the past, younger people escape the past. In a similar vein, Connerton (1989: 12) mentions the lack of memory of the Holocaust in the early years of the Israeli state and contends that the need to commemorate the Holocaust occurred much later, in the 1950's, when it was not taken for granted anymore.

The examples of Proust, Gagliano, Boro, and Israel indicate that the idea of a 'moratorium' is not only a useful concept for exiles, but also for people who stayed in the places where they had lived before the advent of war. It seems to be a fruitful insight for understanding why people who experienced violence delve into their past at an old age and not when they are young. Again, the term "dormant transnational" seems adequate here, as people put their stories at rest in the productive years of the life cycle and re-invent themselves at an old age, when political crisis hit the homeland once again. Furthermore, the Serbian material as well as the example of Gagliano indicate that this moratorium could last well beyond the 'first years of exile.' After all, it took Saša and Mira almost fifty years to put the past center-stage, and in Gagliano it was well into the 17th year after the end of the First World War that the people still avoided the topic of the war.

105. Considering that Boro was not at ease with telling me about his experiences, including torture, the killing of his best friends, and starvation, and rather did so because he wanted to do me a favor, I decided to not quote from the interview with him. This was the case with several other refugee families and the talks I had with them.

Unsettled Accounts and yet new unsettled accounts

> "The war is like a wanderer, even after the war is over.
> (Balkan Blues)"[106]

Unlike the silence of the newcomers who upon arrival tried to get over their often traumatic experiences by resorting to incredibly ambitious work-days which left hardly any time for remembering, the political exiles of the Second World War were ready to bring their stories to the fore. In a way then there was a time-lag, enabling the stories about Ustaša massacres to loom like a shadow over the present, putting "unsettled accounts" (Bornemann 1997) that were fifty years old at the center of attention, as if the recent violence had not 'arrived' in the diaspora yet. With reference to all post-socialist East European states, Bornemann (ibid.: 6) contends "that a successful reckoning with the criminal past obligates the state to seek retributive justice and that a failure to pursue retributive justice will likely lead to cycles of retributive violence." While Bornemann addresses the state level, the salience of a failure to reconcile a violent past is of equal importance on the individual level of memory.

A poignant example for the way that the recent civil war is viewed as the continuation of the Second World War is provided in the "One hundred irrefutable facts" about the violent disintegration of Yugoslavia, a little pamphlet published by the *Serbian Unity Congress* (SUC) in 1994 in San Francisco. The first fact runs as follows:

> "The current civil and religious war in the former Yugoslavia is but the resumption of the 1941-1945 civil war in which the Croatian Fascists, collaborators of the Nazi regime, and Muslim religious extremists murdered between 600,000 and 1,200,000 Serbs. The issues are the same, the battlefields are the same, even the flags and army insignia are the same."

Of course, both wars were incredibly more complex and did not parallel a cyclical progression of events at all as smoothly as the authors suggest, but for the construction of a timeless "Croat aggression" against Serbs this summary was apparently meant to suffice.
But not only nationalists have indulged in the thesis of the repetition or continuation of history, other scholars, too, have noted the striking similarity between World War Two and the Third Balkan Wars, e.g. considering

106. See Žbanić's documentary *Was uns bleibt sind unsere Bilder* ["What is left are our images," translation from the German mine] 2003.

that many of the villages that saw destruction in the previous war were again the places of intense fighting in the 1990's. [107]

At this juncture I shall make clear that memory is always as much about what is absent as it is about what is present – this example lends itself perfectly to point this out in a most lucid manner: "Recollection [...] is both selective and interpretive" (Kerby 1991: 83), including and excluding aspects of a past. In the pamphlet text though it is remarkable to what degree facets of a Yugoslav past are met with silence. The narrative indirectly implies that the relatively peaceful and prosperous forty-five year long period of socialist Yugoslavia was totally irrelevant. Old unsettled accounts resulted in yet new unsettled accounts, leaving the prospective of a better future more than dubious.

Instead of present stories temporal distance provided old and young with the freedom to construct stories from the safe heavens of the past by fusing fact and fiction, a mixture which "good" stories require. What anthropologist and gerontologist Myerhoff (1992: 231) observed with regard to the storytelling of East European Holocaust survivors living in a Senior Citizen Center on Venice Beach in Los Angeles, California, can be equally true for elderly Serbian survivors of World War Two:

> "They 'make' themselves, sometimes even 'make themselves up,' an activity which is not inevitable or automatic but reserved for special people and special circumstances. It is an artificial undertaking, this self-construction."

Myerhoff continues:

> "Since these constructions are intentionally designed, they are not only reflections of 'what is'; they are also opportunities to write history as it should be or should have been, demonstrating the culture's notion of propriety and sense" (ibid. 233ff.).

But is not *all* imagining an 'artificial understanding' and a 'self-construction'? Instead of stating the obvious, what is at stake here is *how* our imagination – collective and individual – helps to construct these imaginaries. What is crucial about these stories is that though people assume responsibility for inventing themselves, partaking in distortions, contradictions, re-

107. As Barbara Jančar-Webster (1999: 71) contends: "If the West is appalled by the ethnic cleansing, rape and mass atrocities that have occurred in Krajina and Bosnia during 1991-1994, the sober truth is that all this has been a déjà vu. The similarities between the wartime statistics and those from the region's latest civil war is striking [...]" (Jančar-Webster 1999: 71)

versals, exaggerations and even lies they maintain their sense of integrity and authenticity, exercising power over their images. With regard to Jewish Holocaust survivors, Myerhoff emphasizes the role of memory for elderly victims whose fear of oblivion increases acutely. She remarks that the fact that Jews spent so much of their history as pariah people surrounded by hostile outsiders and the Holocaust further intensified their awareness for their distinctiveness (Myerhoff 1992: 235). Thus, telling stories becomes an act of self-definition, history-writing, or even the search for justice, the latter pointing clearly to Mira Pesić's outstanding activism for the Čelebići trial.

Never reaching international recognition for the hundreds of thousand of dead between 1941 and 1945, Serbs in exile became determined to speak out "the truth" about the "Balkan Holocaust" (MacDonald 2002), and by doing so claimed to embody the Serbian conscience against Tito's Yugoslavia since World War Two.

Important in this endeavor was the attempt to parallel the fate of Serbs with that of the Jews: "Another central theme in Serbian writing was the image of the Serbs as a long-suffering, persecuted people, often likened to the Jews" (MacDonald 2002: 69). An aspect worth exploring at this point is the metaphoric referencing and thus the latching on by the Serbs and those representing 'their' story to the imaginary of the Holocaust, which arguably has received the public attention that the Serbs so long for. Note, that through Myerhoff I am reproducing this act of latching on, inferring the unspeakable cruelties that Jews were exposed to in Europe to be similar to the massacres against Serbs, Jews, and Gypsies in Croatia.

According to MacDonald (2002: 4f.) in the 1980's and 1990's, a 'victim-culture' emerged in international affairs, characterized by an increasing number of NGO's which helped to define which group "is a victim and how victimized they are." No allegation of guilt could be stronger than charging the other with having partaken in a 'holocaust.' To claim a likeness to the Jews became an important verbal tool in ethnic conflicts all over the world, if one looks at Rwanda, the Armenians, or East Timor. In the former Yugoslavia, Croats, Bosnian Muslims, Kosovar Albanians and Serbs all took part in this 'contest of suffering,' demonstrating their awareness of the considerable power in determining the identity of the aggressors. Political leaders of Western democracies were no less cautious with applying the term 'holocaust' to the Balkan wars. As Ballinger (2003: 146) states, "the Holocaust is the West's central morality story." From Germany to the United States comparisons of the violence in Bosnia with the fate of Europe's Jews became increasingly common. With this simplification of the complex situation it was hoped that a case could be formulated for Western intervention.

In a New York Times article, titled "Does the World still recognize a holocaust?" then British prime minister, Margaret Thatcher is quoted in her scorching indictment of Western inaction toward Bosnia: "I never thought I'd see another holocaust in my life" (Darnton The New York Times 1993: Section 4, page 1). Having entered the discourse about the Yugoslav wars of disintegration, the metaphor of the "holocaust" had a strong and long-lasting impact on how the world viewed the events in the former Yugoslavia. In turn, Serbs, who were usually likened to German Nazis, felt even more encouraged making use of this most powerful term for describing a victim-perpetrator binarism. Of course, their version only likened them to the Jews, not the Germans. Jasenovać lay at the core of the version of the "Serbian Holocaust."

The dismemberment of the homeland met the Serbian diaspora in a difficult position, still not having succeeded with officially recognizing the Serbian victims of World War Two, and with Serbs branded as *the* aggressors in the Third Balkan War possibly loosing that dream out of sight forever. Who wants to listen to cruelties of a time 'long past,' while so many Bosnian Muslims were slaughtered in the present? The Serbs I conversed with never viewed the present without consulting the past. Many of the old developed an often righteous determination to be themselves, as well as to speak "the truth," thereby constructing an explicable, moral universe. According to Myerhoff: "Particularities are subsumed and equated with grander themes, seen as exemplifying ultimate concerns. Then such stories may be enlarged to the level of myth as well as art – sacred and eternal justifications for how things are and what has happened" (Myerhoff 1992: 240).

It is exactly this myth-like enlargement of personal stories, which provides the words spoken with the power to generate collective feelings among people who are living very remote from the homeland and, if they wished, could have hardly any contact with one another. The stories that Serbs tell themselves about Balkan history are a conglomerate of personal details and historical 'facts' as well as 'fictions,' the present local and global context and life in the host country. They are elaborate representations of the Self – and not the Self or a life as such – and the collective. Like Liisa Malkki's (1995) notion of "mythico-history," the life stories told by Serbs resemble "worlds made."

Many (older) Serbs in the Bay Area appeared deeply convinced of the righteousness of their visions of the past and the world. Had they not given their own blood, left their houses, to make a living from scratch in a new, far away country, only to maintain their own credibility? Was their decision to emigrate not a far-reaching step in their lives that was undertaken with great consequence due to the reluctance to accommodate them in a post-war Yugoslav state that seemed to offer them nothing? Whereas life in exile did provide a fresh start and often fulfilled the dream of wealth and social peace, it also nourished an imaginary undertaking that expanded their individual painful past to collective proportions and enhanced the production of a far-reaching antagonistic ethnic universe. Suspended from life in Yugoslavia they were not exposed to anything that would shake their manichaeic "worlds made," until these imaginaries once again seemed to become real.

San Francisco Underground

In his famous movie *Underground* (1995), which won him the prestigious Cannes festival prize, Bosnian film director Emir Kusturica depicted the tragic story of two friends, Crni and Marko. The film's entry is the night between 5 and 6 April 1941, the day when the German occupation started with the Nazi bombing of Belgrade. Both a parody and a satire the foolish gangster Crni and the career comrade Marko get into struggles over the young, blonde Natalja who commits herself to each and none of them, and even accepts the courtship of the blue-eyed German officer Franz. Marko soon proves to be the grand opportunist and manipulator, and when the war is over leads "Crni and his whole extensive entourage, which has gradually piled up in the cellar (including his own brother Ivan, a surviving pet monkey from the zoo, and a Gypsy brass band from Crni's wedding) to believe that the war is not over" (Gocić 2001: 30). From 1945 until 1961 they live in the subterranean, building weapons for the war, which Marko sells for a fortune, listening to the media bulletins falsified by Marko. When Crni breaks free and sees daylight for the first time, he stumbles upon the production of a partisan spectacle about his wartime heroism. "[H]e shoots down a wrecked actor who plays Franz and again creates havoc, this time on the film set – adding a couple of extras to his list of casualties. ... [t]hey also discover the existence of a maze of underground routes which connect the European capitals, with a lively traffic of weapons and refugees – a whole world of people like themselves" (Gocić ibid.: 31). *Underground* contains a couple of brief, tinted documentary shots showing Belgrade, bombed by the Nazis in 1941 and the Allies in 1944. "When Germans are not bombing us, the Allies are," dying Marko comments on Belgrade's „special relations" with the West, almost prophesying the 1999 NATO intervention.

Seen from the perspective of the Serb diaspora in the United States, Kusturica's parodic rendering of the Yugoslav wars in the 20th century is well to the point. Like Crni, Father Dimitrije maintained his World War Two Chetnik ideology almost unchanged since those difficult years. It seems that the manifestation of violence into his very body has reinforced the ideological persuasion underlying the political conflicts in the former

Yugoslavia. The traces of war serve as an origin point and fix star for legitimating his long-distance nationalist claims. Like in the novel *White Eagles over Serbia* (Durrrell 1957), about underground Chetnik men in the Montenegrin Mountains waiting to take over Serbia, San Francisco's retired priest always expected to overthrow the "communist" Tito regime. But like the Serbian undercover agents in London in Durrell's fictive writing, this loyalty could only be maintained by emigration, from where he fought against a homeland which denied him a home. And while he engaged in diaspora politics as a way to stay close to his homeland, "[r]ather than a mirror of the homeland, the diaspora becomes its alter ego" (Hockenos 2003: 265). Thus, participating in the reburial of the dead on his first mission back to his home country can be seen as a direct symbolic continuation of his fifty-year-long dissident practice, which had its peak in the anti-Tito rallies in Chicago and the church split in 1963. And Father Dimitrije, Saša, and Mira still want to convince the Americans, Washington, the International Community and the world how Serbs suffered under "the fascist Croats" as well as under Tito and later Tudjman. And yet, the priest notes: "*Nevertheless, I always say that you have to live beyond history in order to walk forward, otherwise there is no progress.*" What remains is the ambiguity between the insight that history cannot be an end in itself and the adverse practice of presenting the past. But it seems that only Father Dimitrije's world is inhabited by educated, bearded Chetnik men fighting against uncivilized, uneducated and brutal Partisans. In both Mira's and Saša's stories Chetniks are absent, and their diaspora engagement is characterized by a discontinuity that brings us closer to the many Serbs that did not 'wake up' in 1991 and continued to stay away from exile politics altogether.

Not having rid themselves of the 'injustices' of the Second World War, Serb émigrés often lived in a time-warp, with their visions of the homeland staying unchanged from the year they left the country, 1948, 1951, or 1967. San Francisco resembled an underground, a place for ideological warfare against a regime, that in turn provided its citizens with as much peace and prosperity as could be hoped for during the Cold War. And as war broke out again in 1991 a self-fulfilling prophecy came true, with the homeland up in flames. "[I]t was the nature of the émigrés fantasies, not their compromises, that caused the greatest suffering" (Hockenos 2003: 13). These wise words notwithstanding, ultimately, in the former Yugoslavia it was the shadow of the Second World War that made possible the brutal violence, which tore apart the country, this time apparently forever.

Chapter 5. The Architecture of Memory

> "Every attic is an archive, every living room a museum. Never before has so much been recorded, collected; and never before has remembering been so compulsive. ... What we can no longer keep in our heads is now kept in storage." (Gillis 1994: 14)

The dominant themes of the Serbian politics of memory in the United States having been outlined, it is now possible to place these themes in the wider anthropological context of memory. So far I have analyzed life story accounts for their rhetorical strategies and political ideologies, and I have indicated how 'memory is put into practice,' so to speak, meaning in which ways the rendering of one's past is linked to long-distance nationalism in the present. I wish to have made clear the important role of the Second World War in the construction of "worlds made." In this chapter I will go back to the narratives in the preceding chapter and explore in more detail non-discursive, material ways of remembering and recollecting, which have often been overlooked in the study of memory, identity, and representation.

Many ethnographers, by describing the surroundings and interior architecture of their interlocutor's dwellings, only do so in order to achieve a more lively illustration of the informant's personality. In contrast to this, I wish to detail the material artifacts in the houses of the participants in my study and to present them as a building block in the construction of exilic historical consciousness. Below, focusing on the same individuals as above, but including others as well, I will analyze the fashioning of one's home, the location of a residence, and the interior decoration in order to explore the subjectivities of the narrators. I argue that the material side to remembering one's life, the 'housing' or "architecture of memory" is in itself an artistic project weaving together the main elements in an individual's past.

The 'housing' of memory

> "Remembering the house in which an uprooted culture originated and developed involves reversing history and sinking symbolic roots into a vanished human and geographical world. The remembered house is a small-scale cosmology symbolically restoring the integrity of a shattered geography." (Bahloul 1996: 28)

Aleksandar Tišma, Jewish-Serbian author and survivor of the Nazi massacres during the Second World War in Novi Sad, Vojvodina, became *the* Serbian writer about the brutal perpetration against Serbia's population at the hands of German *Wehrmacht* troops. Written at a time when remembering the war torn past was on the rise all over Yugoslavia, in "The Book Blam" ([1985]1997), Tišma provides the reader with a psychogram of a survivor who is wandering through the familiar streets of his hometown. Immersed in melancholic remembrance of his lost world, the former inhabitants of the Jewish quarter, who have all disappeared, including his parents, sister, and relatives, Tišma foremost follows the painstaking question what it means to be a survivor who lost everybody and everything. Interestingly, the book starts with the description of buildings, more meaningful ones such as the main hotel, and the recent socialist multistory residence complexes, the movie cinema, restaurant, bar, and the ordinary town houses in the old city (Tišma 1985: 5). Thus, to reconstruct a life that was, Tišma first delves into the material objects or houses of a lost world.

Borislav Pekić, in *The Houses of Belgrade* ([1978] 1994), depicting one of the prime builders of houses in Belgrade, Arsenie Negovan, takes the figure of the house for keeping a memory of the past even further. In his old age, losing his sanity, the protagonist in Pekić's novel obsessively links the history of Yugoslavia, epitomized by two moments of unrest, the student riots of 1968 and the riots which immediately preceded Germany's attack on Belgrade in the spring of 1941, through the stories of the houses of Belgrade. Arsenie's passionate obsession and love for the buildings is characterized by their description in truly humanizing terms:

> "There was no building which I couldn't describe in detail, especially if it had attracted my attention because of some unusual feature. I could hardly remember Martinović himself, but recalled his house distinctly – most probably because of its color, since it had no other striking feature. It looked in fact as if it had been rubbed with wet ash. And if the house lacked character, this was entirely in keeping with the reputation Martinović enjoyed as a grain dealer in the market place." (Pekić 1994: 112f.)

In the words of Bachelard:

> "Not only our memories but the things we have forgotten are 'housed.' Our sole is an abode. And by remembering 'houses' and 'rooms,' we learn to 'abide' within ourselves." (Bachelard [1958] 1994: xxxvii)

In *The Architecture of Memory* (1996) Joëlle Bahloul explores this 'technique' of remembering through the narration of living spaces among Jewish and Muslim exiles from Algeria in France who were displaced in the course of the independence of Algeria. In order to remember the people, voices, smells, and events that filled a place, displaced persons take great care to mentally reassemble the landscapes, houses, apartments, room arrangements, and streets wherein they can situate their stories. In his work on the "collective memory" Maurice Halbwachs (1980: 130), too, underscored the importance of spatial images in the process of remembering: "The reason members of a group remain united, even after scattering and finding nothing in their new physical surroundings to recall the home they left, is that they think of the old home and its layout [...]. Thus we understand why spatial images play so important a role in the collective memory."

However, in Saša's, Mira's, and Father Dimitrije's cases, 'the architecture of memory' is not only about recalling the old home, it is also about re-constructing a whole life and transforming it through material memory techniques in the new dwelling. "Looking at the house and the land naturally renewed the memory of all events, be they profane or religious, that have taken place there" (Halbwachs ibid.: 64).

In contrast to Bahloul, my focus does not lie on the literal and 'authentic' reconstruction of the houses people left, but rather on the traces of a "lost world" that are decorating the new house in exile. Whereas Bahloul took great care to develop maps of houses and rooms people inhabited before they left Algeria, in the following I will look at the interiors of the 'new' houses Serbs inhabit in the United States. "An entire past comes to dwell in a new house. [...] Thus the house is not experienced from day to day only, on the thread of a narrative, or in the telling of our own story. Through dreams, the various dwelling-places in our lives co-penetrate and retain the treasures of former days" (Bachelard 1994: 5). At once referring to the narrative act of a lost place, that place itself is sunk into the new living space of the migrant, where it is represented on photographs or paintings. As Allen Feldman (1991: 14) states: "Narrativity can be invested in material artifacts and relations that have a storytelling capacity of their own."

Re-creating Serbia in their new dwellings

Many exiles attempt to relocate and re-create Serbia not just mentally, but also spatially in their new dwellings. Like Saša, Father Dimitrije, and Mira I met many other Serbs who furnished their homes with photographs of parents, grandparents or other family members, and birthplace houses or paintings of villages and homes.

Danilo Milošević for example, who as a young man fought as *dobrovolji-ci*[108] in World War Two and since immigrating to the U.S. in the early 1950's never returned to his homeland, decorated his walls with various watercolor paintings made by himself. One depicts the village church of his hometown. During World War Two, Ustaša soldiers forced Danilo and other villagers to burn down their church and the priest at their own hands. In 1995, the holy building had just been restored with the help of émigrés, with Danilo playing an active role in sending remittances, when the church was destroyed again, this time by Croatian army shelling. Therefore, the painting of the church, which Danilo passes a few times every day when walking through his house, became a symbol for two horrible events and two visual proofs for "the never-ending Croatian brutality" against Serbs. Furthermore, the painting symbolically restores the holy building, thus (re-) constructing it a third time in Danilo's far away house in exile.

Eighty-two-year-old Budimir Mihailović, a former Second World War Chetnik fighter and like Father Dimitrije and other old men a member of the Serbian National Defense, Serbian Unity Congress, and Serbian Benevolent Society – multiple membership being common among Serbian émigrés – lives in the foggy Sunset district of San Francisco, near the Golden Gate Park. Upon arrival in the United States where he had an uncle who helped him with this immigration, and speaking only a few words of English, Budimir immediately started working in a can factory up to the closing down of the company and his retirement. After a few hours of interviewing in the pinkish colored living room, filled with Victorian sofas, chairs, and cushions with a rose flower pattern, 'Buda' asks me to go downstairs with him to get a drink. Leaving the first-floor with its obviously female traces we descend to the basement of the house, Buda's terrain and male world, where in the afternoon he offers me *rakija* at his bar.[109] He sits behind the counter like a bartender, showing me old newspapers and telling me stories of his life. On the wall hang awards from the St. John's Serbian Orthodox Church for his decade long commitment to the parish – in the 1950's Buda belonged to a group which built the church in its leisure time –, a SUC badge, and one black-and-white-picture of the smiling, bespectacled Chetnik leader Draža Mihailović and another one of King Peter Karadjordjević, Yugoslavia's exiled last monarch. Draža Mihailović and King Peter appear like political icons in Budimir's private worshipping shrine. Sipping at his rakija he shows me a dusty 1913 newspaper from Montenegro a friend of his gave him. In the basement of his

108. Serbian Orthodox volunteer unit during the Second World War that was neither Chetnik nor Partisan and leant towards the Chetnik side.

109. Note, that the metaphor of the cellar used in Kusturica's movie *Underground* 1995 can be found in the example of Budimir's 'male world' in the basement of his house.

house, where he hosts his male guests, old male friends and his sons and thrives in the memories of his past over a glass of plum brandy, there seems to rest the center of his house and his home 'away from home,' carefully watched by the 'wise' eyes of his dead heroes. While explaining the photos to me the old man gets ever more lively and excited.

Keeping photos, paintings, awards or little items from the house they left seem to be common practices among Serbian exiles and other displaced people all over the globe. In *History in Exile* Pamela Ballinger (2003: 172) discusses similar mnemonic practices whereby Istrian exiles in Trieste keep more tangible bits of Istria in the form of stones, fragments of their family home's foundation, or vials of seawater. She refers to a man who noted that it was a common practice among Istrians to take the keys to their houses with them when they departed from Istria. I heard of the same practice among Bosnian Muslim and Bosnian Serb refugees, who when they were expelled by the enemy's army, carefully locked their houses and put the keys into their pockets, "in case they returned soon." Similar examples can be found in the case of Cuban exiles in Miami who re-create their homes with soil and seawater, particularly by incorporating them into diasporic shrines (Tweed 1997). Studying neighborhoods in a Greek town where refugees from Asia Minor lived, Hirschon ([1989] 1998: xviii) underlines the perceptual geographical territories, the imbued meanings attached to 'spaces' transforming them into 'places.' In the case of Palestinians who have been uprooted within Israel and live as refugees in neighboring countries, Edward Said notes the excess of decoration, photos, and other objects.

> "Wherever there are Palestinians, the same signs of hospitality and offering keep appearing ... the same displays of affection and of objects – replicas of the Mosque of Omar, plates inlaid with mother-of-pearl, tiny Palestinian flags [...]. Naturally, they authenticate and certify the fact that you are in a Palestinian home" (Said 1999: 58).

The decoration of houses appears to be especially crucial for refugees and exiles in their endeavor to create a mental as well as a physical memory of the homes they lost.

When Saša enters his house in Stockton, he can imagine the house he *should* have had. As he contends, the number plate on his living room wall is

> *„[t]he only thing that I got out of my house last year – a number of the house. You see where the bullet went through? 35 Jezero, jezero, up the lake. When I went to the house, the only thing you can see is the walls, there is no roof, there is no floor, you could walk into the house and pass by the number, you know,*

> *how in Europe the numbers are right above the door? You can go in and everything is destroyed."*

The little item of his childhood house symbolizes the whole house in its absence which is incorporated into his new dwelling, at once a homage to the place where he comes from, a reminder of its destruction and an attempt to cross the temporal and spatial distance separating him from his birthplace. Saša's fashioning of his home is literally mnemonic, pointing to the material side of the "art of memory" that pays tribute to his lost world. Likewise, from the appearance of Mira's huge, massive house I can imagine the house she had to leave sixty years earlier:

> *"The house in which I grew up was an enormous house which sometimes in the 1700's or 1800's was actually a center for the military, for the officer's club and things like that. We belonged to people who owned big houses and business, like hotels and restaurants, we were people whose children went to Gymnasia. We even had a radio in the kitchen and people would come and sit around it to listen to the news."*

Karl Schlögel (2006: 321) points out: "Houses are the most personal, intimate, that one can think of. They are the places of memory. They resemble "property." That in itself is the most intimate and strongest relationship that exists." Quoting from Konstantin Paustowski, Schlögel (ibid. 314) explicated: "Sometimes the history of the house is more interesting than the life of a human being. Houses live longer than humans and are the witness of several generations." [translation mine]

As Ballinger (2003: 183) contends: "Remembering lost houses is a powerful way of symbolically restoring the integrity of a shattered geography." Perhaps, Mira's residence in the Berkeley Hills is as "enormous" as her birthplace house in Croatian Slavonia which she describes as 'housing' or embodying history. The countless books on Balkan history that Mira stores in her living room not only represent the high level of education which imbues her personal experiences and political struggles with the authority of knowledge, indirectly claiming: "We are Europeans, we are educated people, and we study our history" – they also provide her narrative with an objective "truth" that underscores her historical and political claims.

The 'housing' of religion

By surrounding themselves with icons, paintings of monasteries and churches in their homes Danilo and Father Dimitrije move the sacred into their exile dwelling, recreating a nostalgic Orthodox world of peacefulness and harmony. Passing Danilo's painting of the destroyed church of his hometown, he implores: "*We need religion! If we only had followed religion Yugoslavia could have been saved!*" The old man who suffers from a serious heart disease whispers his main message intensely and repeatedly into my recording machine. That religion seems to have enhanced the ethnicization of the conflicts in no way disturbs Danilo's imploring advice. And, of course, not a multinational Yugoslavia that did exist between 1945 and 1991 is implied here, but the interwar period of the Serb-dominated monarchy. "*I tell you, if people had followed the true religion which is in themselves instead of following communism, all this evil could not have happened.*" For Danilo, religion has been lying at the center of his life, ever since his brother was killed by Partisans on the flight out of socialist Yugoslavia and through the years he spent in German and English prison camps. And the belief in Orthodoxy provides a guiding line for Danilo's understanding of the Yugoslav tragedy. In his leisure time he is busy painting icons, the Moraga church being decorated with several one and a half meter large icons that he made.

Transferring the religious into the private realm not only grants the inhabitant a saintly character – as is best shown in the case of Father Dimitrije's icon-like bust of himself. It also mirrors the link between the family, the house, the nation, and Orthodoxy in Serbian culture, exemplified by the annual celebration of the *Krsna Slava*, the patron saint, which is transmitted patrilineally from the father to his sons. The family Slava is always performed at home, with a ritually clean woman or a girl, or (today in exile) even a man, as I observed, carrying the *Slavski Kolač*, the holy bread which is adorned with the holy seal, a small serpentine candle and a sprig of sweet basil, and then placing it before the *domačin* (head of the house) to perform the bread-breaking ceremony. As Joel Halpern in *A Serbian Village* ([1956]1967: 232), one of the first ethnographies by a Westerner in postwar Yugoslavia, points out the individual home is of major importance for religious observances, "with the church itself of distinctly tertiary importance. Religion, like so many other village institutions, is a casual thing, taken for granted, and intimately bound up with the whole way of life." Most family households I visited in the United States maintained the tradition and performed the Slava ceremony at home. An icon of the saint with a *kandilo*, the golden candelabrum, hanging on the living room wall attested to the owners' religious observance. Whereas many younger immigrants do not follow the custom and were not used to do so in Yugoslavia, some of them come to appreciate the exclusively Serbian Orthodox religious observation and take up the family ritual in their new homes.

Furthermore, icon painters seemed to enjoy a revival in the Serbian church community. During the one and three quarters of a year that my fieldwork covered there were several instances that pointed to the attraction of iconography at the turn of the millennium. I met two friends, one thirty and the other thirty-five years old, who were icon painters from the Pančevo monastery in Serbia and worked periodically for the reconstruction of the Saratoga Serbian Orthodox Church in the Silicon Valley, which so far was housed in a modern building with only its icons and altar reminding of a church. Plans for constructing the church completely anew, following the classical church form were underway.

During my stay, the Moraga church in the East Bay of similarly unpretentious architecture received a new cupola in the church hall, decorated with colorful icons made by a young female icon painter from Serbia who was flown to the U.S. on a special series of contracts to embellish a number of Serbian churches in various states. One Sunday morning in spring 2002 the San Francisco parish congregated for the weekly Divine Liturgy, this time for a special occasion. After months of construction, icon painting, and goldsmith work, the new altar, made of pure marble, was blessed in a ceremony led by the bishop of the Western Northamerican Serbian Orthodox diocese, Father Longin. Hearsay disclosed that the noble floor material and the gold paint and golden lighters cost the parish a total of one million dollar. Behind people's backs I heard voices ridiculing the enormous amount of money spent on an altar, which the parishioners cannot even see – since in Orthodoxy the altar is located behind a wooden separation consisting of icons – while new refugees were suffering severe economic problems in a city with mounting living expenses that only well-to-do people could afford. Others were proud of the 'dignity' which was reflected in the newly painted and specially lighted cupola, with a deep heavenly blue and yellow stars radiating warmth and self-esteem.

And the Serbian Orthodox Church "Assumption of the Blessed Virgin Mary" at Fair Oaks, Sacramento, too, launched a Fresco restoration project. On September 28, 2003 the church organized a fundraising banquet with NBA basketball stars Vlade Divać and Peja Stojaković from the "Sacramento Kings," costing between $150 and $500 per person. In short, eleven years after the outbreak of the wars in the former Yugoslavia all the churches in the San Francisco Bay Area were busy at improving their visual appearances, investing considerable financial capital, in order to achieve a more precious, dignified outlook of the worshipping place. The churches which figure as a marker of Serbdom and represent a singular place for Serbian communal life in the United States, were invested with both money and meaning, aiming at enhancing a positive image of Serbdom to the outside world.

In the former Yugoslavia, too, the construction and restoration of religious buildings has taken place with great zeal since the mid 1980's and again at the beginning of the new millennium. As the number of newly built mosques, Catholic, and Orthodox churches in Bosnia goes into the thousands, mirroring the competition for territory which was fought militantly in the recent war in the quest for religious power. As Miosić (2003)[110] has shown, in the Mostar area huge crosses were erected on the highest mountain overlooking the divided city, to symbolically claim the landscape. In the United States, however, the lively religious imagery deployed in both public and private locations was still surpassed by political imagery, whereby the religious and the public were often blurred.

The private "worshipping shrines" I discovered in people's homes appeared to be of crucial importance in people's immigrant lives. And yet the Serbs in the Bay Area are not *physically* attached to the objects that surrounded them in their Yugoslavian domestic life. As Bahloul (1996: 128) contends: "Memory has stored them in its oral archives, as if their materiality could exist only in remembrance. [...] Thus memory effects the shift from the practical to the symbolic". But is the relationship between the practical and the symbolic not more complex than Bahloul's causal linkage suggests?

Maintaining a photograph of the 1947 executed Chetnik leader "Draža" Budimir not only commemorates the dead hero: More than anything else the symbol of "the first guerrillas of Europe" (Achin 1963) serves as legitimization of Budimir's own past and present struggles by way of identifying with the movement's leader. After all the old man's sacrifice to the Chetnik cause is not little: while fighting against the Partisans he got shot in the neck and barely survived the months long period of hospitalizations and surgeries, leaving a life-long huge scar which he shows me somewhat proudly. Father Dimitrije whose nose and chin were broken by torture during one of the police interrogations in Tito's prisons, gave a similar bodily commitment to the Royalists.

Mira's brother, Budimir, is another example of the intensity of suffering. Since the war, when still a young man, he suffered from chronic heart disease and has undergone repeated heart surgery, often with meager prospects for recovering. That he got so old nevertheless, as Budimir states, is a 'miracle' and a 'triumph' of his will to live. The stories of violence inscribed in their very bodies attest to the claim of victimhood. In fact, Budimir's and Father Dimitrije's worshipping of Mihailović makes up for a dominant current in the post-World War Two diaspora. Interestingly, as

110. See *Willkommen an der Grenze*, documentary about Mostar by Sylvi Miosić 2003.

Ballinger observed (2003: 107) a year after Tito's death, an outpouring of revisionist histories, most of them originating in Serbia and centering on Mihailović occurred. It can only be speculated if there were links between the Royalist Chetnik émigré organizations and their journals "Sloboda" or "Byronica" and the revival of revisionism in Serbia. What is certain is that a great many former Chetnik émigrés greeted these developments with enthusiasm.

For the old men and survivors, the presence of dead heroes, whether in stories or on the wall are strong traces indicating the crucial dimension of certain life events for the present. And they twisted their life stories once again, this time not by falling victim but by carefully participating and administering events on the ground from the safe distance in exile.

Likewise, the decoration of Saša's home with a large Serbian flag, awards by Bosnian Serb leaders Karadžić and Plavšić can be understood as the legitimization of a personal story by the top ranking nationalist leaders' support. The pictures and signatures on the wall testify to the long-distance nationalist activities of their owners and witness the transformation of what is meant by the house, or 'home,' the people I talked to inhabit. While preceding the outbreak of war in the homeland, Saša was not involved in diaspora politics at all, he now furnishes his living room as if to provide proof of his new activism, which also marks a 'new' life, or the transformation of the private (suffering) into the political.

It remains particularly pronounced for groups such as the Serbs, who preserve a literal vision of a shattered home as they focus on architectural monuments, churches and houses in legitimating their historical claims. By linking semantic discourse to physical landscape, the exiles offer powerful "evidence" of Serbia's destruction, evidence that resists various efforts to silence the story of the massacres of the Second World War. In a variety of ways then, the émigrés (re)construct memories of their lost world, which remains open only to those "authentic" Serbs with roots in the lands where Serbs lived. The ultimate sign of this rootedness is the presence of dead ancestors and burnt down houses in people's new homes, thus materially linking past and present.

The politics of location

The dramatic, negative, images of home and its devastation, as inscribed in the material side to memory, is complemented by an architectural antipode which the three short descriptions of houses revealed. The individuals I focused on in this and the previous chapter, and many others I met and interviewed own well-to-do (upper) middle class houses. If gazing at the sweeping cityscape from Father Dimitrije's living room window or at the green UC Berkeley campus from Mira's house, Serbs defy the classical stereotype of poor, marginal immigrants and in their residences manifest their fulfillment of "the American dream." Moreover, not so wealthy individuals like Dragana Smith or Dragan Jovanović, although not being able to afford to buy a house in Berkeley or San Francisco, nevertheless own spacious homes in El Cerrito, Berkeley's neighboring town, where their huge living room windows offer precious views of the East Bay, the Golden Gate Bridge and San Francisco. Another example is Dragana Gajković. A few years ago she moved from her San Francisco residence to the upper-class area of Marin County across the Bay from the city. In Sausalito she and her husband own a hacienda-style house, complete with swimming pool and barbecue section.

Generation, time of arrival, and economic status seemed to be the indicators for both the successful acquisition of wealth and the obtaining of (leading) positions in diaspora politics. It was more likely that leaders of émigré organizations were older, belonging to the Second World War refugee group, and had spent their 'productive' years making money outside the spheres of ethnic circles. The younger immigrants who arrived in the 1980's and 1990's often didn't participate in diaspora politics, and, of course, many of them didn't have the money to afford to buy a house. Still, they seemed to be eager at renting apartments or houses in the prestigious neighborhoods of Berkeley or San Francisco, although they could have found less costly ones in Oakland. Andreja for example rented a spacious apartment in the valley of the pricey Berkeley Hills, in a house owned by Mira, who helped the younger immigrants by offering her apartments at a low rent. Surrounded by old trees and large Victorian houses, Andreja's home is located in a typical white neighborhood that becomes less and less affordable not only for young immigrants and families but also for middle-class families.

Upon arrival, quite a few people told me of how they were helped with finding housing by families in the church, and sometimes were even hosted by those who had enough space to offer. This was the case for Ljiljana and Vlado, a young couple arriving from Belgrade in 1999, a few days after the bombing started. Upon arrival, they were first hosted by Dragan Jovanović in El Cerrito, who then helped them find the place they reside in now. The computer designer and researcher inhabit a small apartment on Solano Avenue in Berkeley, a small shopping street with restaurants and boutiques. Andreja, Ljiljana, and Dragan testify to the significance that diaspora networks have for creating support systems and social cohesion between people of various age, and time of arrival. Very often, the contact with Serbs who have lived in the U.S. for decades already also changes the outlook the young hold towards the homeland, usually contributing to their Serbianization. These examples also indicate how variables such as generation and economic status loom large in the world of diaspora life.

Not only private houses, but also communal buildings such as the San Francisco Saint John's Serbian Orthodox Church and the Serbian Cemetery in Colma run by the 1880 founded *Serbian Benevolent Society* (SBS) accomplish the ideal of success in real estate acquisition. The former is located on the top of a hill on Turk Street, overlooking the city, while the latter is in a South San Francisco suburb couched in the green upper valley on a mountain range. Considering how important graveyards and churches are in Serbian culture,[111] the two properties demonstrate the concerted effort with which the Serbian community invests in making the United States its home. Time and again, one finds in the mere observation of the location of a residence, the narrative reversal of negative to positive similar to Bahloul's description of the exiled members of an Algerian household now residing in France (Bahloul 1996: 39). What the immigrants strive to generate in this alternation is the emphasis on the human dimension of exile and an immigrant's life. "We have made it!," is a message delivered in a number of ways, one of them being the acquisition of real estate and property as is manifest in the outlook and location of residences. To have lived in Yugoslavia becomes an adventure, a triumph, and a heroic deed. To live in a good location in California, one of the states with the most expensive real estate prices and highest living costs, if possible on one of the San Francisco or Berkeley hills turns the narrative of suffering into a victorious quest.

Most houses in the hills cost at least half a million dollar, many cost much more (Ong 1997: 87). Many Serbs are well-educated professionals who live in upscale neighborhoods, attend American universities, work in high-tech companies, and buy expensive real estate. What Aihwa Ong in *Flexible Citizenship* (1997), an ethnography of Chinese transnationals in the Bay Area, calls the "politics of location" is equally apt for Serbs: "They try to maintain their Victorian homes and upscale English gardens, collect Stradivarius violins and attend city operas, play tennis in formerly white clubs, and dress up by dressing down their noveaux-riches appearance" (Ong 1997: 103f.). With reference to Pierre Bourdieu's (1977) theory of "symbolic capital" and "social habitus" she contends that by recurring to economic practices such as the logics of real estate the migrants effectively manage to compete with other American citizens, and still invest in their family and homeland ties.

But the success that Ong pictures is only one part of the story. Likewise, the deep feeling of failure when not succeeding in the "politics of location" underlines the centrality of status which was expressed by the acquisition or renting of a certain residence.

111. See Halpern [1956]1967: 225-231.

Is it only the rich émigrés who can afford to maintain ties to their homeland? Or, can only the wealthy finance a corporative way of doing so? The success-story Ong tells of the Chinese transnationals whose trade links China with Southeast Asia and California, easily lets the reader forget about the adverse cases of lack of wealth and symbolic capital. Are there not thousands of Chinese immigrants in the Bay Area, who inhabit cramped, little apartments in the city or its suburbs, struggling in low-paying positions, and often working more than one job at a time? Or what about the middle-class neighborhoods Richmond and The Sunset which surround the Golden Gate Park and during the last ten years have seen a remarkable increase of Chinese and Filipino residents? And the migrants who do not materially succeed in the transnational enterprise of emigration? Are only wealthy immigrants able to feel close to their homeland and actively maintain ties to family and friends "back home"?

Ong's focus on "elite Chinese subjects" (Ong 1999: 4), "Chinese cosmopolitans" (ibid.: 24), or „elite transnationalism" (ibid.: 24) emphasizes that transnational practices, the "flexible citizenship" of owning several passports and belonging to more than one market, more than one nation-state, is bound to a high status in the world of finance and business. On one hand, my own findings support Ong's selection of interlocutors, since those Serbs who owned the biggest houses and had acquired the most economic success were the once who also traversed space most frequently. On the other hand, I find it interesting how immigrants who occupy very diverse positions in the class-systems, from managers and former managers, to priests, students, carpenters, and refugees take part in the development of imaginaries of the homeland, historical visions, and the politics of location.

Old men like the two Budimirs who lost almost a decade through war and sickness only achieved moderate incomes in low-paying technical jobs or doing menial labor. Budimir Pesić, e.g., inhabits a tiny one-bedroom-apartment in the basement of his sister's Berkeley house, underneath Andreja's apartment. The scarcity of his residence is striking, simple furniture, bookshelves with a large number of books, and a little kitchen corner. A few times I met an older Bosnian Serb couple, refugees from the Banja Luka area, both of whom were close to retirement. Boris was employed in unskilled, underpaid construction work while Ivana was unable to work due to sickness. Visiting the two in their tiny two-bedroom apartment in Oakland, bordering Fruitvale, they could not help but complain about the poor living conditions and the "bad, black" neighborhood they called "slum." Located in a gray, four-story apartment building, the windows and doors behind metal bars pointing to an equally gray asphalt yard, where children played and laundry hung out to dry, the couple seemed to suffer from the overcrowded living arrangements. Living of welfare they could barely make it and sometimes were short of money already at the beginning of the month, not knowing how to pay the month's rent. Meanwhile they dreamed of their house in the Bosnian countryside – a photo of it decorated the wall –, where Ivana was busy all day long, caring for her four daughters and, later her grandchildren, feeding the pigs and cows. Ivana and Boris are only one example for the great economic strains on newly arriving semi- or unskilled refugees from rural Bosnia whose stay in the costly Bay Area would prove utterly disillusioning. Indeed, many of the Bosnian Serb migrants who were permitted to enter the United States as political refugees only after 1997 and often inhabited one-bedroom apartments with a whole family in the Tenderloin slum in Downtown San Francisco, recently called "Little Bosnia," have moved to the suburbs of the city or to the Sacramento area, where the rents can be up to a fifth from the ones in San Francisco.

I got acquainted with a young Muslim couple from Velika Kladuša[112], living in a one-bedroom apartment in the Tenderloin with their one-and-a-half-year old son. Working as a wood carpenter since his arrival in 1997, the 27-year-old Mehmet earned enough to pay the $1000 rent and his family's living expenses. In addition to his income his 25-year-old wife Jasmina has recently started working night shifts in a copy shop for six dollars an hour. One afternoon they showed me a video of their last visit to the family back home. Dozens of people gathered in a spacious living room, smoking cigarettes and drinking coffee. Outside the house I could see several brandnew red cars. Mehmet proudly told me that he had six brothers and sisters, and they all had children, from one to four, Jasmina was the oldest out of seven, and her siblings, too, had children. Asking them how these big families made a living nowadays, and could even afford to buy new cars, they remarked matter-of-factly that very few had work and that they sent them money. In fact, almost his whole family is actually dependent on the remittances he sends: "*I think I support about 14 people from the money I send home,*" said Mehmet. Although Mehmet did make a relatively good income, the role of remittances in this family's budget nevertheless amazed me. Family obligations and networks seemed to be of utmost importance, relegating even individual safety concerns to a secondary place: the parents were quite concerned about their hyperactive son's well-being, since they didn't dare to walk on the dirty street with him. Eventually, in

112. I had first met this couple at a folk concert in the Serbian Orthodox church, although they are Muslims. They explained to me their 'closeness' to Serbs instead of other fellow Muslims by recurring to the regional characteristics of Velika Kladuša. In the Bosnian war, a rich industrialist and influential politician, Fikret Abdić, decided to split from Izetbegović's Muslim nationalism and opted for remaining with the Serbs in the multinational Bosnia of former Yugoslavia. The expression "Abdić Muslims" refers to this random faction among Muslims in Bosnia, which was limited to the area of Velika Kladuša.

2002 they had saved enough money to look for a house in the Daily City area, close to the Pacific.

Ivana and Boris, however, stay where they are. They are too old and sick for dreaming of the upward mobility Mehmet and his wife so energetically and remarkably strive for. Instead of raising hopes for themselves, the couple puts all their aspirations in their 18-year-old daughter Maria who is an A-student at UC Berkeley and whom, by emigrating, they wanted to enable to obtain a good education. Now they merely wait for her to finish until they can return. Therefore they legitimize their uncomfortable and unsettling experience in the United States with the investment in their youngest daughter's future. In doing so they take part in the practices of transnationalism, and they reify the politics of location, if only by aspiring to the dream of leaving the Fruitvale neighborhood and being able to afford to live in Berkeley. Without Ivana and Boris, Maria would never be able to one day become a well-earning professional in the U.S.

Acquiring a greencard, buying a house, earning academic credentials and taking up a professional position is not only the manifestation of personal success, it is also an investment in the family here and back home, who by receiving remittances benefit from their relatives' migration. Moreover, wealth abroad is the fundament on which diaspora activism for the homeland rests, be it the funding of Serbian children, the work with the Čelebići trial, or Chetnik lobbying for the resurgence of the monarchy in Serbia. But without the imaginaries of the homeland and narratives of victimization this wealth wouldn't lead to the cultural practices that my interlocutors pursued. While it is often from comfortable residences in which they live not only as Americans but as wealthy Americans that old and young can lean back on and invest in their homeland ties and their narrative of the Self, wealth is not the exclusive entrance key into the world of transnationalism.

Conclusion

This chapter has been animated by the challenge of describing and accounting for the striking historicity of thought and social action among elderly, politically active Serbian exiles in the San Francisco Bay Area. Neither their stories of suffering nor their long-distance nationalism are singular; many displaced people all over the world try to come to terms with their nation's tragic past, present, and future, of which they, although residing far away, perceive themselves to be an intrinsic part. However, what is especially significant in the Serbian case is the explosive power of a past that has never been reconciled, as it unfolds itself in the memories of people at a moment when another major tragedy, another war intrudes deeply into the present. Analyzing both discursive and non-discursive practices of remembering I wish to have made clear how narratives and social actions are closely interconnected, bridging both time and space. Saša, Mira, and Father Dimitrije certainly belong to a determined tradition of diaspora activism that has in the last decade become emblematic for many other peoples moving across the globe (see Tölölyan 1991). While state-of-the-art technological advances in communications and transportation have dramatically transformed the relationship between the homeland and the diaspora, it was the occurrence of war starting in 1991 that resulted in a major change in how émigrés thought about and undertook actions for the homeland. That a decade later the academic literature is still remarkably silent about the diaspora's role in the recent Balkan Wars is disturbing. Not only after 9/11 should it be more urgent than ever to investigate closely the political ideologies, memories, and nationalist aspirations which exiles develop about their homeland. With this study I aim at contributing to a critical rethinking of place making as suggested by Gupta and Ferguson (1997), Marcus (1998), Clifford (1997), and others. As my material indicated, political upheaval and war in the homeland can drastically change the ways that migrants in the U.S. relate to their country of origin. Therefore, scholars should pay close attention to the role of diasporas and their fluid nature at the time of crisis in the homeland. The specific Serbian case indicates that a strict reading of diaspora as a people that is forced into exile makes sense, instead of resorting to an inflationary use if the concept for all migrants that is common today. For anyone trying to understand Serbian long-distance nationalism, the crucial role of violence lies at the core of a memory of the past, which is instrumental in shaping long-distance nationalism.

Furthermore I wish to underline various forms of agency, as well as complicity with power, in state-building processes in the former Yugoslavia. Just as teleological accounts of capitalism and globalization's progressive march forward through time wrongly assume that the objects of these processes rid themselves of the 'burden' of history, so does the belief in a fixed but submerged past, waiting to be exhumed, imply both a given history and a pre-constituted community that is the subject and bearer of that past. I have instead shown how particular individuals who are also representative of collectivities on whose behalf they speak have been continually (re)constituted through practices of remembrance and contests over history which actors phrase in terms of singular and exclusive historical truths. Simultaneously, actors such as Mira, Saša, and Father Dimitrije may urge us to rethink scholarly conceptualizations of fluid or "deterritorialized" identities (Appadurai 1996), such as the hybrid and the borderland mestizo/a. Too attractive is the longing for fixity, belonging, and roots that only a collectivity such as the nation seems to promise.

As we have seen, the legacies of World War Two and the Cold War are increasingly read through a narrative of genocide privileging ethno-national identities over other identifications. In an age that has supposedly witnessed the destruction of metanarratives (Lyotard 1984), an account of World War Two privileging the Holocaust of Jews has become the ultimate reference point and source of moral capital for many political actors, such as the Serbs, contesting power. The identification with the suffering of the Jews, for instance, figured in media representations on all sides of the Yugoslav wars (Živković 2000), which in turn contributed the phrase "ethnic cleansing" to the semantic arsenal for discussing violence, retribution, and redress. Many people who participated in this fieldwork stake the claim to work through the jungle of Yugoslav history and the immense suffering, but when it comes to the means for confronting the past (a truth commission, official apologies, the Criminal Tribunal at the Hague?) a plethora of diverse viewpoints prevail. Without addressing the past on many levels, considering the contrastive claims of the different ethnic groups to the "truth" of the Second World War, the accounts of the recent violence at the end of the millennium cannot possibly be settled.

Part III. Conspiracy theories, future visions, and the International Community[113]

Chapter 6. Conspiracies in the age of globalization

> "The evil is more connected than the good."
> (Steve Tesanović, 58 years old)

> "History *is* a conspiracy, set in motion by demonic forces of almost transcendent power, and what is felt to be needed to defeat it is not the usual methods of political give-and-take, but an all-out crusade."
> (Hofstadter 1979 [1952]: 29)

Investigating the long-term consequences of the Serbian experience of displacement, memory, and identity politics for those who lived through it either in the Second World War, the Third Balkan Wars, or both points to the eagerness with which historical and political explanations for the tragic events that cut through everybody's lives are sought. As has been outlined in the preceding chapters, whether in coming to terms with one's (changed/ing) identity, in reconstructing one's life story, or in elaborating on historical visions for understanding the past, grand explications of the Yugoslav wars loom large. Explaining the violent events in terms of broad, externalized power structures is a prevalent practice among Serbs in Serbia (Živković 2000) as well as in the US (Bock-Luna 2002)[114], examples ranging from an Islamic conspiracy, an Albanian and Croatian expansionism to the idea that the Vatican and Germany had long stood in the waiting to break up multinational Yugoslavia. While the images of an extremely bloody war were distributed by the media and provided the global public almost simultaneously with what went on, as if to make transparent what nobody could really understand, many Serbs strongly doubted these visual representations as well as the official explanations of the Yugoslav disintegration, instead developing their own analyses of events. What is common in

113. The notion "International Community" is in itself highly politicized, as it seemingly refers to all nations world-wide, while in its in actual term covering only powerful Western nation-states (Chomsky 2000: 2). However, I will use this term, because exactly this same notion of a Western International Community is referred to by my informants.

114. This part and especially chapter seven is an extended and revised version of the Bock-Luna 2002 publication.

these narratives is that what most people in the world thought went on, to many Serbs isn't the 'truth' at all, but has been produced by a gigantic "propaganda machine" aimed at eliminating the Serbs. These narratives, as will be explored in the present chapter, often come along in the fashion of conspiracy theories. But what exactly are conspiracy theories? What does it mean to call somebody a traitor or conspirator? Which structure of the political does the form of conspiracy imply? What insights in how people perceive themselves and the world do they provide? Which role do they play specifically in the Serbian case of long-distance migration? And, what does conspiracy thinking among Serbian migrants tell us about the broader phenomenon of the rise of paranoia in late modernity?

Recently, not only following 9/11, conspiracies and conspiracy theories have aroused much interest in the general public and also in anthropology and related disciplines (Barkun 2003, Todd and Sanders ed. 2003, Malkki 2000, Melley 2000 et al.). In this part of the study I confine myself to describing and analyzing a few selected conspiracies that interlocutors told me during my fieldwork. My goal is not to judge these visions of the world morally, and to either denounce them or to assert their "truth" value, but instead to explore two dimensions. First, I am interested in their political content, what they reveal about the way that Serbs in the diaspora view the world around them in relationship to their homeland. Second, by focusing on the temporal dimension of conspiracies I investigate the striking aspect that conspiracies were told to me in the future tense, providing expectations and prospects for times to come which derived from the recent and more distant past. Considering that the past plays such a huge role among Serbs in the U.S., it seems necessary for me to address the temporality of conspiracy theories and their potential of linking past and present by constructing 'timeless' global visions. Below, I shall start with giving an example for opening up the relevance of conspiracy thinking in contemporary Serbian migrant life in the United States.

Tito, the Trojan horse

"Tito was the Trojan horse for Communism actually. He was really a Trojan horse. Who knows really what was Tito? Still it is unclear. There are so many biographies of Tito, and who is Tito? Many biographers definitely refuse his Yugoslav or Croatian origin," the gray bearded Father Dimitrije Aleksandrović tells me conspiratorially in one of our interviews, sitting in a comfortable armchair in his living room in Diamond Heights, San Francisco. After having read several biographies of Josip Broz Tito, born in Kumrovec, Croatia, to a Croat father and a Slovenian mother in 1892, I was rather stunned to hear this information. The retired priest and historian, who only recently received his Master's degree in history at the Catholic University of San Francisco, con-

tinues his revelation by offering 'proof' to this allegation in the hybrid form of historical study and witness account:

> *"His latest biographer personally believed that he was a Polish Jew. He was definitely not Croatian because when Belgrade was captured, I mean 'liberated' – I say captured by Soviets – we went to Belgrade and came to the main square, Terasije they call it, and there is a theater, opera, and national theater with a balcony. Tito was there and thousands of partisans and those I call partisan mob at that time. They killed everybody, like in a revolution. I was young, I was with that partisan. We came to listen to Tito, but I didn't understand him! Very hardly, very hardly, he doesn't speak Croatian accent, he speaks some strange... to me today it sounds like Polish accent, I feel that. It was my impression. So, one of those partisans just looked at me, as if he was saying: 'I didn't understand him well, very heavy accent, not Croatian at all.' And it was through years that Tito improved to speak Serbo-Croatian language, long time after that. That's what they say, a couple of authors of Tito, Djilas, Nora Beloff, British author, they all accept him as most claim that he is from Kumrovac, whatever, but some other new are coming mostly from Serbian part, they say he is not Croatian, he is not Yugoslav at all."*

Why delve into a Tito conspiracy? And what would the rumination about the former Yugoslav leader's ethnic background tell about conspiracies in general and in the specific Serbian case? I chose Father Dimitrije's narrative on Tito's allegedly mysterious identity, because, I believe, in many points it is characteristic of conspiracy thinking today and in specific illuminates Serbian views of the past and Big Power politics. As the authors of *Transparency and Conspiracy* (West and Sanders, ed., 2003: 12) claim "ideas that power operates in hidden ways" enjoy strong support by people world-wide. Conspiracy theories are a symptom of our age which is characterized by global transformation, military intervention, international terrorism, and the power of multinational capital, leaving ordinary citizens in a state of anxiety and with the feeling of loss of control (Harding and Stewart 2003: 258). Instead of "transparency," a term that today is widely employed by politicians, business men, and NGOs alike, to attest for the official fight against opaque power structures, corruption, and political scandals, many people seem to rather believe in the invisible, disguised, and corrupted ways that power works.

George Marcus, in *Paranoia within Reason*[115] (1999: 5), notes that nowhere does this desire to prove that "something is 'out there,'" or, a "duty toward knowledge in the absence of compass" (Marcus 1999: 5), thrive better than in Eastern European countries where "the cold-war era itself

115. Curiously, the book has been published in a series called by the matching title "Late Editions. Cultural Studies for the End of the Century."

was defined throughout by a massive project of paranoid social thought and action that reached into every dimension of mainstream culture, politics, and policy" (Marcus ibid: 2). Likewise, in the United States, with the heavy influence of anti-Communist Cold War politics the climate for paranoia was ideal, as Timothy Melley in *Empire of Conspiracy* (2000) claims. From a belief in UFOs to the Iran-Contra affair, the assassination of John F. Kennedy to the Waco affair – postwar American politics are ripe with scandals which are believed by many citizens to have been manipulated for the public and the 'truth' of which are elaborated in conspiracies. The 2000 election of President Bush and the attack on the World Trade Center (WTC) in New York are two of the most recent examples for how widespread conspiracy thinking is throughout a broad cross section of Americans today (Sanders and West 2003: 4). Conspiracies surrounding the death of Princess Diana in 1997 which haunt Great Britain at present are one more example for the popularity of the belief in hidden, disguised actors in the Western world at large. But whereas American authors almost exclusively point to the more recent 20th century as the age of conspiracy thinking, German historian Dieter Groh (1992) refers to the historical depth of the phenomenon, which ranges from the beginning of the witch hunting at the time of the inquisition in the 13th century to the French Revolution, and conspiracies surrounding Marx's concepts of communism in the 19th century.

San Francisco's retired Serbian Orthodox priest, Father Dimitrije, is not the only one who was not satisfied with the established historical accounts of Tito's early life and language qualities in the Slovenian-Croatian Zagorje borderlands where instead of a bilingualism he acquired "a curious mongrel dialect" (Beloff 1985: 32). Rumors in the Serbian community doubting Tito's ethnic background were tantamount and to a great many his person opened up a riddle that they were eager at resolving. According to Beloff, Tito spoke neither Slovene nor Croatian without an accent, and "during the time he was working for Moscow, some of his Serb associates hearing his accent took him for a Russian agent" (ibid.). Richard West (1994: 28) notes that Tito spoke Slovenian better than Croatian. If Tito's local dialect or "Zagorje twang" (Beloff 1985: 32) had been documented for so long already, why should people like Father Dimitrije still delve into conspiracies surrounding the former Yugoslav leader's language and ethnic background? Why was there such a discontent with some minor biographical detail surrounding Tito's person?

A possible answer may be given by historian Richard Hofstadter who in one of the earliest texts on conspiracy theories, the 1952 essay *The Paranoid Style in American Politics*, lays out what he discerns as the general features of conspiracies:

> "A feeling of persecution is central to the paranoid style, but whereas the clinically paranoid person perceived a world hostile and conspiratorial against him or herself, the spokesperson for the paranoid style finds it directed against a nation, a culture, a way of life whose fate affects not himself alone but millions of others ... His sense that his political passions are unselfish and patriotic, in fact, goes far to intensify his feeling of righteousness and his moral indignation". (Hofstadter 1979 [1952]: 4)

Written during the McCarthy era, Hofstadter's classic statement of conspiracy as a mode of 'social thought' was meant to show that "the paranoid style" has deep roots in American culture. Drawing from psychoanalysis, Hofstadter intended to elaborate on a political conception of conspiracy theory, acknowledging the similarity between paranoid social thought and rationality and logic. While his treatise was conceived as a sharp critique of right-wing mentality in its perception of the danger of communist infiltration in the American government, he had some sympathy for the "reasonableness" of thinking in terms of conspiracies. Nevertheless, in the eyes of scholars today he set the tone for later scholars by suggesting that conspiracy theories were collective "paranoid delusions" (Sanders and West 2003: 13). In contrast to this, for Hellinger (2003: 204), Hofstadter "laid the groundwork for dismissing conspiracy theory as pathology," a view that is still common. I view conspiracy as both a rational and emotional response to political circumstandes, e.g. to the feeling of being "under attack," by the media and the public which so many people mentioned throughout this work. Farfetched as it can be, conspiracy thinking is based on very real perceptions of injustice and misrepresentations that many Serbs have shared throughout the 1990's.

Conspiracy as historical explanation

In Father Dimitrije's world view as for Hofstadter, the Cold War was *the* determining political constellation imprinting itself on his life trajectory in emigration and marking his strong anti-Titoist persuasion, nourished by the tumultuous events he experienced as a young Chetnik at the beginning of Tito's coming to power (see chapter 4). In *What was socialism, and what comes next?* (1996: 4) Katherine Verdery proposes to look more closely at the Cold War, instead of celebrating the victory of capitalism. Contending that "the Cold War was also a form of knowledge and a cognitive organization" (ibid.), she urges anthropologists to explore the old and new imaginings of socialism which not only affected intellectual publics in East and West, but also private idealizations of possible futures (ibid.: 11). In other words: socialism is not irrelevant and there is certainly a great deal that can be learned of it today, in America and in Eastern Europe. Father Dimitrije and other Serbs who lived through the Second World War or Tito's Yugoslavia and now reside in the United States have in important ways either participated or been influenced by the Cold War, their narratives still revealing the ramifications of the two competing ideologies, capitalism and communism. Ultimately, the conspiracies elaborated by many participants of my study can be understood in the light of the longest latent conflict in the 20th century.

What is significant in Father Dimitrije's conspiracy is that it starts with questioning an established fact. Throwing into doubt one of the most basic information about the former socialist leader, the narrative plays with historically scientific data, on one hand grounding itself on historical insights and on the other hand discarding historical findings by the witness' skepticism. Far from resembling an irrational, groundless fear, the Tito conspiracy is constituted like a detective story, following the rules of the search for evidence and empirical knowledge. In Hofstadter's words, conspiracy theory "not only starts with certain moral commitments that can be justified to many non-paranoids but also carefully and all but obsessively accumulates „evidence"" (Hofstadter ibid.: 36). But why Tito, who has been dead for twenty years already? And what does it help to 'know' that Tito may be a Polish *Jew*? Was it not enough for Serbs to claim that due to Tito's Croatian background the Yugoslav 'experiment' had always 'suppressed' Serbs?

Along the grain of the new revelation, accusations against Tito could be easily enlarged to the proportions of a Jewish world conspiracy, meant only to destroy the Serbs.[116] But these last questions in relation to Jews didn't seem to interest people much about the Tito story. Rather it seemed to suffice that there was the *possibility* of a disguise, a secret origin of Tito, a fact that would change the whole story and history as such. In a nutshell: what was officially the 'truth' about Yugoslavia and its demise was not the

116. The belief in a Jewish world conspiracy can be uttered in many contexts and in the light of very diverse political ideologies. In the Serbian case, it is related to various outstanding Jewish personalities in the United States. Concerning the vehement condemnation of Serbian violence in Bosnia by many prominent American Jews, some people stated that they were very disappointed with how easy Jews were 'manipulated' by the media and committed treachery against their 'co-sufferers' during World War Two, the Serbs. Many of my interlocutors pointed out to the power of Jews in the media and political landscape. One of the central Jewish target of Serbian frustration was minister of foreign affairs, Madeleine Albright, who under the Clinton administration was responsible for the bombings of Serb positions in Eastern Bosnia in 1995 and Yugoslavia in 1999. As a little girl during World War Two, her father had served with the allied troops in Belgrade: "she knows how to speak Serbian," some informants claimed. According to rumors, friendly Serbs hid the young Madeleine in a closet from being found by German soldiers, thereby saving her life. Fifty years later her "contempt" for Serbs and "evil" character was met with much anger, calling her a traitor of Serbdom.

'truth.' But Serbs like Father Dimitrije were eager at uncovering the "hidden" meanings, finding a clear-cut answer to why "the Serbs always have to suffer" not in politics per se, or in his political acts, but in the *person* Tito.

Daniel Hellinger (2003: 208), in his analysis of paranoia in American politics describes conspiracy theories as introducing "subjectivity and individualized forms of accountability into the otherwise impersonal, structural forces that, according to social scientists, journalists and historians, move our world." In the story of Tito one finds exactly this search for subjective and individualized accountability. In accordance to the belief in the limitless power of one person/dictator who is made responsible for what happened to the country, the priest formulates a view of power that reduces the complexity of institutions and states to the simplicity of only the main political protagonist. Indeed, this reduction of complexity is a core aspect of conspiracy theory. But why didn't Tito's ideological, wartime and post-World War Two actions, or political deeds serve Father Dimitrije's aim of explaining his view of Yugoslav history well enough? For which reason did he have to resort to Tito's language and ethnic background?

I propose, that while during the Cold War Tito's communist persuasions sufficed to construct him as *the* enemy to émigré Serbs in the U.S., whose fight against communism became their main goal, with the demise of the Iron Curtain ideological antagonisms weren't up-to-date anymore. And by the turn of the millennium Father Dimitrije has exchanged ideology for ethnicity, delving into a discourse of personification and ethnicization for explaining Yugoslavia's more recent past. He does so by locating the reasons for the war not only in the Croatian-ness of Tito but in his being entirely 'Other,' an external enemy of the country. In a way, according to the plot, Tito 'went global', crossing the boundaries of the Yugoslav state and making Tito a non-Yugoslav, a migrant, someone from outside. Poland stands for a Catholic country with strong ties to the Vatican, and Jews figure in association with 'the Jewish American lobby' in the United States as an adversary of Serbs during the Bosnian war. Attributing the evilness of the former country's leader to an outside, antagonistic power thereby resembles a displacement of responsibility and guilt, encoding several historical narratives in the scapegoat Tito, with the allusion to him being an external, ethnic 'Other' ranging highest.[117]

As Harding and Stewart (2003: 261) state with reference to another popular conspiracy theory of today: "The dual slogans of *The X-Files* "Trust no one" and "The Truth is out there" – express a heady yet unsettling wedding of a deep skepticism of officially sanctioned truths and the seductions of the sensualization power/knowledge." Searching for facts

117. In the following chapter I will look more closely at the role of external powers and the International Community, which plays a huge role in contemporary conspiracy thinking among Serbs.

and secret interconnections, they combine a skeptical mode of thinking with positivism's methods, while their motivation is entirely sensual – emotional, full with anger, disturbance, and a deep feeling of injustice. Therefore, one could conceive of their conspiracy theories as "mass response of ordinary people to impersonal forces that they cannot control and do not understand" (ibid.). Indeed, this psychological approach to conspiracy theory as a way of coping with an overwhelming reality seems quite adequate with regard to Serbian paranoid thinking, since many Serbs feel that their suffering is undeserved and try to find a cause for it. "Thus the world around them is no longer as it should be. It becomes more and more an illusion, a semblance, while at the same time the evil that has occurred, or is occurring and is becoming more and more essential, takes place *behind* reality" (Groh 1987: 1).

Conspiracy and Pathology

Forty years after Hofstadter's writing the public still views conspiracy as pathology, juxtaposed to the mainstream's trust in 'officially sanctioned truths.' This is reflected in how Serbs comment on conspiratorial thinking among themselves, for example old Budimir Pesić from Croatian Slavonia who warned me: "*They [Serbs, B.B.-L] like conspiracy theories and suffer from persecution mania! No, serious, some of them have had bad experiences with being misrepresented, so you should be sensitive about it.*" Linking together 'wrong' representations of 'them' with conspiracy thinking, it becomes clear how sensitive political issues are for many Serbs.

Another example of the view that conspiracy is a mere delusion is a Wall Street Journal article, called *Paranoid and Vengeful* (1992). In their report on a visit to Bosnia-Herzegovina, Roger Thurow and Tony Horwitz, upon exploring Bosnian Serb views on the Bosnian war in the town of Bjeljina, contend:

> "In stark contrast to their menacing image on the evening news, Serbs today are a defensive, self-pitying and paranoid people. Whether they are dug in on the front lines, or waiting in the gasoline lines that snake through Belgrade, Serbs' abiding conviction is that, like Jews, they have been persecuted through centuries of European turmoil and now are under threat again." (Thurow and Horwitz 1992: A1).

Whereas the authors illuminate many important aspects of Serbian history, from the battle of Kosovo, via the First World War to the Second World War, in order to explain the feelings of Serbs during the Bosnian war, the article's subtext is that of an irrational, pathological people. The text thus implies that there is a 'truth' to the war, and that Serbs certainly don't own a bit of it, dismissing their 'paranoia' as mere delusion. In contrast to this view, I argue, that conspiracy thinking is not too different from historical and political practices of reasoning and truth production.

Budimir, in his opening remark on Serbs' "persecution mania," followed the same course by latching on to the discourse of dismissal. After all, many people involved in the Balkan war, including Budimir, my readers, and I who followed the events on television screens or in newspaper articles were made to believe that the war was primarily about a "Greater Serbia" nationalism, which was paralleled even with the Nazi Holocaust.

If one looks closely at Hofstadter's definition of the term he has certainly pointed out some core aspects of conspiracy thinking which are helpful for the analysis of Serbian visions of the Balkan wars and the New World Order. According to Hofstadter "[what] distinguishes the paranoid style is not, then, the absence of verifiable facts [...], but rather the curious leap in imagination that is always made at some critical point in the recital of events" (Hofstadter ibid.: 37). Furthermore, the form of conspiracy thinking is that of accumulating facts towards an "overwhelming 'proof:'" "It is nothing if not coherent [...] in fact the paranoid mentality is far more coherent than the real world since it leaves no room for mistakes, failures, or ambiguities" (ibid.: 36). Father Dimitrije, I suggest, takes part in creative discursive interventions not only to cope with reality, as Groh has proposed, but to reconstruct history and to actively shape reality.

Nowhere does the frustration with public media and academic discourse and occur more poignantly than in the case of Serbs in trying to make sense of the Yugoslav wars, and thus the drive to interpret reality differently. Father Dimitrije's attempt to externalize the reason for Yugoslavia's troubles, by 'Othering' Tito's person fits into this general pattern of searching for outside powers that conspire, a theme that I will explore further below.

Ethnography and Conspiracy

On a late afternoon in August 2001, I entered the San Francisco apartment of a popular Blues musician, Steve Tesanović, in his late fifties. Upon arrival, standing in his cramped kitchen, bearing the signs of a bachelor household and receiving one of the tasty "Turkish" – or, in my interlocutors' terms "Serbian" – coffees in a white, stained enamel cup, I was thrown straight into a world of conspiracies. After an introduction, which was very short considering that we had never seen each other before – another participant gave me his contact – besides the coffee he offered me a detailed monologue about a Vatican conspiracy against Serbia. The disintegration of Yugoslavia, the middle-sized bespectacled man wearing a

French cap argued, had been planned long before and followed a clear pattern, continuing the German-Croat-Catholic alliance from World War Two, when Croatian monks and priests willingly participated in the Ustaša massacres against the Serbian population in order to achieve the elimination of Croatia's Orthodox minority. Although Tesanović, who is somewhat famous outside, and not so much inside the Serbian immigrant circles, spent most of our three hour long conversation on the popular Vatican conspiracy it was not the only plot he envisioned, although this theory seemed to be most important to him. While talking he grabbed the book *Unholy Trinity* (1991) from his bookshelf full with records, waving it to me as if to vehemently prove his claims. Among the other plots the immigrant from Montenegro who came to the U.S. in the 1960's indulged in, were the not so well known conspiracy surrounding the public stabbing of Yugoslav tennis star Monica Seleš, a Serb from Novi Sad with an American passport now residing in Florida, during a tennis match in Hamburg in 1993. Whereas the undisputed version of the event ran that a mentally disturbed East German man who was a star of Steffi Graf committed the attack.[118] Steve had something else to say: "*She was on the top of her career when they stabbed her in the back so she couldn't ever be the same again. That's what they do to the Yugoslavs. And the guy who did it never got arrested.*" According to his motto "Think of the worst, it will be true," Tesanović suspected a grand conspiracy led by a secretive "they" behind the attack on Seleš, whose ethnic Serbian background almost automatically turned her into a victim. It simply couldn't have been a single, crazy villain who nourished some personal hatred against the tennis-star, simply because Seleš was the most serious competition for his beloved number One, Steffi Graf. In the fashion of conspiracy thinking, where everything is connected, Tesanović links the attack to the Yugoslav war, and the "anti-Serbian" news coverage of the Balkan conflicts. After all, Seleš had repeatedly received death threats in the wake of the dismemberment of Yugoslavia.[119] If John F. Kennedy was the victim to a government conspiracy, why should not have been more behind the Seleš attack, which was never investigated closer?

This day in his San Francisco Sunset residence Steve could hardly stop feeding me with conspiracy theory. He passionately delved into the theory of the manipulation of American Blacks by some invisible forces in America, and a Hitler-conspiracy, claiming that Hitler is still alive somewhere and that his death in a bunker in 1945 was staged by a German grocer double, a plot researched by the conspiracy theorist Mate Brussels. "*Who would know what really happened in history? We don't know,*" says Steve and shrugs his shoulders. While I was drawn into elaborate conspiratorial schemes, I had

---

118. According to the BBC news article *Attack on Monica Seleš* at http://news.bbc.co.uk/onthisday/hi/dates/stories/april/30/newsid_2499000/2499161.stm
119. ibid.

never thought of before, many of which were undermined by numerous video-tapes of news interviews made during the Bosnian war and Internet publications Steve showed me to manifest his points, it became increasingly difficult for me to not believe in them, too! Perhaps, if Hofstadter had met Steve he may have matter-of-factly diagnosed a "paranoid style" in the musician's world view.

"Most academics," Keeley has concluded, "simply find the conspiracy theories of popular culture to be silly and without merit" (1999: 109, n.1). In this vein one could easily discard Father Dimitrije's and Steve's 'theories' under the rubric of senseless, irrational ruminations of old, frustrated men. The emerging interest in the topic of conspiracy theories is, as Brown (1997) tells, often greeted with raised eyebrows. However, anthropologists with their interest in 'exotic' places and 'strange' customs, have curiously ignored the topic of conspiracy theories. Sanders and West note that anthropology had a pioneering role in the social sciences with discovering "sense" in the religious practices of "primitives," pointing out to Evans-Pritchard's work on the Azande ([1910] 1985), whose thought he found not to be so "irrational" once he had adopted their "idiom." Nevertheless, the belief in conspiracy theory in our own societies that the official public view discards as "irrational" has been left untouched until recently. According to Sanders and West (2003: 13f.):

> "Anthropologists might be expected to show more sympathy than social scientists working in other disciplines, but, even in a time when the discipline has embraced study in familiar places, anthropologists have manifested their indifference to occult beliefs and conspiracy ideas among familiar natives [...] We can only speculate on the reason for this. Anthropologists are, after all, social and political beings in their own rights. 'Close to home,' where the research subjects' beliefs actually have the potential to affect the anthropologist as a fellow member of society, it is perhaps harder to establish methodological empathy and easier simply to disagree with Other views of the world [...] Perhaps, in part, for such reasons, no anthropologist (that we know of) has yet undertaken ethnographic study of right-wing militia movements in the United States."

With regard to Sanders' and West's allusion to the hardship of "establishing methodological empathy," I wish to point to a crucial aspect of Steve's conspiracy thinking which makes it easier to understand, if not to empathize with, the workings of conspiracy, and that is the use of books and other texts in the imagination of conspiracies. How my interlocutors use books, I argue, can serve as a key to uncovering the logic of conspiracy thinking in the Serbian diaspora, relegating the claim of pathology or mania once and for all.

“Ratlines“ and “textual communities“

Helpful for the exploration of the use of books in Serbian conspiratorial thinking is Keith Brown’s (2003: 51f.) discussion of “textual communities,“ a term he borrowed from Joanne Rappaport in her work on Columbia (1990). With regard to Macedonian narratives on identity and history, Brown (2003) is interested in the concern with documentary evidence, be it journalistic, travel, political, or scientific accounts that “have helped mold enduring ideas about the region and the issues at stake“ (Brown ibid.: 52). In referring to Rappaport, Keith explains that the notion “textual community, comprised of a group of people whose activities revolved around the interpretation of key texts“ (1990: 183). For the purpose of my argument it suffices to say that certain books, some of which will be discussed in the following, did not only play a crucial role in undermining historical claims to truth and justice, but they also served to link together individual people and provide collective answers to contemporary political questions.

Steve’s favorite book, *Unholy Trinity. The Vatican, The Nazis, and the Swiss Banks* ([1991]1998) by Mark Aarons and John Loftus, is significant in the regard that like other publications Serbs refer to it forms a crucial element of conspiracies, like a building block nourishing the political visions my interlocutors construct for understanding the past. For the researcher, looking at the books Serbs read can provide guidelines for analysis, in finding out which knowledge informs their ideas. Ultimately, the specific knowledge of diaspora Serbs has to be conceived as “situated knowledge“ (Haraway 1991), produced in a certain social, historical, political, and lastly “textual“ context. Here I will delineate the main thesis of *Unholy Trinity* and show the “curious leap in imagination“ which is undertaken in order to produce a conspiracy out of a well-known historical study.

Aarons and Loftus investigate the Vatican’s role in rescuing 30,000 Croatian Ustaši from Tito’s communist troops and helping them travel in secret to Argentina and Northamerica following World War Two. Among the Nazi criminals ferreted out of Europe so that they could be used in the supposedly greater fight against Communism was also Ante Pavelić, leader of Germany’s Nazi puppet state, who became an advisor to Argentina’s dictatorial president, Perón. While the Vatican was under pressure of Mussolini’s Italy and the allies and didn’t support the Holocaust, Pope Pius XII and other leading Vatican clergy were instrumental in the “Ratlines,“ as the secret smuggling network was called. In their book, Aarons and Loftus provide rich insight into previously inaccessible Vatican archives and British and American intelligence information, laying open how a number of Vatican officials – not *the* Vatican – were deeply involved in hosting war criminals in Italy and helping them escape from Europe, instead of assisting Jews.

First published in 1991, the book was a timely document for opening up old wounds in the ethnic conflicts surfacing in the same year. For many Serbs it became a long-awaited source of evidence for the genocide against Serbs, the infamous World War Two Vatican-Croatia connection, and the role that highest Vatican officials played in the endeavor to support fascist Croats. Moreover, many Serbs, like Steve, refer to this work in order to emphasize the Vatican's stand not just during the Second World War, but also with regard to the recent breakup of Yugoslavia. "*Germany and the Vatican were behind the war, as always they tried to destroy Yugoslavia, this time successfully,*" claimed a great many of my interlocutors. When I conducted an interview in the house of Drago Milicić, 70-year-old electrical engineer from a village near Belgrade, who had traveled with Saša Gocić to Bosnia and was a big fan of Radovan Karadžić, I found the book lying on his toilet water tank, as if it were a daily newspaper. And Mirko Stanković, sixty-seven-year old engineer from San Jose, upon meeting in the San Jose train station, and conducting an interview while sitting on one of the wooden benches from the turn of the century, claimed that 'all you need to know' in order to understand the recent war was *Unholy Trinity*. Thus, when I later bought the book myself, what I expected was a straightforward pro-Serbian nationalist text, but I was soon taught the opposite was true. As Aarons and Loftus (1998: xi) state in their preface to the second edition, Serbian attempts to legitimize Serbian nationalism by using the book's ideas were immediately brushed aside:

> "The detailed account provided in the first half of this book of Croatian fascist atrocities against Serbs, Jews, and Gypsies engendered considerable interest amongst Serb nationalists around the world. Some Australian Serbs even approached us seeking support for the nationalist cause being pursued in Bosnia in the 1990's. Needless to say, and in light of the detailed research we had undertaken in Bosnia and Croatia, this overture was rejected as an attempt to secure our support for the Serb genocide of the 1990's as some sort of 'just' retribution for the Croat genocide half a century earlier."

Extending the book's claim all the way to the present, Serbian migrants purported the thesis of the continuity of history, constructing a cosmology of good and bad, friends and enemies. In doing so they could in fact draw from an event that was regarded significant, Germany's and the Vatican's premature 1991 recognition of Croatia's and Slovenia's independence, which stirred up old fears of a Catholic-Orthodox divide splitting up the region as it had done centuries before. But obviously, there were no “Rat-lines“ during the 1990’s, and the Vatican didn’t help war criminals from Croatia to flee to Argentina in recent times. Nevertheless, many a Serbian reader did try to “prove“ that Germany and the Vatican were as guilty as in the Second World War, thereby attempting to relieve guilt from the Serbian side. And they implemented their specific reading of *Unholy Trinity* to undermine their claims. What did remain as a constant variable in the 20th century, thus, was the perception of a world divided into separate political blocks according to religious criteria, reducing the political to the categories of “enemy“ and “friend“ (Schmitt [1932]1996)[120].

Considering the relevance of *Unholy Trinity* in Steve’s and others’ conspiracies I suggest to look closely at the literary and not just life historical or historical sources that undermine the claims my interlocutors stake. Far from crazing for path breaking personal ideas or obsessions, they are well read and participate in an intellectual public debate, which they turn to their own ends. In this they profit from their specific position as professionals and university educated citizens in American society, where unlike for Serbs in Serbia, Western publications by journalists and academics are easily accessible. Interestingly, the talks were often characterized by allusions to authors, if political scientists (e.g. Michael Parenti, Susan Woodward) or anthropologists (e.g. Robert Hayden, Andrei Simić), thereby manifesting the degree to which ‘our’ interlocutors, instead of simply offering their culturally and socially informed ‘world views,’ provide the researcher with a view which is pregnant with the repercussions of ‘our’ own scientific writing. In the words of Renato Rosaldo (1989: 21): “Social analysis must now grapple with the realization that its objects of analysis are also analyzing subjects who critically interrogate ethnographers – their writings, their ethics, and their politics.“ As a consequence I suggest to look at the twists people make when reading certain texts and grounding their claims on them. In this vein, below I will turn to one if not the central event for many Serbs during the 1990’s, the NATO bombing of Yugoslavia, and investigate how academic writing figured in constructing conspiracy theories for explaining the three-months-long war.

1999: The “realness“ of conspiracy

Hundreds of upset and angry Serbs gather at the downtown San Francisco tourist spot Powell Street, carrying banners with the Serbian nationalist royalist flag, two dangerous

120. What is interesting in this regard is that Schmitt has been analyzed as pursuing a typical conspiratorial analysis himself, mainly due to his simplistic view of politics as a permanent struggle between good and bad, friend and enemy. See Groh 1992: 278 ff.

looking white eagles on black background, and voicefully paroling "Kosovo je Srbija," "Kosovo is Serbia." It is the 26th of March, 1999, and my family visit to the United States draws to a close. My friend Andreja invited me to join the protest, organized by the American socialist organization "International Action Center." It is the first public march after the onset of the NATO bombing of the rump state of Yugoslavia, Serbia and Kosovo, two days before. The night preceding the beginning of the war we watched Kusturica's "Underground." I still had in my mind the film's final message: 'There will always be a reason for war. Maybe next time NATO will bomb us?' So the war did start again. That afternoon I find myself in the middle of the outrage, pain, and desperation of crying older women who on their family visits in the United States are afraid for their sons serving in the army in the homecountry thousands of miles away, young men and women who furiously debate the pros and cons of Milošević's political moves, and people who solemnly march along, with sincere and determined faces, holding signs saying "Clinton=Hitler," "Demographic genocide against Kosovo Serbs," "NATO and the new world order," with a swastika in the background, and target signs known from the Belgrade protests. The war that takes its course in a far remote place seems to move touchingly close, forgotten are the busy shoppers and honking cars hustling through the city center. There are quite a few older women and men, immigrants who had left Yugoslavia more than forty years ago, and who since long have been American citizens.

A few years later this and other protests that took place throughout the spring and summer of 1999 are still the topic of emphatic talk, in which mixed emotions such as frustration and enthusiasm are revived. The priest's wife tells me about a protest in June, organized partly by the Serbian Orthodox church in San Francisco, where she appeared in traditional folklore fashion[121]*. Showing me a photo of herself, face held up and looking content, holding in her hands in front of her corso a banner with the sentence "I am proud to be Serbian." "I always feel as if I am there," she states, "I share their pain. My heart has never left Serbia."* [Fieldnotes and recollections]

To many Serbs, the NATO bombing figures as *the* central event of the 1990's. For some, predominantly Belgrade Serbs, whose hometown had been spared the years long violence in Croatia and Bosnia the bombing of Yugoslavia's capital even marked the beginning of war, instead of the last episode of the country's dissolution. 1999 thus became the epitome of the Yugoslav disintegration, ringing true to the widely held belief in Serbian innocence and the image of the defenseless nation, a David struggling against an overwhelming Goliath. Once again, a loss in battle was twisted into a "heavenly victory," turning Serbs into the pure victims of a decade of lies and big power games. What many people had criticized concerning the Croatian and Bosnian wars in the first half of the decade, a one-sided

121. Curiously, at no other occasion have I seen Serbs dressed in folklore costumes. The congruence of folklore, politics, and nationalism as is evident in this example has been studied in detail by Ivan Čolović 1993.

blaming of Serbs now reached its peak. With nineteen NATO countries undertaking military action against Serbia, the 'unjust' persecution of Serbs manifested itself blatantly, being widely read as a punishment and revenge, instead of a 'just,' 'humanitarian' intervention as NATO named its operations. The NATO war against Yugoslavia reasserted all conspiracies, characterizing the realization of long held speculations and nationalist fears, namely "that the whole world" conspired against "them." And while the International Community officially undertook its military actions in order to chase away Milošević, and not to punish the Serbian population, with every single "collateral damage" the intervention proved to nourish nationalism even more, providing Milošević with a last round of the population's support. This time, the enemy so clearly attacked from outside, exemplifying that Serbs were singled out univocally out of the complex muddle of warring parties in the Yugoslav conflicts. Therefore, in they eyes of many of my interlocutors, the war against Yugoslavia became a self-fulfilling prophecy, giving credence to the widely held belief that the 'evil' comes from outside and not from within – and that it is very well connected.

In the diaspora, as has been pointed out in earlier chapters, the bombing became *the* nation-building event, turning even those who had persistently maintained their Yugoslav identity during the 1990's into Serbs, thus producing a level of (superficial) unity that was unknown in the years before (chapter two). Especially for migrants from Belgrade who had less likely identified with the regions of war, Bosnia and Croatia, the bombing of their hometown meant an unforeseen affront against "themselves," as the priest's wife alluded to in the above passage. Somehow, the bombing also seemed to bring together Serbs originating from all regions, by linking them through a collective suffering that had been less feasible before, when Serbia had remained the region which was excluded from armed struggle and lay behind the frontlines. Not surprisingly then, the event brought about a massive interest in conspiracy theories.

In Belgrade, a series of war postcards was distributed on the main shopping street. On one of them, showing the map of Europe with Serbia in the center, the Serbian capital was marked by a Roman bastion, with a flag sticking out and Asterix and Obelix exclaiming: "We are the last country holding out against the foreign invaders." In the U.S., a flow of e-mails, telephone calls, and Internet sites brought home the fear and anger of loved ones suffering under the bombardment and sanctions.[122] The San Francisco Bay Area experienced a series of talks and debates in book-

122. Aleksandar Zograf's *Bulletins from Serbia* 1999 is a collection of cartoons depicting very well the role of e-mail during the bombardment. In 2001 I met the cartoonist at the opening of his San Francisco exhibition.

shops, university campuses, and public libraries, one of them by Michael Parenti, professor of political science with a degree from UC Berkeley.

Together with Noam Chomsky who in *A New Generation draws the Line* (2000) dealt with the double standards of the West regarding Kosovo and East Timor, Parenti, himself a Berkeley resident, was a 'late-comer' to the Yugoslav wars. His book *To kill a Nation* (1999), purporting the thesis that the International Community had from the beginning aimed at splitting Yugoslavia apart, and now undertook the "humanitarian" intervention to achieve its goal of economic hegemony over the Balkans and Eastern Europe, came out just on time to express the views and sentiments many Serbs held. And since Parenti was not of Serbian descent, his political position and selection of data, mostly English speaking newspaper articles, was welcomed all the more. The opening page reads like a manifest of conspiracy thinking:

> "This book deals with the lies our leaders have been telling us for more than a decade about events in the former Yugoslavia, and how these events fit into the broader context of US global policy. In the pages ahead I investigate the conflicts leading to the dismemberment of that country, and the interests motivating US leaders and their NATO allies" (Parenti 1999: 1).

Since its publication in the wake of the three-months-long Kosovo war Parenti's study has almost become a must to read among Serbs in the Bay Area. Very soon I had two copies of it, both were gifts of people I worked with, and in the many talks I had with my interlocutors Parenti's name was mentioned with great frequency. The book stands in line with other U.S., German and Austrian publications, such as Yossef Bodansky's *Some call it peace* (1996), Klaus Bittermann's *Serbia must die!* (1994), and Hannes Hofbauer's *Balkankrieg. Die Zerstörung Jugoslawiens* (1999) that claimed to discover the 'truth' behind the 'lies' offered by the West about the Balkan wars. In the U.S., the California based political scientist Parenti may be the most exposed proponent of the 'pro-Serbian' reading of the wars.

In the fashion of conspiracy thinking, Parenti claims that "Western policy" vis-à-vis Yugoslavia has not been misdirected, confused, or contradictory, as many observers argued, but that behind Washington's at times changing stance stood a program, and that was to break up the country and to enforce privatization and "Third Worldization" on the hitherto independent, socialist Yugoslavia. Parenti's treatise presents the ambitious task to tell "the whole story, the true story about the relentless attack on Yugoslavia" (ibid.: 8). As a leftist political scientist and political activist Parenti shared sympathy from both the leftist intellectual spectrum, as well as liberal and Republican minded Serbian migrants who saw their case supported by someone who had gained recognition in other fields before and turned his attention to the Yugoslav conflicts well a decade after its inception. But an economic reading of the wars, which fits into the popular conspiracy that the U.S. wants to build an oil pipeline from the Caspian Sea all the way to Western Europe via the Balkans, fails to explain why the West shouldn’t have found to achieve this without shedding the lives of hundreds of thousands. Furthermore, it doesn’t ring true that anything be gained economically from the breakdown of infrastructure and economic activities in the region, at least as of now.

As for Chomsky (2000: 21), in addition to the economic level, the military dimension is crucial: NATO with the U.S. as the leading world power, used the Kosovo war as a test case in order to stake a new role for the hitherto defense system of the North Atlantic alliance. The theory runs that with the pretext of fighting for peace and human rights, NATO instrumentalized the conflict to carve out a more encompassing structure of the alliance, which had lost its clearly defined role of defending Europe against the Soviet Union with the demise of the Cold War, and as to not lose its raison-d’être now gained a position of leading “humanitarian interventions“ worldwide. Therefore, Milošević was only constructed as the main evil to follow the new military line, whereas other areas of violent conflicts, such as Turkey, East Timor, Sudan, were left out. “Some places were bathed by the light of the West’s concern – Bosnia and Kosovo, for example,” though “others were obscured by our lack of interest“ (ibid.).

In addition to the economic and military reading there is the focus on the religious underpinnings of the conflicts. As for Bodansky of the International Strategic Studies Association (ISSA) the “global Islamist jihad“ (Bodansky 1996: 2), or “Iran’s strategic offensive into Europe“ (ibid.: vii) are the conspiracies underlying the war in Bosnia. Why else should NATO have supported Muslims in Bosnia and now (Muslim) Kosovo Albanians, many Serbs inquired, although they were known for criminal activities and the drug trade in Western Europe? “These Islamist activities, including the manipulation of the Clinton Administration, are the primary destabilizing factor threatening the chances for a lingering peace in the former Yugoslavia,“ Bodansky contended (ibid.: 3). The West had allied itself with “the Islamist world“ in order to smash Serbs, a secret move that was seen to be made visible once again with 9/11. In this vein I can understand my friend Andreja’s reaction to the terrorist attacks in 2001: “*Now it’s pretty clear to everybody how Bosnia and Kosovo are connected to Afghanistan and the terrorists. If you look into German prisons there are a lot of Albanians, 90% of the Heroin drug trade is undertaken from Central Asia to Europe via the Albanians. The Mudjaheddins in Bosnia and Bin Laden and so on. This is important, you should research that, it is important financial flows.* “Following the destruction of the World Trade Center a great many people I talked to felt that their warnings of an Islamic threat in Bosnia in the 1990's suddenly were confirmed by the El-Qaida attack. And even the Wall Street Journal reported that Bin Laden had been to Bosnia and even held a Bosnian passport![123] Therefore, what Sanders and West laid out as the main feature of conspiracy thinking, the belief that "power works in hidden ways," is confirmed by the example of the NATO bombing of 1999. What does the glance on a few selected writings which are popular among Serbian migrants teach us about conspiracy thinking in the Serbian diaspora?

The reading of a few selected texts concerning the bombing of Yugoslavia shows the scientific (and pseudo-scientific) underpinning for the thesis that everything is connected, from a Vatican conspiracy to an Islamist plot reaching as far as 9/11, via the NATO strategy of "humanitarian rightism" (Hayden 2000). Germany, Afghanistan, the U.S., Kosovo, and Bosnia are all linked by the secret project of Islamist expansion, paired with anti-Serb hatred, and topped by U.S. imperialism – a hodgepodge of factors, which is a striking paradox in itself. But in conspiracy thinking there's no contradiction left in the scheme, only a concerted effort of various powers to conspire against Serbia. Furthermore, what the works of Parenti, Chomski, and others share is that their focus lies *only* on the International Community and geostrategy, as if *internal* reasons for the war and local actors did not exist. In this they differ vastly from other political scientific studies, for example Susan Woodward's *Balkan Tragedy* (1995a), shedding light on a plethora of political and military events in the former Yugoslavia, while also taking into consideration the respective impact that the diplomacy of the International Community had in each of the events. Finally, Hellinger's argument that conspiracy is not so different from political science is confirmed, since the Kosovo war shows the degree to which the feeling of persecution among Serbs is mirrored by certain writings of leftist political scientists.

After all, and this may indeed be a revealing detail, Hellinger, in order to make his argument about the similarity between political science and conspiracy theory, has recurred to the same author as many Serbs have: Michael Parenti (Hellinger 2003: 226). Arguing for an integration, not marginalization of conspiracy theories as "explanations of a structural and historical character" (ibid.: 205), Hellinger also foregrounds the possibility of using conspiracy thinking to serve popular resistance and empowerment. Quoting Parenti, Hellinger invites scholars to embrace conspiracism, because "one is likely to be called a conspiracy theorist, not only if one believes that ruling-class leaders sometimes use conspiratorial methods, but if one thinks that there is even such a thing as a ruling class that seeks to

123. See "Bin Laden's Balkan Connections" at www.balkanpeace.org, Internet publication Sept. 2001. In the article the author also points out to Bin Laden's contacts in Albania and Kosovo.

maintain hegemony" (ibid.: 226, Parenti 1994: 160). In the case of the NATO bombing of Serbia, I argue, that the politics of resistance and nationalism are as mixed up as they are in the example of the Vatican conspiracy, and that the potential is at least twofold. On one hand, as a leftist myself I believe in the potential of popular resistance against "humanitarian interventions," since the war against Yugoslavia was certainly a test case for future world-wide military interventions and a new arms race. On the other hand, marching under the white eagle on black any participation in a Serbian, or any other ethnic, protest, would necessarily bring with it not only a spatial but also political closeness to a radical long-distance nationalism. Unfortunately, the only protests one could find in the U.S. and Germany in 1999, after the peace movement had been corrupted by the new NATO concept, were those organized by Serbian migrants. Thus we can conclude that political agendas are rarely orderly put apart from each other, and to draw the line between nationalism and resistance has never in the history of nationalism been an easy task.

By focusing on what one could call 'pro-Serbian' academic readings of the Yugoslav wars I have attempted at shedding light on the discursive context in which my interlocutors found themselves. However, while the search for literature which Serbs use to manifest their claims may appear too deterministic, it is necessary to address the various ways that different people view the situation of their homeland in the light of a violent past. In the next chapter, I wish to move away from textual manifestations of conspiracy thinking and explore conspiracy thinking 'in action,' by focusing on the visions of the world and the International Community by a number of Serbian migrants. Moreover, I will add another dimension to the reading of conspiracy thinking and that concerns the temporal level of conspiracies.

Chapter 7. Imagining the Future in the Light of a Violent Past

> "Exile can produce rancour an regret, as well as sharpened vision. What has been left behind can either be mourned, or it can be used to provide a different set of lenses. Since almost by definition, exile and memory go together, it is what one remembers of the past that determines how one sees the future. (Said 2001: xxxv)"

I did not come to San Francisco to study conspiracy theories. My intended research interest was neither history nor memory, but these issues were developed in my writing as I realized how central they were for the people I talked to and interviewed. In the world of Serb exiles history, memory, identity, and conspiracies seemed to be of utmost importance. The previous chapters have described the pervasive historicity of identity and memory among Serbian migrants in the Bay Area. The role of history was so powerful in the U.S. that one is tempted to think of it as the central and constitutive feature of the Serbian migrants' consciousness, the symbolic core of their life world (Gilroy 1991: 17). The conspiracy theories I have analyzed in the preceding chapter have pointed to the fact that for many Serbs in the diaspora events occurring in the distant and recent past ask for grand explanations, with conspiracies filling the void by providing timeless global visions. In the present chapter I will follow my interlocutors one step further, by asking what comes next?[124] What do people expect of the future?

That I have decided here to focus on visions of the future and the International Community seems to me worth doing because the insights that the interviews with displaced Serbs in the U.S. produced seem particularly timely and important at this moment – in the political context of the former Yugoslavia and in a global context where apocalyptic fears, predictive crisis management and the projection of future scenarios tend to interject themselves into people's lives with a heightened intensity. In addition to speaking rather excessively about history, conspiracies, and political events in the past, informants were very eager to unfold to me their expectations for the future as perceived from the perspective of a still turbulent present, when the latest wars in the 1990's were still fresh and conflicts, in their view, far away from being settled to a satisfying degree for

124. This question is inspired by Katherine Verdery's important inquiry in her book title *What was socialism, and what comes next?* 1996.

all sides. What comes next after the wars in Yugoslavia? How does life "here" and "there" continue after such terrible times? And, in which ways do people imagine their future lives?

In this chapter, I will locate future visions of my interlocutors and their relationship to historical time. I will quote extensively from four persons – all of these have been quoted at more or less length in earlier chapters – with whom I have been in close contact and on especially warm, friendly terms with while staying in the U.S.: Andreja Marković, a young carpenter who deserted the army and fled from Sarajevo in 1991; Dragan Jovanović, an economist and immigrant since the sixties; Budimir Pesić, a lay historian and philologist who was exiled in the early 1950's; and Father Dimitrije Aleksandrović, San Francisco's retired Serbian Orthodox priest (see also chapter four).

The choice to focus on a small number of interlocutors, like I did in earlier chapters, and to include life historical background information here has the advantage of understanding better the individual and social context of conspiratorial thinking. I have chosen these narratives because they cover a range of historical viewpoints representative for a majority of my informants and elucidate the differing and often in themselves contradictory positions of a diasporic national consciousness and nation-building in a very concise way. First, using insights of Malkki (2000), Ricoeur (1998), and Wachtel (1998) I will argue for a revised approach to temporal dimensions which instead of looking at time as a linear progression of events takes into consideration the overlapping of past, present, and future. Second, in referring to a few future scenarios as elaborated by displaced Serbs I will ask: In which ways do people imagine their future lives? What do these at times personal, at times far reaching political visions mean to the understanding of national imaginings in a diasporic place? Which insights into conspiratorial thinking does the discussion of time and temporality provide? What can we as anthropologists learn from the ideas people who have left their homelands develop about their future in a transnational space? Ultimately, the following material presents another dimension of long-distance nationalism, and that is a reconciling, conciliatory, and optimistic vision of the conflicts in the homeland.

Realism and the Dismissal of the Future

As the historical lines of "ethnic" conflicts have been paid much attention to by anthropologists and deserve even more careful interlocution, those visions and narratives of the future which I encountered have been hardly examined at all yet. One exception is the work of the Finnish-American anthropologist Liisa Malkki on future visions of Hutu refugees. In her article *Figures of the Future* (2000) Malkki explored the expectations of the future and the International Community among refugees from Burundi in Montreal, Canada, a project which followed her earlier work *Purity and Exile* (1995), based on her fieldwork among Hutu refugees in Tanzania. Malkki explains the relative inattentiveness to visions and narratives of the future in the study of national identity and national thinking with the linear and deterministic concept of history in which time is viewed as progressive and the past used as the most decisive:

> "It is common to see the imagination of the future dismissed as daydreaming, fantasy or merely indulging in crackpot schemes; imagined futures deemed insufficiently "realistic" are likely to be classed as utopian. The term utopia, deriving from the Greek word for "no place," is often understood to refer to a pleasant fantasy with little purchase on "real life." History, on the other hand, presents itself as "real"." (Malkki 2000: 3)

With regard to influential works on the history of nationalism (Hobsbawm and Ranger 1983, Anderson 1983, Smith 1995) Malkki remarks that history is, of course, not just what happened, but rather a continuous process of social production, an invention, or imagination. "That people struggle so mightily over narrative visions of the past and the future and over what the categorical, historical subjects of such stories shall be" (Malkki 2000: 3) implies that instead of a neat succession of past, present, and future, temporal categories rather overlap each other. The future as such is already implied in the past and present and vice versa. In a similar vein French philosopher Paul Ricoeur in Das Rätsel der Vergangenheit[125] (1998) offers a fresh view on the relationship between the temporal dimensions. He believes "that undone deeds of the past can form expectations to a high degree, which enable to orient historical consciousness towards the future anew" (Ricoeur 1998: 66, 129)[126]. He further continues: "Humankind of the past, how we imagine it in its lived presence, has not only designed itself towards a certain future, but its actions had unwanted consequences. These consequences would not only rarely but often destruct plans and frustrate dearest hopes" (ibid.: 64). In conflating past, present, and future, Ricoeur draws from Heidegger's Sein und Zeit (1993) to stress that Dasein as Being could only have *been* if it were oriented towards the future. But in Ricoeur's, view Heidegger is more concerned about historicity than with the future, thereby holding to the more established category, the past (Ricoeur 1998: 60). In contrast to Heidegger, Ricoeur attempts to demon-

125. In English this roughly means *The riddle of the past* [my own translation].
126. My own translation from the German into English.

strate the opposite, that the presenting of the past influences the vision of the future (ibid.: 56).[127]

What service does this insight do to us when studying visions of the future among displaced Serbs? Malkki and Ricoeur, both on very different footings, but for my purpose in a similar vein, explore what is beyond a mere polarized commonsensical opposition between past and future. As "imaginative constructions" built out of people's perceived realities, these visions of time depend on discursive productions, on certain kinds of narrativity. Malkki suggests: "Different political factions, for example, may well set themselves apart not just with different versions of history, but different future-stories" (Malkki 2000: 3). Both versions can be meaningful and formative for not only present alliances and actions but also future political decisions.

I will argue in the following that designs of the future are part of the memory of the past, which is also shown in a brilliant work by Andrew Baruch Wachtel, *Making a Nation, Breaking a Nation* (1998). Analyzing literature and cultural politics in Yugoslavia from the early 19th century till the 1990's, Wachtel traces the very beginnings of the Yugoslav idea of numerous South Slav authors among the then colonized Balkan peoples, different versions of the nation and political visions. To Wachtel, the texts he portrays are part of a "cultural production" of Yugoslavia, as they not only theorized on an idea of a common nation for all the South Slav people, but were also built into the practice of the educational system and cultural politics of the country. In stark contrast to many of the works on the breakup of Yugoslavia, Wachtel argues that it is not politics, economics, or history that brought Yugoslavia into being and destroyed it in the end, but culture and cultural politics. Whereas I am critical of any monocausal explanation of the Yugoslav wars and do not think that the economy, nationalism, or cultural politics could be solely blamed for the breakup of the country, the focus on cultural politics is nevertheless promising, since 'culture' did certainly play a great role. But what are these "ideological mechanisms" and "cultural productions" about if not the imagination of a national future?

As he travels through time and investigates what became of the idea of a common nation-state for the South Slavs in the literature, it is clear to me that what is at stake in the literary creativity to come to terms with a nation, Yugoslavia, is that most of the authors throughout the history of Yugoslavia portrayed by Wachtel struggle for a vision of the future of the South Slav people, take for example Ivo Andrić's well-known *Bridge on the*

127. That the future and the past are interacting concepts instead of separate entities has also been pointed out by the historian Eric Hobsbawm 1997 in his latest work which in the German edition is titled *Wieviel Geschichte braucht die Zukunft* 2001, or "How much history does the future need?" [translation mine]. See also Friedman 1992 for some reflections on anthropological work which takes serious the overlapping of past, present, and future.

Drina (1977) written during the Second World War. In Wachtel's view Noble Price for Literature laureate Andrić, "chronicled the difficult interaction of the peoples of Yugoslavia through historical time, while yet holding out hope for a supranational union that might bind them together" (Wachtel 1998: 157). Such positive visions for the future are not just successors of the past, but the past is well built into the future, laying out a conception of the future that has learned from the past and seeks to overcome it. What seemed all too unrealistic in the light of the terrible massacres in World War Two and the massacres against Serbs, Jews, and Gypsies that raged between 1941 and 1945, later on proved "real:" ideas of the future and hopes for a common political framework did indeed precede a relatively successful Yugoslavia with all its problems and conflicts.

This is not to say that literary works are a prophetic 'machine' for envisioning and thereby realizing the future, but rather it serves the purpose of this chapter to show how closely intertwined versions of national histories and the expectations of the future are, leaving open no simple chronological or progressive time. In my interpretation, the intellectual endeavors of authors from all the main Yugoslav nations, Wachtel depicts in much detail, are intellectual designs of the future, or literary laboratories of (im)possible futures. Andrić's work rather belongs to a positive vision, but there are also apocalyptic imaginations that entertained sinister and nightmarish visions of the future. Wachtel draws extensively from literary Yugoslavian texts that envisioned a rather horrible, morbid, and nightmarish future, not at least the „last Yugoslav writer", the Jewish author Danilo Kiš, who like Miloš Crnjanski before him, specialized on the subject of death (Wachtel 1998: 227).[128] Both are future visions and according to Malkki they can be called "utopian" or "dystopian." However, I will retain from these notions as they subvert the actual meaning they supposed to imply, namely that these visions are *not* impossible or utopian. It would therefore be unwise to jump to early conclusions as to where the line between rumor and fact, and fiction, subjectivity and objectivity might lie. Indeed, it might contribute to a better understanding of the present situation Serbs find themselves in to suspend the search for such a line altogether. For the question "Is it fact or fantasy?" may not be the best question posed in this study at all. In the words of Paul Rabinow (1986: 237) "[w]hat Foucault has called the regime, or game, of truth and falsity is both a component and a product of historical practices. Other procedures and other objects could have filled the bill just as well and have been just as true." With regard to anthropological work on violence a few authors have alrea-

128. Literary projections of the future are not emblematic to Yugoslavia only, if one looks at influential Western works, for example George Orwell 1949, Ray Bradbury 1985 or Aldous Huxley 1932, it is obvious that the history of our own cultural production is full with millenarian future-scenarios.

dy pointed out to the necessity to take a closer look at rumor, how rumors work and how they resemble the chaos of the present moment and shape people's life. In this vein Anna Simmons (1995) in her study on violence in Somalia argues that rumors composed knowledge and were manufactured in a specific social context, thus contributing to the situational composition of reality of which rumor played not just a side part (Simmons 1995: 43). This is not to pose that tracking any falsification or empirical observation be left aside completely. But taking serious rumors as integral factor in the course of violent events and in their aftermath, that are charged with immense confusion and secretiveness open up channels of communication for those not in positions of receiving closed-door politics information.

In my view the focus of literature as a cultural vessel for transporting the national idea is illuminating and challenging, however in this chapter I want to point out to the importance of ordinary people's visions of Yugoslavia and its tragic end. Whereas literary texts provide a powerful mechanism for channeling national thinking, it was *people* from all different social backgrounds whom the "real" national endeavors actually affected in their everyday lives, and who formed and are forming their subjective views around the experiences with the former socialist country. Real people in Yugoslavia and the diaspora are now envisioning not just the making and the breaking of the nation, but they also participate in a certain discourse of making the nation anew and forming stances in long-distance nationalism. If, as Marko Živković in *Telling Stories of Serbia* (2000) argues, rumors and conspiracy theories tended to proliferate in Serbia in the 1990's, my findings among the Serbian diaspora come to a similar conclusion. "Faced with the situation where events where slipping away and would not stay still for me to make up my mind, I decided to give up the ambition of finding out what was *really, really* happening" (Živković ibid.: 52). As Hellinger (2003: 209) sums it up, conspiracies are subjective, secretive and "stand in contradiction of generally accepted moral behavior." In delving into conspiracies people discard a reality that has been explained to them by established modes of knowledge, such as journalism, politics, or scientific thought, suspecting power. In the following I will try to not only embark on what Serbs tell about Serbia and the former Yugoslavia, but what stories they tell about global politics and transnational identities and how these reflections reveal the struggles over national history and a fragmented, diasporic national identity.

The Future can only get worse

While I had not expected to find optimistic scenarios of a better future, the very dark and pessimistic visions nevertheless surprised me. My friend Andreja told me by way of an anecdote:

> *"What I think of the future? When the war broke out in Slovenia everybody said: 'It can't get worse than that'. It did get worse. When the Serbs were bombed in Bosnia in 1993 they said: 'It cannot get worse than this!' It did get worse. When NATO started bombing in 1999, they said: It can get worse than that. That's what they learned from it: It can still get worse."*

One conspiracy theory ran as follows:

"Milošević, Tudjman, and Izetbegović acted in accordance with their plans, they were directed by Washington. They want to weaken Yugoslavia by splitting it into small pieces and then control it more easily."

In support of the 'truth' of this theory many Serbs recounted the famous meeting between Tudjman, Milošević, and Izetbegović in Bosnia at the beginning of the war, when during a lunch Tudjman took a napkin and drew the future border of Croatia and Bosnia on it, following exactly the territorial limits of the 1941-44 NDH Ustaša state.

While the recent past was marked by disintegration and the present rather by the integration of territories into small states, I had not expected to hear about yet new processes of breakup and disintegration. But Zoran Martić told me otherwise. Claiming that the process of dismembering Yugoslavia hasn't been finished yet, he revealed to me the following conspiracy:

> *"The first time I went back was in 1997. For me it was shocking to come to Belgrade, I stayed in a hotel, next to a MacDonald's – a MacDonald's in socialist Yugoslavia! I was afraid of the police, and they did come to interview me. But I had a question for them, I said: 'Why is it that Yugoslavia had the telephone number 38, and Serbia after separation 381, Macedonia 385, and Bosnia 386 – what about the missing numbers?' And I explained to them that those numbers are for the future independent states Montenegro, Kosovo, Vojvodina."*

What this narrative illustrates is Hofstadter's notion of a deep feeling of persecution, based on the personal political background of Martić, who belongs to the *Ravna Gora* Chetnik organization in the U.S., and whose father and grandfather had also been Chetniks. Upon analyzing the federal telephone codes on his visit to the homeland, his conspiracy of a planned further dismemberment of the rump state of Yugoslavia, Serbia-Montenegro, appears like a self-fulfilling prophecy: in the telephone system at least the country has already been split up to even smaller pieces, only to secretly announce events of tomorrow. Politics does not occur in public, but in hidden channels, often at earlier points in time than is officially announced.

Michael Djordjevich, president of the SUC (see chapter three), presented his future vision with much oratorical eloquence and pathos, forgotten are the difficult present-day diaspora-homeland relations:

> *"It's a new century, new world, let's move forward, and don't look behind where the graves are and the battlefields and the Turks. Otherwise you'll never get in peace with yourself, and then you can never get in peace with the world."*

This motto seems to guide Djordjevich's political activism, despite the fact that in his pamphlets and open letters he makes repetitive allusions to the Serbian suffering during World War Two in order to legitimize Serbian violence in Bosnia during the recent wars. History remains the Serbian lobby's biggest asset, opening up contradictions between a modern global world à la U.S. style and what is coined as a cornerstone of Serbian identity.

The future stories differed as different social and political actors set themselves apart with diverging attitudes towards a Yugoslav versus Serb identity or towards the Partisan versus Chetnik national history from World War Two which implied communists/socialists and royalists/capitalist dualisms.

In conclusion, even in the rather small community of people, there were marked differences in political visions of the future. There was, it seems, more consensus about what had already happened than about things to come. People did not appear to argue as much about the correct interpretation of past events, there was a shared consensus of Serbian victimization and an outspoken stance against one-sided and explicitly "anti-Serbian" views on the wars in the former Yugoslavia. But the future was another matter. What is to happen? What is to be done? What will become of "our homeland"? What will become of "us" in the U.S.?

The Green Border[129] and the Designs of the International Community

An extraordinarily timely contemplation – in the light of the fighting between Albanians and Macedonians in Macedonia from 2000 to 2001 and the renewed killings in Kosovo in spring 2004 – was suggested by my friend Andreja Marković, whom I know since 1996 when a student at an

129. In the former Yugoslavia and at present the original term „Želena Transverzala" or the short form "Žetra" is used. Translated into English it would mean "Green Transversal." It is the area that in the East-West connection connects Muslim nations in the Balkans, i.e. Bosnian Muslims, with the other Muslim peoples (e.g. Albanians, Turks etc.) in the Peninsula. However, as my friend didn't mention the Serbian term but translated it into the simpler version "Green Border" I will also keep the English term.

American university. Since then I had undertaken quite a few trips with Andreja and my husband, who has also been a close friend with Andreja from before. Retrospectively, our travels seem to me like gradually creating imaginations of Yugoslavia. After going to Arizona together and listening to Goran Bregović's soundtrack for Emir Kusturica's movie "Underground" while driving, the following year we met in Budapest, the place of his first exile and residence of his sister, and in 2000 at the Montenegrin coast, to visit his mother who is exiled there from Sarajevo. Those private connections and political discussions preceded and formed the path to my ongoing interest in the dismemberment of Yugoslavia, and cannot certainly be imagined apart from him. Knowing Andreja for his political and military strategic interest, following all the up-to-date news on the Balkans and ardently discussing his historical insights and views on military moves with his friends I will quote from parts of an interview which followed a lively discussion we held before recording our conversation. The section I selected is relatively long, as I believe the course of his argument on the "Green Border" to be important and needing more detailed attention.

B: What was it you said before to me, the "Green Border," the "Turkish" border? I just thought about it, and I wonder if you think that is going to happen in the future? Do you mean by that the West with the Albanians establishes this Green Border again through Yugoslavia? Like the old Turkish... How did you call it?
A: Well, if you look at the borders now, and if you compare this border with what it looked like before Yugoslavia, you see that it is pretty similar, you just look at the border of World War Two, who was associated with what, who is getting what part, you know, just measure every inch and you get a pretty good idea of what is going on there.
B: So this Green Border is like the old border of the Ottoman Empire?
A: Yeah.
B: Why is it called Green Border?
A: You know, green is the official color for Islam.
B: So you think that the Albanians will get Macedonia, Kosovo, maybe Montenegro, and the West will help them?
A: I don't think anything, but I definitely think that Kosovo-Albanians had never achieved anything by themselves. That means every achievement they can have there, everything, even arms or bullets, whatever they have will be sponsored by the West, got paid or watched or whatever, something else. It's ridiculous! If you look how five years ago Americans happened to have the troops between Serbia and Macedonia, and Macedonians side patrolling fearing that Slobodan Milošević is going to invade Macedonia, and they had peace-keeping United Nations troops throughout the border, and now Kosovo – who knows how they get arms? Running through the border and attacking the same country that happened to be protected against Slobodan Milošević and now they say: We cannot do anything? Like these Albanians simply are armed there and they

allowed them to carry the arms. What kind of agreement is that, when they can carry the arms anyway? It should be a demilitarized zone.

Andreja's not very rosy future predictions have not been proven altogether wrong, as in 2001 we could daily follow in the news media that a war apparently was rapidly evolving in Macedonia and a third NATO military engagement was passionately discussed in Europe at the time. While in 1991 Macedonia did not experience a violent secession as did Croatia and Bosnia, the U.N. presence for the pacification of Albanians and Macedonians in the young nation-state as well as pertaining Greek claims to the country demonstrate that rivalries are still adamant (see Brown 2003, Danforth 1995). The interview passage I quoted is rich in detail on ideas of the collective national narrative of Serbs and the heated issue of International Military Intervention. While glossing over the power relations between the warring parties during the latest Balkan wars in order to explain a historical continuity spanning from the Ottoman empire to the present, Andreja seems to unfold a clearly defensive vision of the Serbian role in Yugoslavia's autonomous republic, Kosovo. The impression of an expansionist Albanian strategy which resembles the nearly 500- year long Ottoman grip on the country, termed symbolically "Green Border" and entailing large parts of Serbia, Bosnia, Macedonia, regions of Montenegro, and what is now Kosovo, feeds perfectly into the picture of 'paranoid' Serbs, whose sense of history comprises of the idea of its endless repetition.[130] In the thick of this personal future-scenario one can read a number of different lines, I want to try and clarify below.

The narrative is heavily informed by events of the recent past which are not directly addressed but indirectly they are lying at the core of the argument, that is the interpretation of recent political history. Obviously, Andreja refers to the Kosovo war in 1999 when NATO bombed Kosovo and Serbia as an answer to what they termed „police oppression" against Kosovo-Albanians by the regime in Belgrade, as has been outlined in the preceding chapter. Here, the narrative opens up a very complex topic, the question of Kosovo, which to many Serbs symbolized a central event in the Balkan wars and stands for American foreign intervention which was strongly rejected by all Serbs I spoke to. What Serbs perceived of as a civil war, based on violence from both sides, the Albanian Kosovo Liberation Army (KLA) and Serbian paramilitary and police units, was in their view unjustly reinterpreted by "the West" as only one-sided "Serbian aggression." Fueling into a climate of victimization that had already lasted for al-

130. It should be clear that the obsession with the repetition of history is not ungrounded. In connection to the Green Border, the Muslim nationalists themselves are publicly talking about their national/religious strategy of connection the whole Muslim world, as Ayatollah Khomeini has said, from Indonesia to Bosnia.

most ten years, including the country's isolation due to economic sanctions, NATO engagement in Kosovo is analyzed by Andreja from the present perspective as the main component for strengthening the Albanian faction in Kosovo and forging ways for a further Albanian expansion. This view mirrors a prevalent attitude among Serbs in the U.S. which, wrongly or not, views Western intervention and the Serbian loss of control over Kosovo, which by now is almost completely in the hands of Kosovo-Albanians, as a great military punishment and moral defeat. Employing derogatory stereotypes of Macedonians and Albanians "who will be sponsored by the West" in order to juxtapose the 'fighter mentality' of Serbs (see also chapter one), Andreja constructs a cosmology of 'strong' nations, like Serbs, who fight without the help and against the West, and 'weak' nations who can only fight when supported by external powers.

Foremost Andreja's account addresses the inconsistency underlying the diplomatic moves of the International Community, at one time arming a warring faction (Croatians, Kosovars), and at another time disarming military rivals (Serbs and Albanians in Kosovo), whereas he believes that Kosovo Albanians had been armed by the same governments a few years earlier. Such politics on the side of the intervening countries, in addition to putting Serbs at a disadvantage, in Andreja's view has not only devastating consequences for the constellation of power in the region, but also ridicules the West by undermining its own credibility.

With regard to the future of Yugoslavia the regions of Bosnia and Kosovo again play a crucial role:

B: What is your vision for Yugoslavia? For the Serbs in Yugoslavia?
A: Oh, we got screwed up how it is going right now, it's going deeper and deeper, but we will pull back.
B: You will pull back? Where and how? In Kosovo or in Bosnia, too?
A: Well, that might look really kind of too nationalistic, maybe, but we are still the strongest ethnic power regionally, and as long as we don't have this international kind of make-ups around and pressure, we will recover like that from the time that the big powers just let us alone so we can make allies with them. We will immediately be again who we were before.
B: So do you think the future is rather war? Like more successful war?
A: No, we have... no, if you talk about successful war, we win every war, we never lose a battle, that's just a war, we just lose everything else, we lose the country, we lose the identity, we lose everything, except the war. Nobody beats us up, Muslim never beat us up, they are always screaming: NATO, come to help the poor Muslims! You know? They bomb us to some negotiation terms, but nobody really forced us with a military kind of power that beat us up. All this war right now, I don't know any case that really, we have like a couple of stories, everything else is just political decisions. Because we can maybe avoid a bigger tragedy of the region, we just need to do some consent, but you know

Muslims never, never beat us up. They had like all these zones, peace zone, no fly zone, no [laughs] and so on, they would never be successful to run a war against the Serbs. Or Croats neither. The story between Croats and Serbs is that Croats are more competitive than Muslims.
B: I mean, I guess the Muslims also, now that they got their state...
A: No, they cannot succeed! If they were for 24 hours without international support, 24 hours and this state will be just cut into pieces, from now if this U.N. or whatever just pulls out from there and just says: Do whatever you guys like, they don't care anymore, that state would just stop to exist the same minute. The next day it would be a completely different flag, different president, everything will be like this [laughs], this is not a real state, that state cannot support itself. And that's the bottom line.
B: So do you think it will disappear?
A: It doesn't exist right now!
B: When will it disappear? Like in the next 50 years or 10 years?
A: When somebody got tired to put the money in.
B: But that would be again kind of bloody, because you have to draw another border or to...
A: No, it will just simply be divided, no more borders, as simple as that.
B: Just between the ethnic groups?
A: Just between the ethnic groups, it will be just divided.
B: Like Kosovo, too?
A: Kosovo is a different story, Kosovo will be bloody.

As Andreja admits himself in an almost self-censoring way – later on he is aware of not speaking "politically correct" – this passage does reflect a "nationalistic" view of a hypothetically hegemonic position of Serbs in the Balkans. To note, Andreja, too, employs a tautology similar to the "Obstinate Otherness" discussed in chapter one, when mentioning: "*We will immediately be again who we were before.*" Having witnessed four military losses[131] under former Yugoslav president Milošević, how can he still maintain with ardor that Serbs were "invincible" by stating that "*we lose everything except the war*"? Here, I don't want to participate in an equally censoring anthropological discourse on the danger and "falsehood" of nationalism, rather I want to ask for the specificity of certain nationalisms, counterinventions of narratives, and subtle recasting of official, "Western" discourses without deeming people's fears and visions wrong or illegitimate. Andreja's insistence on the invincibility of Serbs stands in stark contrast to the critique of another informant of mine, who stated polemically: "*many Serbs maintain*

131. By these he means the withdrawal of the then Yugoslav troops from Slovenia in 1991 following minor clashes between Slovenian forces and the Yugoslavian army JNA; the retreat from Croatia after heavy fighting in 1992; the outcome of the Bosnian war with the Dayton Peace agreement in 1995; and the bombing of Kosovo in 1999.

the mythic power of a people that assembles it national success story out of a lost battle." In the famous battle on *Kosovo Polje* of 1389 Serbs and their Slav allies were defeated in a major fighting by the Ottoman Empire, which later resulted in the loss of control of the territory and the end of the medieval Serb kingdom. Subsequently, poets, politicians, statesmen, and diplomats until today have been constructing the heroic "persistence theory" which claims that despite the loss Serbs are the "heavenly" people, similar to the Jewish victimology of the "chosen people."[132] Repeatedly mentioning "nobody beats us up," Andreja explicitly alludes to Milošević's famous nationalist speech on the Kosovo Polje in 1989. Especially noteworthy in this regard is his use of the collective pronouns "we" and "us" – "we will pull back," "we are still the strongest," "we will recover," "nobody beats us up" – one of the most basic rhetorical strategies of nationalist imageries (see Čolović 2002). And yet, his outlook is also realistic, given the outbreak of violence in Kosovo in spring 2004. Without going into depth of the complex and multi-faceted history of Kosovo Andreja's statement about Serbian hegemony in the past and future is highly contradictory.

In numerous other conversations Andreja has claimed his pro-Yugoslav and non-nationalistic attitude which he maintains until today. Andreja's 'in-betweenness' resembles very much the ambiguity I discussed about Lena at the beginning of this study. How can he reconcile such ambivalent political ideas? As has been demonstrated in chapter one, nationalist and non-nationalist standpoints can coexist in one and the same person, being derived both from the politically correct official anti-nationalist context in the West as well as the actual strengthening of ethno-national entities and the right to self-determination world-wide. In the specific Yugoslav case this contradiction has been most acute, since the West has favored ethnic homogeneity (in Croatia) and multiculturalism (in Bosnia) simultaneously.

On a personal level, I suggest that Andreja's dilemma is comprised of his experience of escaping a country and army which he as a 19-year-old was serving as true believer in its multinational constitution, whereas the troops were falling apart due to the forming of separate Croat, Slovenian, Bosnian Muslim, and later Serb armies. The end of Yugoslavia meant a total breakdown to him personally and displacement of him and his family. Andreja fled from Sarajevo early on in the war and thereby became a deserter. How could he continue being a Yugoslav, if most of the South Slav groups didn't belong to the category anymore and the country officially stopped to exist? The breaking of the nation required as a next step the making of the nation, this time e.g. as the Croatian and Serbian nation. By the favoring of Slovenian, Croatian, and Bosnian independence NATO

132. For more details on the role of the Kosovo myth, see Anzulović 1999, Mertus 1999, Petritsch et al. 1999.

states such as Germany and the U.S. had supported the death of Yugoslavia and its multinational reality. At present there is no alternative left except to imagine out of its ruins new, ethnically homogeneous nation-states, such as Serbia whose state formation is still in the process of becoming. After a decade of nation-destruction and nation-building, instead of stability Andreja foresees another round of nation-destruction, this time with regard to Bosnia. Not acknowledging the Muslim-Croat federation's existence, Andreja puts into disbelief the act of nation-creation as such. In short, Andreja's future imagination is that of utter pessimism, disbelief, and cynicism and reflects the troubled experience of somebody who has fled his homeland and has not really arrived in another country yet, which then bombs his home country. To him the struggle of Serbs is not one for a "Greater Serbia," a concept which he calls "nonsense," but a struggle for mere survival and existence on the geographical map on which a "Green Border" is drawn slowly. In the fashion of conspiracy theory the past projects itself onto the present, redrawing geopolitical maps following the geostrategy of the Ottoman Empire. A struggle too seems to be his attempt to create a consistent narrative in the course of our conversations. Long-distance nationalism, as Andreja's example shows, is a fluid phenomenon, and it doesn't need to be taken for granted as a 'primordial' fact by its believers. In the light of his pro-Yugoslav life history and a revitalized pro-Serbian national story the incompatibility of the two can only lead to a highly contradictory discursive formation. What seems clear is that to Andreja the famous "state of emergency," Benjamin addressed, might remain to be not the exception but the rule.

The Quick Sand of History

> "War always repeats itself, you have never in the history of war resolved anything, cultural assimilation and education is to resolve differences." (Dragan Jovanović)

> "Guilt is the burden which the past transfers to the future.
> (Ricoeur 1998: 56)"[133]

The next interviewee I will refer to is Dragan Jovanović, whom I know from my first visit of a Sunday service in the Serbian Orthodox church, where he proved an invaluable help introducing me to other Serbs. Recently retired, married to an American, and father of two adult daughters, he came to the U.S. as a young man from the Hercegovinian town Trebinje in the "flower power era" at the end of the 1960's. California's political cli-

133. My own translation from the German.

mate and the remarkable landscapes made it easy for him to decide to stay immediately. An economist, with a degree from the University of Belgrade, he didn't agree with the socialist model of "self-management" but believed in the capitalist market oriented economy he encountered in the U.S. While he was not attending church in his home country because it was a "taboo," as he explains, from the beginning on, he was an active member in the Serbian diaspora church. Dragan stresses his religious "roots," since he has been able to practice religion freely from the very first day in the California. Both his father and grandfather were Orthodox priests who were killed by the Croat Ustaša in the 1940's. Whereas he is very much in favor of many social and economic aspects of the United States and likes the people a lot, he doesn't agree with American foreign policy as most Serbs don't. Nevertheless, in contrast to Andreja, who stresses the political influence of external powers on the breakup of Yugoslavia and the future, Dragan reasons quite differently. While on this sunny afternoon sitting in his living room, sipping tea, looking out of his window in El Cerrito, overlooking the East Bay with the San Francisco city skyline in the background, he explains the war to me as follows:

> *"At the beginning of the war they used the poetry and religion as a tool – don't tell me that was implemented by the U.S., like turbo-folk, my stomach turns upside down when I hear that – it's culture, they destroyed culture. The Croatians answered with the chessboard and the past of the Kings; it's pushing all the glory of the puppet state. That's not preservation of cultural identity, it's unearthing the evil."*

In this passage Dragan indirectly discards conspiracy thinking among fellow Serbian migrants, when arguing that cultural nationalism was not "implemented by the U.S." The economist thus presents an outspoken critique of conspiracy theories and their inherent denial of inner-Yugoslav cultural and political processes leading to war. With his statement "*it's culture, they destroyed culture*" he adheres to Wachtel's theory of cultural politics as the reason for war.

Although a very active member in the church community, Dragan is present at almost every service, and at parties and celebrations he stands behind the counter and serves beer, wine, and *rakija*, the Yugoslavian plum brandy – he also distances himself from nationalism and the blaming of the West for the tragedy in the Balkans he encounters among many parishioners in the church. He is aware of the guilt of the recent past and far away from denial. With much fervor he poses: "*I doubt that anybody can mastermind anything like it outside of Yugoslavia. That's [Yugoslavia] where I personally put the largest blame for all that happened in Yugoslavia.*" The above quoted passage reminds one of Wachtel's argument I referred to before who emphasizes not political, social, historical, or economic factors for the wars but the "cultural production" of ideas, be it literature or in this example "turbo-folk," a mixture of folkmusic, Turkish sounding beats, and techno, a contemporary musical genre which led to highly controversial debates in Yugoslavia. While some celebrate it as an innovative, powerful version of new Yugoslav folklore, others attack its "Oriental" character and nationalistic impetus (Živković 1996:1)[134]. Dragan's opinions are often gestures of self-critique and the rejection of cultural nationalism in Serbia and Croatia, which for him focus on destruction and bring about an "unhealthy" and "morbid" culture. History is there to be remembered but not to be repeated or celebrated for its own purpose. The latter he calls the "quick sand" of history, "*to delve for 500 years into defeat and death, that's not healthy.*" His analysis of the destructive potential of his home country is informed by his version of the past which he sees as a repetition of history, a cycle of wars and violence:

> *'Morbidity is part of that quick sand, Serbia isn't away from it yet, first see the river, then build the bridge... If you are an alcoholic and you don't admit that you are you can't get cured. The same with Serbia, if you don't admit that you are guilty, you can't get out of it. In this time of the year we are going to ask for forgiveness in Christianity, but that means something. It's not really what you put into your mouth, it's what comes out of it. Extremism breeds extremism and leads to frustration. I just hope for the best part of religion that teaches us to be good humans."*

The "destruction of alternative" thesis, Eric Gordy, in the *Culture of Power in Serbia* (1999) established finds striking resemblance here: Serbs are equated with sick people, they are guilty but "can't get cured," because like an alcoholic who is addicted, they cannot recover unless they admit they are guilty. Without acknowledging the guilt the future will look dark in the same way as the past. This is a very devastating judgment about "the Serbian people" and assumes that ethnic nationalism is the ground for the trouble in the Balkans, a dominant explanation in academic writing. How is he managing the present and designing the future in the light of such a critique? Instead of sinking into the "quick sand" of extremism himself Dragan develops three solutions for a better future: religion, education, and cultural assimilation, which symbolize a true combination of American (cultural assimilation) and Serbian (education, religion) values. He is sure that he can master individually not to fall into the trap of nationalism. In order to contribute to a better future one has to find a careful and so-

134. See also Gordy 1999.

phisticated balance of the version of the past, Dragan illustratively describes:

> *"I don't want that to be my quick sand, so I stay great and the same as a saint could be. Sometimes an excellent foundation to build is you put a lot of water, and then you compact sand, so it forms almost a concrete like strong base, and you build big buildings. That's what I am trying to do with my past. How successful, I don't know, we will see."*

This picture of using one's past constructively in order to provide for a better future is a highly optimistic vision of the future. Then, how does such a hopeful future-scenario look like when avoiding the "quick sand" of history? What does a "concrete base" of history implicate in practical terms? His positive expectations for the future lie in the realm of religion, to be a "better" person, "as a saint could be." As such it is a very personal and spiritual attitude, not political in the sense that he would engage in the *Serbian Unity Congress.* In addition to his engagement in the church, Dragan is an active member in the *Serbian Benevolent Society*, one of the earliest end-19th century organization dedicated, e.g. to sponsoring university studies of Serb students and maintaining the Serbian cemetery. Although his past is quite bitter – many of his close relatives were killed, he grew up without a father, his grandfather was starved by Croatian fascists, his mother had to change her passports five times in her long life, and a number of family members fled the recent wars to Sweden, France, and England – he refuses to *be* bitter. Praising his Muslim childhood friends and recalling past anecdotes about growing up together in Trebinje, he still meets these friends when visiting his old mother as well as maintains contact with other Muslims and non-Serbs. He attempts to draw a clear line between memory and remembering historical "facts" and the production of enmities, the political manipulation of collective memory. What was lacking in history according to his view was forgiving, and here he clearly attacks the rediscoveries and reburials of victims of 1941-44 wartime massacres, as emblematic for the "quick sand of history."

To him, the victim category is highly problematic because it easily leads to hatred and "unreflected" actions, and it makes people "grab a gun," which maybe, he, Dragan, admittingly would also do, were he not in such gentle, far-away retreat from all the heated and bloody events. His praise for cultural assimilation makes him contemplate what has gone wrong in the history of Yugoslavia and what should be changed, if ever a new Yugoslavia would exist, and that he like others indeed hopes for:

> *"Cultural assimilation leads you to regions. Bavarians are more similar to Austrians than to Germans, Slovenes are more like Austrians than Yugoslavs,*

> *Southern Serbs are more like Macedonians, Southern Croats like Italians... King Alexander should have said: We are not countries or states, but cantons, like Switzerland, regions gravitate, are cohesive, that's much smarter.*"

This thought play is very global and cosmopolitan in nature, Yugoslavia like a mixture of Switzerland and the United States! Again, it is cultural ties, cultural similarities between groups like Bavarians and Austrians, Slovenes and Austrians and so forth, "cultural assimilation," not "by design" which results in a melting-pot of culturally similar peoples, but spontaneous, fluid, and "flexible." In fact, Dragan refutes the idea of the nation-state with clear territorial borders once and for all, thus demonstrating that, not unlike scholars of nationalism, he regards the very idea of nation-states as the primary problem, not the solution. Understanding the problem of Yugoslavia as a dilemma of nationalism and the historical imagining of the Yugoslav nation he draws his future visions from the contemplation of past political developments. At another point of our conversations he opines that Sarajevo instead of Belgrade "*should have been*" the capital of a united country, and not republics based on the national category of Slovenes, Croats, Muslims, and Serbs, but regional attachments are to form an imagined future "Yugoslavia."

When stating that „*Alexander should have said...*," he likewise employs the conditional form, for contemplating the "undone deeds" mentioned by Ricoeur, which best exemplify the intertwined temporal dimensions. This future-scenario throws into stark relief the idea of nations all along, as the borders between Slovenia and Austria, Serbia and Macedonia are senseless due to the cultural affinities which make them regions, not nation-states. As a foil with which he perceives his own country he views the U.S. as a success-story, thereby in contradiction to other statements favoring the nation-state: "*Open the door and let them mix!*" Dragan's belief in cultural assimilation stands in stark contrast to Andreja's cynical and negative expectations of the future. In this, Dragan appears more successful in imagining a consistent life history and formulates an utterly "political correct" and pro-American future scenario, turning history to optimistic ends.

Between Anglophony and Germanophony

Overall similar to "geopolitical imaginings" in Serbia itself – which try to make sense out of a chaotic and "muddy" situation by way of blaming internal factions for what went wrong[135] – future visions in the diaspora are based on perceptions of the International Community and the complex interactions between the powerful Western European countries and the

135. See Živković 1996, 1998.

United States and Yugoslavia. In order to achieve a better understanding in a transnational political setting Serbs I talked to in the U.S. often use a highly coded and symbolic imagery of national stereotypes and binaries. Herzfeld, in *Cultural Intimacy* (1997) describes cultural nationalism in Greece as "cultural intimacy" or "disemia" (ibid.: 14ff.). These stereotypes and essentializations, such as the "Serbs," the "West," the "Muslims," and so on, can be interpreted as "social poetics," i.e. the uses of categories that make sense in the context of the nation-state, or in my study, in-between the nation-states and in a transnational arena. Applying fixed categories to informal speech as we have seen here doesn't mean that the content is necessarily fixed as well, as Dragan's and Andreja's narratives already demonstrated. I argue instead that seemingly static categories are used to express simply and straightforward the chaos and sufferings in-between the dissolving nation-states.

One more example to analyze the struggle for a consistent personal history in the light of a violent past and present is Budimir Pesić, an 80-year-old immigrant from Croatia who came to the U.S. in the mid 1950's.[136] Having experienced encampment in and expulsion from fascist Ustaša Croatia in 1941, which was followed later on in the war by perpetration and imprisonment under Tito's communism – although himself a socialist ever since –, before fleeing to Hungary and getting imprisoned there for eight years without a trial, Budimir embodies the contradictory and painful events from the (dis)order of the (post) World War Two past. Living just a few streets away from my American home and an inhabitant of the same house Andreja lives in, owned by Budimir's sister, Mira Pesić Connor, we had frequent chances to meet and talk. We were often sitting in his tiny apartment in the basement of the house, with living room, kitchen, and bedroom all in one compartment, surrounded by large numbers of books on Yugoslavian history, Russian history, poetry, art-history, and dictionaries of a variety of different Romanic languages, but also Japanese and Albanian which he just started to learn. Proud as he is of his cosmopolitan style of life and knowledge of languages, these skills were also the reasons, as he explains, for the long turmoil of imprisonments in Tito's Yugoslavia and Hungary: in both cases he was suspected to be a spy. During our talk he constantly offered me sodas, bread, German jam, Yugoslavian *sarma* (cabbage rolls filled with pork), and cakes – just so much on the topic of the legendary Yugoslavian hospitality.

In our extensive conversations, which could last up to five hours or longer, if I hadn't interrupted Budimir's amazing memory to recall past experiences and attitudes towards historical events in minute detail, he soon

136. Budimir has been mentioned randomly several times before. To note, the life story of his sister Mira Pesić Connor I discussed in part two, of course, refers to the same events Budimir experienced as well.

came to accept my sincere interest in Yugoslavia and regarded me "worthy" of hearing his life-story, as I had demonstrated that I proved quite some familiarity with Yugoslav history. Born in 1921, Budimir grew up in a town in Slavonia, where both his father and mother were well-off merchants and knew the imperial languages of the time, German and Hungarian. The multi-ethnic character of the place and his contact with Germans, Austrians, Croats, Hungarians, and other groups from early on left traces on his personal and national narrative, e.g. his claims to be "Serbo-Croatian," say a Serb from Croatia. Such a designation is very unusual in my overall sample and indeed officially non-existent, and symbolizes his outspoken refusal to use the exclusive national category "Serb." Contemplating the events of the World Wars he explains "the Serbian" attitude towards international powers as follows:

> *"Most of us, we had a certain admiration for the English, for England. We knew that we were pushed into those two wars. Then, in World War One, Austria overreacted to that murder in Sarajevo. There were so many statesmen murders before that and after in very different places of the world, people didn't go to war for that. [...] You know, you can have a friend, but suddenly you discover he couldn't be my friend, because he is doing so many terrible things. And he is flattering you, he needs you, because you admire him. And he is a son of a bitch. You don't approve anything of what he is doing. And later on you discover that that flattering is also not sincere. That's what the Serbian people learn about the English. And then what the Serbian people learn is that the Germans are sincere, that we quarrel, we quarrel, I hit you, I am going to give you back. [...] Even during World War Two when Hitler was really mad at Serbs he tried to prevent the slaughter of the Serbs by Ustaša."*

This is a historical narrative embedded in a complex commentary on events in Yugoslavia and the collective mentality of "the Serbian people." Resenting the "inconsistent" and changing English stance towards Serbia, which was supported by Great Britain in the first and the second World War, Budimir rejects the "dishonest" behavior of England and lack of "sincerity." Germany, instead, is a sturdy partner, in times of friendship and hostilities. What used to be a relationship of alliance and support in the last fifty years is now a climate of distrust to him, since the English government held Serb forces solely responsible in the last Balkan war. This was reflected also in a personal sense, when Budimir with some reluctance at the beginning and many talks without recording, after which I wrote down notes at home, then spoke quite freely into my recording machine. "*You know, I wouldn't tell you this if you were English, because you know why? I have met some English women who were as pretty as you, but they are not trustworthy, they turn their back against you. But with you it's different.*" Why this positive attitude towards Germans, considering how much damage the German *Wehrmacht* has done to Serbs and other peoples in Yugoslavia during the Second World War? While acknowledging that Germany's favoring of Slovenian and Croatian secession played a crucial part in the breakup of Yugoslavia in 1991, he attributes the greater blame to England and the U.S., what he explained to an American professor in a public discussion during the wars and recalls to me as shown below:

> *"No, you [the Americans] should have prevented the war. You could have done it. Now you blame the Germans for favoring Croatia, I said: 'Look, there must be eventually some character in it. They lived together for centuries with the Austrians, there were animosities, they were the ax of Croatian rebel against the Habsburg and so on, but their mentality is Western.'"*

Again, as Ricoeur remarked undone deeds of the past, or the future in the past, can shape the ideas of the present and future. By granting legitimacy to Germany in general to play out her "old alliances" with Croatia the "Anglo-Saxon gang," as Budimir explains, has had more responsibility to overpower not just Germany but the eventual path to secession and war. Thereby, he appears to speak Germany free following her historical alliance with Croatia, because of which they couldn't have known "better" or done differently. He even assumes that "Anglo-Saxons," which to him are both the English and the Americans in an ethnic sense, originally stirred up the hatred that was to break the nations apart: "*So we are denying the propaganda of Anglo-Saxon labels, that we hate each other to death. This is a big lie. But they want us to hate each other.*" This is an elegant reversal of the popular explanation of Yugoslavia's collapse in a deterministic fashion with "fiendish-political" potential, or "age-old" religious and ethnic hatreds which prevailed in the media and beyond[137]. Explaining the wars along ethnic lines is very widely done, in academic literature and elsewhere, but such monolithic reasoning is too simple. Not only has the ethnicization of the conflict among the people in Yugoslavia occurred much later, as some scholars argue, it has also been analyzed that the West undertook quite some effort in projecting the 'ethnic-ness' to the turmoils, which for Woodward rather lied in the questions of community (Woodward 1995a: 17ff.). This problematic external ascription of ethnicity as the foundation of the conflict is here sharply addressed by Budimir. In describing his relationship towards Germany he clearly distinguishes between political viewpoints and personal attachments. Repeatedly he emphasizes the "good character" and honest behavior of Germans, notwithstanding all the unfavorable actions of Germans against Serbs specifically:

137. See Kaplan 1993, for a critique, see Wachtel 1998: 14ff.

> *"They brought us Pavelić and all these things, but the average German is a good man, he has character. Maybe the new generation will make it possible to make normal friendly relationship, what we had for thousands of years with them. We are definitely not against it, we could get along with the Germans, not with the Nazis, but we know we have personal friends, many of us we grew up with them, so we are all right with the Germans."*

Budimir's narrative is ripe with hope for the future. Why this positive attitude towards "Germans" considering how much damage German troops have done to Serbs, Gypsies, and Jews during World War Two? Partly, the old man who loves to speak German to me, may have wished to be polite to me, the German anthropologist, and produce an image of solidarity which he may not have produced to an American researcher. But I propose that the level of empathy between interlocutor and researcher does not alone explain Budimir's pro-German stance. It appears that Budimir, in order to keep his positive memory of life in Croatia before the war coherent feels an urge to advocate a friendship with Germans in the future. He distinguishes clearly between negative political events on the one hand and positive human interactions on the other. His major goal is to resist creating personal enemies out of the government's official political enemies, and in this vein he underlines not having anything against Croats, Germans or Albanians. Budimir proves a remarkable resistance against the manichaeic or cosmological world view of "good" and "bad" actors in history, which so many other participants in my study have voiced throughout the conversations.

In order to advocate such peaceful coexistence, I suggest that Budimir's narrative of the past contains what Michael Taussig (1992) has called "dream-work." Recalling the meeting with an old Indian friend in front of Machu Picchu, Peru, Taussig tells of a rather curious twist in historical narration. As opposed to the official version of history following which early Incan craftship construed the marvelous architectural site in the Andes, the Indian holds the unsettling claim that it was the Spanish who with whips beat the Indians to build the monuments. "To my old Indian friend at least, there was no mystical secret of Indian technology [...]. For him these glorified ruins were monuments to racism and the colonial authority to wield the whip" (Taussig 1992: 42). The Indian's statement could, of course, be easily discarded as being a farfetched distortion or joke. In Taussig's interpretation though the story has deeper underlying layers. For the Andean native clearly employs the image of the famous ruins to project a violent colonial past on it, the untold story of Peruvian history which deals with the Spanish oppression of the 'Indios' which lasts until today. Thus, holding the ruins as a curing image to colonialism's past is based on an evasion which twists history to different ends. In a way then, the Indian uses the fictive plot in order to make a creative intervention to the writing of history.

Now, let me turn to a very different narrative Nikola gave me when talking about his victimizing experience in Jasenovać in 1941, which I suggest resembles the plot Taussig described in one aspect, that is its "dream-like" quality:

> *"When we were in the concentration camp one woman spoke up and talked to the Ustaša guy Pero, who was a nice man. Brave as she was in a situation were they had captured and threatened us she said: 'I have an honest dream. I dreamt that a big flood will come and pour all over Yugoslavia. Just a few mountaintops will last like little islands. And these islands then have the different peoples on them and, when the flood resides, will get together again later.' The Ustaša guy Pero listened and then told her: "You should keep on dreaming."*

In this dream, manichaeic visions of the world, which have such a central place in Serbian long-distance nationalist imaginings, are crisscrossed and suspended. The dreaming quality of the storytelling entails cunning humor as well as a subversion of common knowledge and fixed boundaries. The "bad" Ustaša is not only bad, since he is pictured as the listener who against his violent calling consents to the dreaming of the speaker. History in Budimir's narrative is not only what was, but what could have been or should have been. In this vein, history can be expressed in explaining the past as the old man loves to do, or by telling a dream, projecting an optimistic future onto a twisted past. The rather exceptional case of Budimir demonstrates that the experience of perpetration does not necessarily lead to nationalist activism, as was the tenor in the preceding chapters. Instead, his narrative reveals a conciliatory and reconciling tone.

Going back to Budimir's Germanophony, as a matter of fact, I suppose that his pro-German position is also related to a more general phenomenon of the cultural imagination of Germans in Serbia as a symbol for "civilization" (van de Port 1998: 53f.). Culturally the Germans influenced the Balkans a lot over many centuries, and Budimir's recital of Goethe's poem "Kennst du das Land, wo die Zitronen blühen?"[138], symbolizes an impulse to see the German and Serbian culture as close and on overall friendly terms with each other. In doing so he can draw on actual positive personal experiences before the war and after, when staying in Germany as a DP for about a year. Budimir's Germanophony expresses a hope for a future alliance with Germans. In his future-scenario – and he is reminding us

138. "Do you know where the blooming lemon trees are?" [translation mine].

vaguely of Dragan’s hope for “cultural assimilation“ – all people will unite and mix:

> *“De Chardin! The great French anthropologist, Jesuit by the way, he discovered the Peking man, he was in China. At the beginning the Catholic church official wanted to eliminate his teachings, but they couldn’t succeed in it, and he used to say a beautiful thing, he said: ‘Mankind is like a tree. For thousands or millions of years the tree is growing its roots and the branches. But the branches will not go down toward the roots, the branches are going to make a beautiful crown, when mankind is by mother nature reunited. And then as a Roman Catholic I cannot say that, but the thing is: Who knows how many Adams and Eves were or appeared in different parts of the world? Because anthropologists try to explain everything, but the anthropologist is caught in contradictions, in the holy scriptures there are some parts that are blank, and science has to fill it in when they reach the position that they will be able to answer.’ So I do believe that nations are going to stay, but they will not be constantly waging war. They will be like lovers in the NATO or like mosaic parts of different colors that create a beautiful image of our existence.“*

Using the metaphor of the “tree of nations“ – “the tree is growing its roots,“ “the branches are not going down towards the roots“ – he refuses the fixation of nation-ness in the soil. Instead he favors a united crown in the top signifying a truly cosmopolitan global society. Budimir’s vision of the future is at this point full of hope. In this narrative he implicitly tries to get rid of essentialisms and fixed rootings, he hopes for a tree of difference and change. While he believes that nations will stay, they might change in that they will not be constantly waging war anymore, and “they will be like lovers in the NATO“ – will they?

“If you don’t have peace in the Balkans you will never have peace in Europe“

So far, I have referred to persons, Dragan, Andreja, and Budimir, who laid out to me their personal and idealistic future-scenarios, be they optimistic, like Dragan’s and Budimir’s, or pessimistic, like Andreja’s. All three presented their expectations as a puzzle of different ideas to me, like a patchwork of visions, and in one and the same person one could find frightful ideas, while others sounded rather positive. In my last example I will turn to a person, who like Budimir was exiled shortly after the Second World War. As opposed to Budimir who was and is left-leaning and a socialist, Father Dimitrije Aleksandrović has always been a strong opponent of communism, as we saw in chapter four. What makes him markedly different from the other examples I used is his active role not only in religious matters, not unlike Dragan, but also in the political realm.

Analyzing the past and developing visions for the future, his contemplation of historical events is a particularly rich foil for a time to come when everything is to be done the opposite way and therefore better:

> *"And that's what we are most of us: patriots without illusions. We see the situation, we know when we have to do it; we try to make Serbian people what they are. They are not what most Serbs think – that they are number one. When some simple Serb talks he thinks that Serbia is number one, everything is around Serbia, most small people think that. But we know that Serbian people have to get together economically to become independent, and then to play smart games with the big powers. We are now very much against these dangerous heroic beliefs and want to do it better than how we did it in 1941. I remember, I screamed the sentence, I was thirteen years old: Better grave than slaves, better war than pact, you know, and that... like crazy about America and Great Britain as Western allies, those illusions we have to overcome, and be intelligent and have intelligent leaders, and help them as much as possible, keep the tie. We figure it's almost about three million Serbian people in the diaspora, so it's tremendous energy."*

Taking into consideration what went wrong in Serbian history, in his view first, the overestimation of their own political and military potential, second, the "illusions" projected on the "big powers" England and the U.S., and third, the loss of connection between Serbia and the diaspora, Father Dimitrije articulates some clear-cut measures of how to do better in coming times. A core aspect of his narrative is "to play smart" games with the Western states, an agenda which he repeats several times during our interview, thereby implicitly addressing how in the last ten years Serbian political leaders were rather failures diplomatically. Besides, in his rejection of patriotic "illusions" and "dangerous heroic beliefs" there is a clear departure from some of the nationalist statements mentioned earlier in this work. I even suggest that the account entails a tone of reconciliation.

His analysis of the present situation is unsurprisingly negative:

> *"Serbia is a chaos, they need 50 years to become one healthy nation, at least. So we think that the diaspora could help with not only money, because if we put all money the diaspora has and send in Yugoslavia, we have calculated very freely, they maybe could be able to live for two months, maybe three months. But we could individually send people, not everybody... Number two, with opening the way for the West for people to build connections, investment, and with advice. When we went to Yugoslavia in 1990, we tried to see what is going on, we didn't find three accountants who know how to operate a modern way. I am not an*

> *expert, but people who are used to the modern type of accounting could see that the economy, everything was of the typical Soviet system which had been introduced to Yugoslavia. It's awkward, it didn't function at all."*

In order to build up the country, he focuses especially on technology and the economy, based on his relentless critique against the socialist system in Yugoslavia, the "typical Soviet system" as he says. That this was not so, he couldn't see himself, as he refused to ever visit Yugoslavia while Tito was in power. Therefore, the assumption he expressed to me in another section of the interview that he "got out of touch" and sees Serbia "under a glass cover" as applies to many of the older generation of diaspora Serbs appears right.

In the first part of the passage Father Dimitrije speaks not as an individual "I," but prefers to use the collective "we," as if his views were representative of those of other Serbs. Moreoever, the personal pronoun "we" forges a unity which he and others wish for but know that they are far away from achieving. Charging his personal viewpoints with a collective form is a rhetorical strategy characteristic of diaspora organization's leaders who are used to speaking on behalf of "the Serbs," as if the ethnic label implied a political consensus. Father Dimitrije maintains the collective form when explaining the main goals of the SUC: "*We* try to make those people there to listen, try and think broadminded, see how *they* live, forget about *me*, Serbs, just try to preserve as much as possible *your* identity" (italics mine). In fact, the singular forms "I" or "you" and the plural forms "we" and "they" could be used interchangeably in the priest's speech, pointing to how 'identity' is always already perceived as a collective, national identity, as has been shown in part one of this study.

As a small country, Serbia has to come to terms with being relatively powerless and not communist Yugoslavia anymore, "and you have to try the best to put yourself in the order, in the row of everything around you – that's what we are working for, that's why we are writing." His is a position of overcoming frustration and past scenarios, forgetting about history as a "guideline" and "glory," but preserving it as a "beautiful history" and going on with the present and towards the future: "*I cannot live off history, history is a very important part of my duša,*[139] *my being, but not as a guideline in modern life.*" His pragmatics of politics reminds me of Dragan's warning of the "quick sand" of history and the repetition of violence. In order to prosper one has to accommodate oneself with the West and not rumble around and specialize in conspiracy theories or the past. In his future-scenario there is no space for resistance against "neo-colonial powers" but the necessity for a smooth accommodation with the New World Order. Father

139. "Duša" means "soul" in Serbo-Croatian.

Dimitrije wishes to build a bridge, to assist economic progress towards modernity, which reminds one of a development agent from the modernization school. Nevertheless, and here he quite contradicts himself in his earlier statement on the need to recognize Serbia's small size, he doesn't seem to give up on nationalistic ideas concerning Serbia's future:

> *"But my prediction for the future of the Balkan to be healthy is that Serbia will take over Montenegro, Bosnia, part of Bosnia – Croatia will take that other part –, because Germany will be there, so far, we may know, and Macedonia. They cannot exist anymore as solitary states. Albania is going to eat them, Bulgaria doesn't recognize them, Macedonia neither, Bulgarians think they are Bulgarian, they think that they should not exist. And Serbs are all over Yugoslavia, even before they called them Macedonian many Macedonians had been Serbs. In the 1990's they said: You are now Macedonian. Fine, but even their church now is coming back and is becoming part of the Serbian church. So, in my prediction, God knows when, 50 years from now, the healthy situation of Balkan will be this: Slovenia will stay alone, Croatia will be alone, Yugoslavia will be the center of the Balkan. Europe needs a healthy European situation, they need peace for prosperity. If you don't have peace in the Balkans you will never have peace in Europe. And the key people in the Balkans not by their greatness but by their position in history are Serbs. And you have to play with them."*

So in the end, Serbs are the ones Europe has to play with, – because everybody, at least in Southeastern Europe, is Serbian anyway – not vice versa! Father Dimitrije's earlier critique of history and call for modesty are finally paradoxically denounced, as this last passage reflects with a gist of enthusiasm the hope for a hegemonic Serbian position in the Balkans and Europe. Macedonians are not really Macedonians but Serbs, Bosnia and Montenegro will be taken over by Croats and Serbs, and a Serb-centered Yugoslavia, without Slovenia and Croatia, but including Bosnia, will prevail. One could call Father Dimitrije's contradictory vision of history a "future-minded history," since at the same time that he like Djordjevic and many others critiques the 'obsession with history' among many Serbs, he still grounds his whole thinking concerning Serbia and its future on the past. In a way then the future is caught up in the past.

As shown earlier in the preceding narrative of Andreja the priest does not construct a coherent national vision, but is caught up in ambivalence, paradoxes, and contradictions. The social imagination of the future is highly problematic. The project of the imagination of the nation from afar appears to be insolubly intertwined with diverging moral imperatives and political values. Dragan obviously did best at forcing the chaotic present into a neat future scenario, but the others are struggling hard between the contradictory expectations of late modernity.

Conclusion

> "We were all deprived of our food: past, present, and future. There was no future, because it had already happened. It happened, because – in its own ways – the past happened once again." (Ugrešić 1994: 17 [transl. from the German B. B.-L.])

If I am to search for the common thread linking the narratives of the four Serbian migrants above, I propose to look closely at the issue of time in the context of Yugoslavia's disintegration. Is the future really so significant? And if it is, in which ways do the interlocutors communicate the future? Quite obviously, as the examples show, Serbs in the U.S. were not "deprived of their food," but 'ate too much' at least of one ingredient: the past. With reference to memory politics in the former Yugoslavia, Dubravka Ugrešić noted: "We live in the past, present, and future *simultaneously*. In the hodgepodge of time suddenly everything what we knew, and all that we will know, has popped up and struggled for its own right of existence" (Ugrešić 1994: 128 f., italics by the author). Reacting to the unmaking of a nation-state, the fifty year long existence of Yugoslavia which shaped her life, and the official history that was taught about that country, Ugrešić is deeply moved and upset about the fervor with which history was manipulated in the service of nationalism. She continues: "The present in which we die, mirrors the permanent rewinding of movies from the past and those from the future" (ibid.). Despite the huge differences in the politics of history, as perceived by Ugrešić and Serbs in the diaspora, the implosion of the past is a common theme. Thus, the future would be primarily about repeating the past, much like Aleksandar Kojeve's Hegelian notion of continuous history (1975) and Mircea Eliade's "cyclical time" (1984). In other words, the model of history as a linear progression of time is utterly futile in the case of the former Yugoslavia.

If objectivism's belief in a neat succession of past, present, and future were met by a common perception of linear history, we needn't worry about the manipulation of history, a repetition of events, or a continuity of time. Future visions, such as Serbs form about Serbia and the world would simply not be possible. But in the case of Yugoslavia's demise, historical memory was transferred to the future, and the Second World War past was projected on the 'present' of the 1990's. The criteria connectedness, claims to absolute truth, and secrecy which authors of conspiracy theories gave as defining characteristics, seem to be equally fitting for the rather millennial or apocalyptic future visions my interlocutors indulged in. Paired together, both the temporal dimension and conspiracies have common denominators. They are built on a timeless, continuous, unchangeable version of the past, producing fixed, untranscendable 'truths'. The message conveyed in this use of time rests on a dark assumption, namely that the 'ghost of history' cannot be contained and that in the Yugoslav case, the past has to be taken more serious than ever. Any premature hope, similar to the hope in the future of Yugoslavia that persisted up to the 1980's, would be oblivious due to the extraordinary relevance of the past in the future, which is, to note, again unreconciled. As Liisa Malkki (2000: 19) concludes:

> "One cannot easily rekindle Bloch's 'principle of hope' without first taking account of the structures of fear and without examining the enormous losses that people have suffered on all sides."

And yet, three of the four narrators in the previous chapter have also formulated optimistic and reconciling visions, which should not be easily brushed away. For they present one more dimension of the phenomenon of long-distance nationalism, as it makes way for conciliatory and empowering thinking, despite the prevalence of nationalist imagery and ongoing political conflict.

As I have tried to exemplify in this chapter the notion "cultural production" adds an important aspect to the analysis of national ideas and the violent breakup of the Yugoslav nation-state. In the diaspora, however, I suggest that the cultural production of ideas concerning the past and future of the nation is not so much based on the cultural production of ideas per se, but rather on the production of "geopolitical imaginings." I assume that the global future visions and conspiracy theories are well connected to geopolitical imaginings in the homeland, described by Živković (1999). As I have shown, Serbian exiles in the United States instead of focusing on the complex local cultural processes in their homeland, regard global political power structures of highest relevance, embodied in the various forms of conspiracy theories of the International Community. Long distance travel, telephone, the World Wide Web, and e-mail are established means by which Serbs in the homeland and abroad maintain close contact and exchange information. Furthermore, it seems that the diversity of perspectives encountered in the four life stories is strongly influenced both by the region of origin and time and circumstances of emigration.

Serbs have historically been scattered throughout the Balkans and formed diasporas before the modern global age and therefore have been exposed to different political empires and cultures.[140] While I cannot draw any specific conclusions regarding the relationship between region of origin and political visions, the four cases revealed some possible tendencies which are representative for a broader spectrum of Serbs. Dragan's memo-

140. See Roudometof 2001: 101-130.

ry of growing up with Muslims in the ethnically mixed Hercegovinian town of Trebinje to a certain degree mirrors the expressed need for a peaceful co-existence between the different ethnic groups. The pro-German outlook of Budimir, while an exception in my overall sample, is not unique among the older generation of Serbs in/from Croatian Slavonia who indeed cherished to be exposed to the multiethnic and multilingual "K.and K." society. Envisioning a hegemonic role of Serbia as the priest exemplified, I suggest, is more likely to be found among Belgrade Serbs than among Serbs from Bosnia. Of course, these regional affinities are neither homogeneous nor static, and, as Andreja has shown can change. Whereas in the past he appreciated his Sarajevan Yugoslav identity, in the diaspora he learned to regard Yugoslavia as an 'illusion' and gradually became more Serbian. Identity change, esp. the departure from being "Yugoslav" to being "Serbian" is very representative for many young migrants who lived most of their lives under socialism (see also chapter two). Nationalist viewpoints are very prevalent in the American Serbian diaspora and Andreja is certainly not the most extremist in this regard.

The material suggests that historical structures of frustration and enmity need to be studied instead of just dismissed as paranoia or extremism, and therewith prematurely silenced. As Malkki formulates: "For it is these [the future visions, B.B.-L.] that are always already projecting forms and structures into the future, as shadows dancing on the wall" (Malkki 2000: 19). Even (or especially) the most paranoid future-scenario can be as important as any national history in shaping the present and political alternatives for the future. What the four informants unfolded to me must be seen in the context of the struggles over history, truths, and knowledge production of which those future visions are a meaningful part. As such they are being developed not in some 'isolated' Serbian town but in the midst of contemporary American society, with which they are intricately connected and which thus to a certain extent bring those imaginations about.

Chapter 8. Conclusion

The wars of the 1990's, which ripped Yugoslavia apart were certainly the most devastating event Europe has witnessed in the second half of the 20th century. The questions and issues that have occupied this study were derived in direct reference to contemporary European and world events, and the Balkan war in particular. A central theme has been the impact of the violent dismemberment on the way of life and identity of people living in the San Francisco Bay Area who ascribe to being Serbian.

This final chapter considers drawing the main themes, methodology, and theoretical implications of the research in a concise way, as to make comprehensible the various arguments of this study and the multiple theoretical ideas that informed it. At the end of this chapter I will point to possible future research on the topic, which leaves ample opportunities for further investigation.

As I have noted in the introduction, my work has not been guided by one theoretical insight or one theoretical 'school' only, but throughout my writing I have introduced various possibilities of reading the extensive material, constantly opening up new theoretical angles instead of limiting myself to a single way of reading. In doing so I have been animated by Roland Barthes' contention that a text consists of "a tissue of quotations drawn from innumerable centers of culture" and that its meaning lies "not in its origin but in its destination" (in Clifford 1986: 51ff.). Important in this approach was also the fact that I developed the writing out of my understanding of the narratives and viewpoints expressed, instead of applying already elaborated theoretical ideas on the material. Thus, my study has been guided foremost by the question, what was important to my interlocutors and in which ways I could understand and interpret the issues they came up with.

The conversations and observations reveal, from chapter one onwards, that the Balkan war was not only a tragedy for its people and the world community, but also a distressing life event for people living thousands of kilometers away. Serbs in the United States were moved through a range of historical, cultural, and emotional processes that involved them in coming to terms with the way they experienced guilt, worry, accusations of the majority society, and above all, their own pasts through the prism of the present. At the beginning of the millennium when this research was undertaken, the recent past appeared to be still fresh.

In focusing not on one category of migrants only, e.g. DPs from World War Two, or "brain drain" émigrés from the 1990's, but by paying attention to the differences between people who arrived at various dates and under very diverse circumstances, my analysis sheds light on the decisive role that certain cultural and political contexts have for the conflicting visions that migrants form about themselves, the nation, and the world around them. The conversations revealed much in relation to the individuals themselves and their visions of the homeland and to a lesser extent, the country in which they are living (United States). However, I have tried to shed light on the specificities of life in the host country which informed the stories told, whenever it seemed of relevance, especially in chapter five when exploring the places where people live and remember, the interiors of houses.

Overall, my study has been animated by recent works on long-distance nationalism (Anderson 1994, 1998, Danforth 1995, Fuglerud 1999, Glick-Schiller and Fouron 2001, et al.) and the significant gap that Anderson's first investigations of the phenomenon produced. The absence of a micro-level analysis in Anderson's approach on nationalism underscored that what was missing was an ethnographically grounded analysis of 'ordinary' people, and their active participation in the formation of national identity. Challenged by this far-reaching critique, my study has encompassed individual narratives as well as social practices and interpreted these extensively.

In the first part, *Identity in Exile*, I have explored the multiplicity of meanings attached to identity declarations by the highly factionalized Serbian "community" in the wake of the Third Balkan Wars. The first chapter, based on interviewing as well as on participant observation also serves as an introduction to the main themes that are of importance to being Serbian, such as 'Otherness,' victimology, and history. Taking into consideration a wide spectrum of discourses broadly ranging from essentializing and Serb nationalist to non-nationalist, "Yugoslav" declarations my focus lies on the way that the recent conflicts have shaped identity abroad. Far from understanding being Serbian as fixed or static, my interlocutors have pointed to the dynamic aspect of identity formation, especially in times of crisis. Important for my understanding of long-distance nationalism is that not everybody who expresses a strong national identity is necessarily a long-distance nationalist. However, national identity certainly lies at the core of long-distance nationalism and is manipulated by political actors. Most people I conversed with perceived the breakup of Yugoslavia as a catalyst for making new choices for positioning themselves vis-à-vis the homeland, but also with regard to the host society. The creation of inter- as well as intra-group boundaries is noteworthy, as interlocutors try to set themselves apart not just from various 'Others,' especially Croats and Americans, but also from other Serbs, or those Serbs who claim to be "Yugoslav." In chapter two, therefore, I discuss the re-negotiation of being Serbian in the light of "Yugoslav" women, who in retrospection speak of the force to succumb to ethno-national categories and to become more Serbian, too, since "Yugoslavia doesn't exist anymore." Partly, through constant processes of "interpellation" (Althusser 1972) of Americans or other non-Serbs in the United States who ask them again and again "who they are" and where "exactly" they are from, the fixing of identity takes place almost inevitably. Thus, the crucial role of external actors influencing the perception of Self and the nation has been taken into consideration. Of central relevance is also the media reporting which was perceived by most to be overtly biased against Serbs and has therefore led to a "demonization" of "them" in the United States, with the result of a strengthening of ethnic identification. In stressing the impact of the media on people's perception of themselves and the nation, I contend with Nicholas Procter (2000: 169):

> "We saw how media journalists and reporters such as Neil Ascherson, Martin Bell, Misha Glenny, Mark Thompson, Mark Traynor, Ed Vulliamy and others, played a vital role in this process. They became, along with their editorial teams in the Balkans, England, and in the United States, the architects of a real and bloodied imagery of suffering and devastation. They became lead figures in what I have called consciousness industry that manufactured particular ways of seeing the Balkan war."

The people I spoke to reacted strongly against most of the mainstream media's reporting about the recent wars. Through being moved by the news they watched, they also perceived of their identity in more pointed ways, often in defense of "their nation." Perhaps, the media became *the* motivation for a great many to engage themselves for "the Serbian cause" or to retain from doing so. And since mass communication, print media, and the Internet seemed to prove their effectiveness so well, in turn the founders and spokespersons of diaspora organizations attempted to make use of these mediums to distribute their opinions in the same way, as has been shown in chapter three. However, these attempts were either too late, too few, not convincing, or they didn't reach enough people, in order to effectively turn public opinion around in favor of Serbs.

While in general the tendency to unify in times of crisis and to view national identity along ethnic lines has certainly increased through a revival of Serbdom in the homeland and in the diaspora (Čolović 2002), still declaring oneself a "Serb" or a "Yugoslav" or else can change depending on the situation and context. I have stressed the heterogeneity of individuals who often don't have much more in common with each other than that they originate in the same country, so that strictly speaking, the term "community" is inadequate. This view has been enabled, too, by my inclusion of those individuals who have very little or no contact at all to the Serbian community – in fact the majority of Serbian migrants! – which officially congregates around the institution of the church.

In chapter three I have analyzed two major diaspora politicians of the *Serbian Unity Congress* and their rhetorics as well as transnational practices of lobbying abroad. In stark contrast to the plethora of meanings that individual Serbs associate with being Serbian, as has been shown in the preceding chapters, the SUC is characterized by the self-confident claim that "we know what is good for us Serbs," thus reducing complexity in favor of a deterministic, static approach to ethnic identity. Again, the media play a huge role, for distributing opinions in pamphlet form and thereby shaping discourses of the recent wars that people all over the world could easily access. Whereas the elitist organization claims to be the missing link between the diaspora and the homeland, a look at the various activities throughout the 1990's and the striking lack of interest among many émigré Serbs has led me to the conclusion that the impact of Serbian long-distance nationalists has overall been ineffective. In order to understand the weakness of diaspora politics, an exploration of the historical precursors to the SUC and factionalism prevailing in the Serbian diaspora is of crucial significance.

Thus, having discussed the dominant themes in the politics of identity among Serbs in the San Francisco Bay Area and the local and global contexts that shape the re-negotiation of being Serbian, part three of this study, *Living in the Past*, has been intended to go deeper into the phenomenon of the past which has been pointed to frequently already. In chapter four I have been concerned with the life stories of three elderly displaced persons, who have been victimized in World War Two and have been taking part in diaspora politics fifty years later. By focusing on a few selected individuals and their detailed biographies I have analyzed in more depth how the present shapes the memory of the past. Inspired by theorists of memory (Connerton 1989, Gillis 1996, Halbwachs 1992, Kerby 1991, Meyerhoff 1992 et al.), my interest was guided by the question how people remember; not in the sense of a passive, 'authentic' recalling of events, but as a mode of comprehension and creative reconstruction of their lives. Despite the various differences in the presentation of their stories, all three individuals have underscored the centrality of suffering in World War Two which motivated their long-distance nationalist activism.

A common phenomenon hereby is that many displaced Serbs have for many decades put their wartime memory to rest and have fully absorbed themselves in life and work in the United States, when with the outbreak of war their stories suddenly came to the surface again and the drive to engage themselves for the homeland started to determine their lives. I have argued that the role of old people in Serbian culture to transmit history, in this case a history of victimology, is of central importance, as "unsettled accounts" of the past led to new "unsettled accounts" in the present. Given the acute position of the past in Serbian culture, the unsettled accounts my interlocutors speak of – stories which are of high relevance also for the young who have not themselves lived through World War Two – need to be taken serious. With regard to the brutal massacres of the Nazi-backed Croat Ustaša against Serbs, Jews, and Gypsies between 1941 and 1944, I personally believe that Western powers, especially the German government, should have pursued a much more careful and balanced foreign policy and diplomatic missions in the former Yugoslavia, from the very beginning. The lack of officially recognizing old wounds has certainly upset a lot of Serbs and provided many with the legitimization of "righting past wrongs," no matter how untimely this attitude appeared to outside observers.

Moreover, in the context of the Third Balkan War similar accounts like the ones I presented were successfully utilized by the Belgrade regime and various writers and poets in Serbia to spread inter-ethnic hatred in the homeland. Furthermore, the role of the past in the diaspora teaches any student of long-distance nationalism a crucial lesson for the impact of exiles on the homeland, since revisionist histories among Serbian and Croat émigrés have always flourished in the United States and with the dismemberment of Yugoslavia were timely re-exported to the homeland.

Chapter five, drawing from the same life stories but taking into consideration other voices as well, explores the issue of memory from another angle. Inspired by my observation that photos, paintings, flags, or little items from the "lost" houses decorate the 'new' homes of my interlocutors, I have analyzed this 'material' side to memory with reference to recent ethnographies (Bahloul 1996, Ballinger 2003, Hirschon 1998 et al.). As opposed to common ethnographic practices, to describe the interiors of dwellings for the sake of mere illustration, my attempt has been to exemplify the role of objects in the recollection of the past and in staking claims to a "lost" landscape. The dwellings and the locations Serbs have acquired in the United States also reflect the success stories people tell. In order to explore the life worlds and current social context of displaced Serbs I therefore shed light on the material side to people's 'triumphs,' but also include adverse cases of people who have not "made it" as recent refugees in one of the most costly areas of the country.

In my choice to present many of the individuals I worked with as personally as possible, my method was in a way to translate the empathy I developed during the conversations to the readers, in order to open them up for understanding, instead of making moral judgments. After all, my intention was to explore the "worlds made" of displaced Serbs, including their anger, their dreams, their personal endeavors, forms of political activism, and also their historical ruminations, in short: their very human everyday struggles. Nevertheless, I did not wish to perpetuate the viewpoints expressed by overt sympathy, and thus did not shy away from representing their efforts at times in a somewhat distanced and ironic way.

The third part, *Conspiracy theories, future visions, and the International Community*, takes up the issue of historical thinking from yet another point of departure. Considering the immense significance of the past for the present of Serbian exiles, I explore the striking prevalence of grand explanations or conspiracy theories surrounding the Yugoslav wars. Many participants of my study were eager to tell me of conspiracies surrounding the breakup of the country, but also other wars dating back to the fourteenth century, world history in general, and Serbian history in specific. Chapter six is to provide the reader with a theoretical understanding of conspiracy theories in late modernity (Groh 1987, Hofstadter 1952, Marcus 1999, Todd and Sanders ed. 2003 et al.) and in the context of the Cold war, which shaped much of Serbian diaspora life in the second half of the 20th century. Similar to the study as a whole, I have put into question the common separation between "fact" and "fiction," "truth" and "falsehood," academic and 'ordinary' knowledge, and instead attempted to understand the way that Serbs develop visions about the world and Yugoslav history as a way of making comprehensible tremendously complex global as well as local processes and events. Important in this regard is the view that "power does indeed conspire" and that politics takes place in hidden ways, thus leaving ordinary people with the challenge to disentangle a highly disorderly world prone with conspiracy. In doing, so they often base their claims on academic and other writings, manifesting the power that certain books hold and the crucial twists made in the reception of these texts.

In the final chapter I have discussed the visions of the Big Powers and the turbulent Balkan history in the narratives of four interlocutors in this study. Inspired by the striking prevalence of the future in these conspiratorial visions, the question "What comes next?" seemed to be of utmost concern among displaced Serbs. Curiously, an analysis of the temporal dimension, based on insights by Malkki (2000), Ricoeur (1998), and Wachtel (1998), has revealed the interconnectedness between past, present, and future, whereby the past appeared to overshadow even the future. As opposed to a common perception of time as linear and history as moving on chronologically, displaced Serbs communicated a cyclical view of temporal dimensions, with the past repeating itself endlessly. This finding, so to speak that the past is in the future, underscores the relevance which the past plays in the life worlds of Serb émigrés and that the repercussions of historical conflicts for Serbs and other people world-wide need to be taken more serious than ever. In the narratives I discovered a glimpse of hope, with my informants disclosing reconciling visions that speak for an optimistic, conciliatory potential of long-distance nationalism.

On a whole my study is intended to provide a transnational view of the Third Balkan Wars, informing about the significant emotional and political investment of displaced people in events going on "at home." The many examples of activism in the Bay Area have demonstrated the role that long-distance nationalists, diaspora organizations, and individuals play in sending remittances, supporting people and politics in Serbia, and engaging in the public debate in the United States. I hope to have made clear the creative interventions that Serbian migrants undertake in their endeavor to comprehend and be part their nation. Migrants are not passively following the news about events in the homeland, but they keep in contact in various ways, from attending public meetings and celebrations, writing letters back home, calling family and friends, engaging in conversations about the homeland, to return visits. In line with Keith Brown's (2003) summarizing remarks in his study of the Macedonian nation I would contend that

> "[t]his book responds ... to the title of the opening chapter of Partha Chatterjee's (1993) *The Nation and its Fragments*: Whose imagined community? I have sought to communicate a sense of how well people in Kruševo apprehend the elusiveness of the past and the contingency of the present. They are not the Balkan zealots beloved by some observers, pursuing age-old grievances with passionate intensity. Nor are they chameleons who shift allegiance with the times for their own advantage. Their stand, instead, recalls that of scholars acutely conscious of the ways in which historical agents cast their own agendas as historic, and those of others as in need of correction. ... They remind us, if we choose to listen, that there are other ways to negotiate the vagaries of the present than by accepting or rejecting master narratives of the past. They offer, instead, glimpses of a world of debate where passionate convictions, often so deadly, are tempered by knowledge of the uncertainties of nation." (Brown 2003: 249)

In the case of Serbs in the San Francisco Bay Area, I suggest, the intensity with which many of them engage in historical narratives and political visions, despite the fact that they are spatially and often also temporally far remote from the homeland, is even more remarkable than in the case of 'Brown's Macedonians' of Kruševo.

My findings leave open many questions for future research into a field that curiously has been explored very little in contemporary anthropology. In my mind, there is still ample opportunity for further retrospection into the recent Yugoslav wars from a transnational perspective, e.g. an investigation of family and friends who stayed in the former Yugoslavia and their view of exiles, migration, return visits, and the like. Possibly, including the views of people in the homeland can enrich and drastically alter the representation Serbs produce abroad, as those "back home" come to terms with migrants and exile in their own ways. Unfortunately, due to time constraints it was not in my power to include this area of research into my present study. Topics for further investigation that comprise more contemporary events are also worth attention. For instance, for the first time in the history of Serbian migration Serbs abroad were eligible to vote in the Serbian presidential elections in July 2004. In the United States, the SUC had led a diaspora-wide campaign for granting voting rights to exiles for years. How significant was this election abroad? Did it change homeland-diaspora relations, and if it did, in which ways?

Among the most interesting areas of further research to me would be an inquiry into the diaspora life and political visions of Serbs and other former Yugoslav groups residing in Europe, a migration which is very distinct in political, historical, and social terms from the Serbian diaspora in Anglo-Saxon countries. As of my knowledge, since the outbreak of war no single study has been published about former Yugoslav émigrés in Europe, although their numbers are substantial. I assume that the relative geographic closeness to the homeland has enabled more intensive interaction between the migrants and people who stayed. Reportedly, during the Bosnian war German Serbs from their *Gastarbeiter* residences in Southern Germany drove their cars on weekends to go back to their villages and, in extreme cases, even took guns with them to help "Serbia."[141] In the words of Tim Judah (2000a: 223):

> "Although the Bosnian and Krajina Serb leaderships often said that every single man aged between sixteen and sixty would somehow be mobilised 'for the defense of the fatherland', there was one class who could escape the draft. These were the considerable numbers of gastarbeiters who worked in Germany, Austria, Slovenia, and elsewhere. Coaches full of them and their families could often be seen crossing the Serbian border with Hungary on their way back to Germany, or glimpses could be caught of their mud-spattered Mercedes making high-speed dashes through the 'corridor'. The Serbs were always short of manpower, compared to the Croats or Muslims, but these people were far too valuable to mobilise. They were a source of hard cash, as they had to pay a considerable sum to be able to come and go. ... The gastarbeiter community provided not only money but refuges for those who had fled the warzones.

141. This information is taken from personal communication with Paul Hockenos.

> More discreetly, and where it was possible to secure visas, they also provided a haven for those young men whose families had no intention of seeing them slaughtered on the frontline for a cause some at least did not believe in."

Vague as Judah's allusions remain, reading these lines, the opening example of this book comes to mind again. Perhaps, the migrants who were shown on the television news standing up to pay homage to Milošević and who were said to have provided substantial financial help to the country in times of need were not the American Serbs who had been too wary about a socialist to be the leader of Yugoslavia? Maybe it was rather Serbs living in Germany, Switzerland, or Austria? These and many other questions have not been answered yet and provide a challenge to anyone interested in long-distance nationalism in general and the former Yugoslavia in particular. In which ways do migrants from the former Yugoslavia residing in Europe view the tragic events in the homeland in retrospection? How do they keep contact with a home they could, if they wanted to, visit once a month or even every weekend? In short, what are the differences and what the similarities between the Serbian diaspora in Europe and in the United States or Australia, where at least some studies have been undertaken already? Is the diaspora connected across national and continental borders?

A final remark on the specific group under study and my methodological choices for representing "them." I believe that the people I have described and tried to understand are not different from anyone else, American, Bulgarian, German, Chinese, or else living under similar circumstances and having been exposed to a similar cultural, historical, and political background. Despite the fact that I limited my research to this particular group, Serbs in the United States, thereby willy-nilly reifying certain ethnic boundaries in my own ways, I wish to point to the humanness inherent in the thinking and practices of my interlocutors. Be they long-distance nationalists, as quite a few are, or not, my conviction is that the type of book I have written should in the strict term be called "anthropography" and not "ethnography." In employing this term, Daniel E. Valentine in his *Charred Lullabies* (1996: 7) dealing with the Sinhala-Tamil violence in Sri Lanka makes a statement that is important for me at this point: "I have called this an anthropography of violence rather than an ethnography of violence because to have called it the latter would have been to parochialize violence, to attribute and limit violence to a particular people and place." Concerning the Yugoslav wars a similar widely accepted perception, namely that 'the Yugoslavs have for ages been violent' and 'that this could never happen to us' is still common. With regard to my topic, long-distance nationalism which is of similarly politically charged quality as violence is, I have tried to counter this assumption by showing the human quest for meaning and belonging that many of my informants follow.

And yet, the challenge to learn from the Balkan Wars something general about the human condition, can be taken too far as well. Stjepan G. Meštrović, grandson to the famous Croatian sculptor provides one perfect example of an attempt to universalize the conflicts in the Balkans. In his *Balkanization of the West* (1994), Meštrović follows the question if what happened in the former Yugoslavia could not also occur in Europe or the United States. Ranging from examples such as ethnic riots in California, the terror of the IRA in Northern Ireland and the ETA in Spain, to the bombings of Muslims in Somalia and Iraq by American forces, but not of Muslims in Bosnia... – Meštrović's *tour-de-force*, recalling all the violent divisions world-wide attempts to show the equally devastating condition of Western countries. In this vein, the Los Angeles riots are just an epitome of the Balkan war! Interesting as his comparisons are, he misses an important point, and that is the very specific historical, social, geostrategic, and cultural background of the former Yugoslavia, as I have underlined above. Human as the violence and suffering are, they are not universal, but tied to the particular local and global contexts of the former Yugoslavia.

Bibliography

Aarons, Mark and John Loftus. [1991] 1998. *Unholy Trinity. The Vatican, the Nazis, and the Swiss Banks.* St. Martin's Griffin. New York.

Achin, Milos K. 1963. *The First Guerillas of Europe: The true stories of General Mihailović 's Warriors.* New York: Vintage Press.

Althusser, Louis. 1971. *Ideology and Ideological State Apparatusses (Notes towards an Investigation).* In: Althusser, Louis. *Lenin and Philosophy and Other Essays.* Monthly Review Press. New York.

Anderson, Benedict. 1983. *Imagined Communities. Reflections on the Origin and Spread of Nationalism.* Verso. London.

Anderson, Benedict. 1998. *Long-Distance Nationalism.* In: Benedict Anderson. *The Spectre of Comparisons. Nationalism, Southeast Asia and the World.* Verso. London: 58-76.

Anderson, Benedict. 1994. *Exodus.* In: *Critical Inquiry* (Winter 1994): 314-327.

Andrić, Ivo. 1984. *The Bridge on the Drina.* University of Chicago Press. Chicago.

Anzàldua, Gloria. 1987. *Borderlands. La Frontera. The New Mestiza.* Aunt Lute Books. San Francisco.

Anzulovic, Branimir. 1999. *Heavenly Serbia. From Myth to Genocide.* New York University Press. London, New York.

Appadurai, Arjun. 1996. *Modernity at Large. Cultural Dimensions of Globalization.* University of Minnesota Press. Minneapolis, London.

Assmann, Jan. [1997] 2000. *Das kulturelle Gedächtnis. Schrift, Erinnerung und politische Identität in frühen Hochkulturen.* Verlag C.H. Beck. München.

Bahloul, Joëlle. 1996. *The Architecture of Memory. A Jewish-Muslim household in colonial Algeria 1937-1962.* Cambridge University Press. Cambridge.

Bakić-Hayden, Milica. 1995. *Nesting Orientalisms: The case of former Yugoslavia.* In: Slavic Review 54: 917-931.

Bakić-Hayden, Milica and Robert Hayden. 1992. *Orientalist Variations on the Theme „Balkans": Symbolic Geography in Recent Yugoslav Cultural Politics.* In: Slavic Review 51 (1): 1-15.

Baldassar, Loretta. 1997. *Home and away: migration, the return visit and transnational identity.* In: Communal/plural (5): 69-94.

Ballinger, Pamela. 2003. *History in Exile. Memory and Identity at the Borders of the Balkans.* Princeton University Press. Princeton and Oxford.

Banac, Ivo. 1992. *The National Question in Yugoslavia. Origins, History, Politics.* Cornell University Press: Ithaca and London.

Barkun, Michael. 2003. *A Culture of Conspiracy. Apocalyptic Visions in Contemporary America.* University of California Press. Berkeley, Los Angeles, London.

Barth, Frederik.1969. *Introduction.* In: Frederik Barth: *Ethnic Groups and Boundaries. The Social Organization of Cultural Difference.* Bergen, Oslo: 9-38.

Basch, Linda, Glick Schiller, Nina, Szanton Blanc, Cristina. 1995. *Nations Unbound. Transnational Projects, Postcolonial Predicaments and Deterritorialized Nation-States.* Gordon and Breach Science Publishers. Australia, Canada... Switzerland.

Bateson, Gregory. 1972. *Culture Contact and Schismogenesis.* In: *Steps to an ecology of mind*, 61-72. Ballantine. New York.

Becker, Franziska. 2001. *Ankommen in Deutschland. Einwanderungspolitik als biografische Erfahrung im Migrationsprozeß russischer Juden.* Dietrich Reimer Verlag. Berlin.

Beloff, Nora. 1985. *Tito's Flawed Legacy: Yugoslavia and the West, 1939-1984.* Westview Press. Boulder, Colorado. London.

Benedict, Ruth. [1934] 1989. *Patterns of Culture.* Houghton Mifflin Press. Boston.

Benjamin, Walter. [1970] 1997. *Critique of Violence.* In: *One-way street and other writings.* The Verso Classics Series. Verso Books. New York.

Bennett, Linda A.. 1978. *Personal Choice in Ethnic Identitiy Maintenance. Serbs, Croats, and Slovenes in Washington D.C.* PhD Dissertation. Palo Alto, California.

Bernard, H. Russell. 1994. *Research Methods in Anthropology. Qualitative and Quantitative Approaches.* Sage Publications. Thousand Oaks et al..

Bhabha, Homi K.. 1994. *The Location of Culture.* Routledge. London/New York.

Bieber, Florian David. 2001. *Serbischer Nationalismus vom Tode Titos zum Sturz Miloševićs.* Unpublished Dissertation. Austrian Research Center. University of Vienna. Vienna.

Bittermann, Klaus (ed.). 1999. *Serbien muß sterbien. Wahrheit und Lüge im jugoslawischen Bürgerkrieg.* Critica Diabolis 45. Edition Tiamat. Berlin.

Blitz, Brad. 1994. *The Serbian Unity Congress and the Serbian Lobby. A Study of Contemporary Revisionism and Denial.* Stanford, at:
www.freeserbia/Documents/Lobby.html

Bodansky, Yossef. 1996. *Some call it peace. Waiting for War in the Balkans.* International Media Corporation Ltd. London, UK.

Bock-Luna, Birgit. 2002. *Imagining the future in the light of a violent past: Displaced Serbs in the United States envision global political futures.* In: Ethnologia Balkanica, Vol. 6: 39-67.

Bogdanich, George and Martin Lettmayer. 2002. *Yugoslavia – the avoidable war.* Hargrove Entertainment Inc.

Bornemann, John. 1997. *Settling Accounts. Violence, Justice, and Accountability in Postsocialist Europe.* Princeton University Press. Princeton, New Jersey.

Bourdieu, Pierre. 1977. *Outline of a Theory of Practice.* Cambridge University Press. Cambridge, New Rochelle, Melbourne, Sydney.

Bourdieu, Pierre. 1984. *Distinction. A Social Critique of the Judgement of Taste.* Harvard University Press. Cambridge, Massachusetts.

Brettell, Caroline B. (ed.). 1996. *When They Read What We Write. The Politics of Ethnography.* Bergin and Carvey. Westport, Connectitut. London.

Brettell, Caroline B. 2000. *Theorizing Migration in Anthropology. The Social Construction of Networks, Identities, Communities, and Globalscapes.* In: C. B. Brettell and J. Hollifield (eds.): *Migration Theory. Talking across Disciplines.* New York/London: 97- 136.

Bringa, Tone. 1995. *Being Muslim the Bosnian Way. Identity and Community in a Central Bosnian Village.* Princeton University Press. Princeton, New Jersey.

Brown, Keith. 2003. *The Past in Question. Modern Macedonia and the Uncertainties of Nation.* Princeton University Press. Princeton and Oxford.

Buchenau, Klaus. 2004. *Orthodoxie und Katholizismus in Jugoslawien 1945-1991. Ein serbisch-kroatischer Vergleich.* Balkanologische Veröffentlichungen, Bd. 40. Harrassowitz-Verlag. Wiesbaden.

Bulajić, Milan. 1996. *Jasenovać. The System of Ustaša ha Death Camps. Tudjman's „Jasenovać Myth".* Strucna Knjiga. Belgrade.

Butler, Judith. 1993. *Bodies that matter. On the discursive limits of „sex".* Routledge. New York and London.

Chatterjee, Partha. 1993. *The Nation and its Fragments.* Princeton University Press. Princeton, New Jersey.

Chomsky, Noam 2000. *A new generation draws the line. Kosovo, Timor, and the Standards of the West.* London/New York.

Clifford, James. 1997. *Routes. Travel and Translation in the Late Twentieth Century.* Harvard University Press. Cambridge Massachusetts, London, England.

Clifford, James and Marcus, George (ed.). 1986. *Writing Culture. The Poetics and Politics of Ethnography.* University of California Press. Berkeley, Los Angeles, London.

Clifford, James. 1986. *Partial Truths.* In: James Clifford and George Marcus (ed.) *Writing Culture.The Poetics and Politics of Ethnography.* University of California Press. Berkeley, Los Angeles, London: 1-26.

Colakovic, Branko Mitra. 1970. *Yugoslav Migrations to America.* unpublished Ph.D. thesis. University of Minnesota.

Čolović, Ivan. 1994. *Bordell der Krieger. Folklore, Politik und Krieg.* fibre Verlag. Osnabrück.

Čolović, Ivan. 2002. *Politics of Identity in Serbia. Essays in Political Anthropology.* New York University Press. Washington Square, New York.

Comaroff, Jean and John Comaroff. 2003. *Transparent Fictions; or, The Conspiracies of a Liberal Imagination: An Afterword.* In: West, Harry G. and Todd Sanders. 2003. *Transparency and Conspiracy. Ethnographies of Suspicion in the New World Order.* Duke University Press. Durham and London: 287-300.

Connerton, Paul. 1989. *How Societies Remember.* Cambridge University Press. Cambridge, UK.

Connor, Walker. 1994. *Ethnonationalism. The Quest for Understanding.* Princeton University Press. Princeton, New Jersey.

Danforth, Loring M. 1995. *The Macedonian Conflict. Ethnic Nationalism in a transnational world.* Princeton University Press. Princeton, New Jersey.

Daniel, Valentine E. 1996. *Charred Lullabies. Chapters in an Anthropography of Violence.* Princeton University Press, Princeton, New York.

Darnton, Henry. 1993. *Does the World still recognize a holocaust?* In: The New York Times, Section 4: 1.

Demirovic, Alex. 1996. *Die Transformation des Wohlfahrtsstaats und der Diskurs des Nationalismus.* In: Bruch, Michael and Hans Peter Krebs (ed.). *Unternehmen Globus: Facetten nachfordistischer Regulation.* Münster: 89-115.

Denich, Bette. 1994. *Dismembering Yugoslavia: Nationalist Ideologies and the Symbolic Revival of Genocide.* In: *American Ethnologist* 21: 367-390.

Denich, Bette. 2000. *Unmaking Multiethnicity in Yugoslavia: Media and Metamorphosis.* In: Halpern, Joel M. and David A. Kideckel (ed.) *Neighbors at War. Anthropological Perspectives on Yugoslav Ethnicity, Culture, and History.* The Pennsylvania State University Press: 39-55.

Despalatović, Elinor. 2000. *The Roots of War in Croatia.* In: Halpern, Joel M. and David A. Kideckel (ed.) *Neighbors at War. Anthropological Perspectives on Yugoslav Ethnicity, Culture, and History.* The Pennsylvania State University Press: 81-102.

Djordjevich, Michael. 1989. *What the Serbs want.* In: Michael Djordjevich. *The Yugoslav Question, What the Serbs want, The USA interests.* San Francisco.

Dolinsky, Lewis. 1998. *Bosnian Serb Leader comes to Saratoga.* The San Francisco Chronicle, May 27: A10.

Dorich, William. 1994. *The Suppressed Serbian Voice and the Free Press in America.* Serbian American Voters Alliance (SAVA). Los Angeles. California.

Durrell, Lawrence. 1957. *White Eagles over Serbia.* faber and faber. Boston, London.

Eliade, Mircea. 1984. *Kosmos und Geschichte.* Insel-Verlag. Frankfurt a. Main.

Evans-Pritchard, Edward E. 1976. *Witchcraft, Oracles and Magic among the Azande.* Oxford University Press. Oxford.

Fabian, Johannes. 1983. *Time and the Other. How Anthropology makes its object.* Columbia University Press. New York.

Featherstone, Mike (ed.). *Global Culture. Nationalism, globalization and modernity. A Theory, Culture & Society special issue.* SAGE Publications. London, Thousand Oaks, New Dehli.

Feldman, Allen. 1991. *Formations of Violence. Political terror and the narrative of the body in Northern Ireland.* University of Chicago Press. Chicago.

Flick, Uwe. 1999. *Qualitative Forschung. Theorie, Methoden, Anwendung in Psychologie und Sozialwissenschaften.* Rowohlt Taschenbuch Verlag. Reinbek bei Hamburg.

Foucault, Michel. [1973] 1995. *Archäologie des Wissens.* Suhrkamp Verlag. Frankfurt am Main.

Foucault, Michel. [1975] 1996. *Die Ordnung der Dinge.* Suhrkamp Verlag. Frankfurt am Main.

Friedman, Jonathan. 1992. *The Past in the Future: History and Politics of Identity.* In: American Anthropologist 94: 837-59.

Friedman, Jonathan. 1997. *Global Crises, the Struggle for Cultural Identity, and Intelectual Porkbarrelling: Cosmopolitans versus Locals, Ethnics and Nationals in an Era of De-hegemonization.* In: Pnina Werbner and Tariq Modood. *Debating Cultural Hybridity. Multi-Cultural Identities and the Politics of Anti-Racism.* ZED BOOKS. London & New Jersey: 70-89.

Fuglerud, Øivind. 1999. *Life on the Outside. The Tamil diaspora and Long Distance Nationalism.* Pluto Press. London, Sterling, Virginia.

Gellner, Ernest. 1983. *Nations and Nationalism.* Cornell University Press. Ithaca, New York.

Gillis, John R. (ed.). 1994. *Commemorations. The Politics of National Identity.* Princeton University Press. Princeton, New Jersey.

Gilroy, Paul. 1990. *Nationalism, History, and Ethnic Absolutism.* In: History Workshop Journal 30: 114-120.

Glazer, Nathan and Daniel Patrick Moynihan. 1963. Beyond the Melting Pot. The Negroes, Puerto Ricans, Jews, Italians, and Irish of New York City. The M.I.T. Press and Harvard University Press. Cambridge, Massachusetts.

Glenny, Misha. [1992] 1996. *The Fall of Yugoslavia. The Third Balkan War.* Penguin Books. London.

Glenny, Misha. 1999. *The Balkans. Nationalism, War and the Great Powers, 1804-1999.* Viking Press. New York.

Glick Schiller, Nina and Georges Fouron. 2001. *Georges woke upe laughing. Long-Distance Nationalism and the Search for Home.* Duke University Press. Durham, London.

Gocić, Goran. 2001. *The cinema of Emir Kusturica. notes from the underground.* Wallflower Press. London and New York.

Gonzalez, Nancie L. Solien de. 1989. *Conflict, Migration, and the Expression of Ethnicity: Introduction.* In: N. Gonzalez and C. S. McCommon (eds.): *Conflict, Migration, and the Expression of Ethnicity: Introduction.* Boulder: 1-9.

Gordy, Eric. 1999. *The Culture of Power in Serbia. Nationalism and the destruction of Alternatives.* The Pennsylvania State University Press. University Park, Pennsylvania.

Govorchin, Gerald Gilbert. 1961. *Americans from Yugoslavia. A Survey of Yugoslav Immigrants in the United States.* University of Florida Press: Gainesville.

Grečić, Vladimir. 2002. *Brain Drain Issues in FR Yugoslavia (Serbia and Montenegro): The Role of Return Migrant Professionals in the Process of Transition.* Unpublished paper presented at the International Studies Association's 43rd annual convention in New Orleans.

Groh, Dieter. 1987. *The Temptation of Conspiracy Theory, or: Why do bad things happen to good people?* In: Graumann, Carl. F. and Serge Moscovici. *Changing Conceptions of Conspiracy.* Springer Verlag. New York, Berlin, Heidelberg, London, Paris, Tokyo.

Gupta, Akhil and Ferguson, James (ed.). 1997. *Anthropological Locations. Boundaries of a Field Science.* University of California Press. Berkeley, Los Angeles, New York.

Halbwachs, Maurice. [1980]1992. *On Collective Memory.* (Edited, Translated, and with an Introduction by Lewis A. Coser.) Harper and Row: New York.

Halpern, Joel M.. [1956]1967. *A Serbian village. Social and cultural change in a Yugoslav community.*Harper Colophon Books: New York, Evanston, London.

Haraway, Donna J.. 1991. *Simians, Cyborgs, and Women. The Reinvention of Nature.* Routledge. New York.

Harding, Susan and Kathleen Stewart. 2003. *Anxieties of Influence: Conspiracy Theory and Therapeutic Culture in Millenial America.* In: West, Harry G. and Todd Sanders. 2003. *Transparency and Conspiracy. Ethnographies of Suspicion in the New World Order.* Duke University Press. Durham and London: 258- 286.

Hareven, Tamara. 1978. *The Search for Generational Memory: Tribal Rites in Industrial Societies.* In: *Daedalus* 107 (4): 137-149.

Hayden, Robert. 1992. *The Triumph of Chauvinistic Nationalisms in Yugoslavia: Bleak implications for Anthropology.* In: Anthropology of East Europe Review, 11: 63-68.

Hayden, Robert M.. 1994. *Recounting the Dead. The Rediscvery and Redefinition of Wartime Massacres in Late- and Post-Communist Yugoslavia.* In: Rubie S. Watson (ed.) *Memory,History, and Opposition under State Socialism.* School of American Research Press. Santa Fe, New Mexico: 167-184.

Hayden, Robert. 1996. *Imagined Communities and Real Victims: Self-Determination and Ethnic Cleansing in Yugoslavia.* In: American Ethnologist, 23 (4): 783-801.

Hayden, Robert. 2000. *Biased "Justice": Humanrightism.and the International Criminal Tribunal for the Former Yugoslavia.* In: Cleveland State Law Review (47): 549-573.

Hearing before the Committee on Foreign Affairs, 103rd congress, 05/ 11/1994. Washington D.C..

Hellinger, Daniel. 2003. *Paranoia, Conspiracy, and Hegemony in American Politics.* In: West, Harry G. and Todd Sanders. 2003. *Transparency and Conspiracy. Ethnographies of Suspicion in the New World Order.* Duke University Press. Durham and London: 204-232.

Herzfeld, Michael. 1987. *Anthropology Through the Looking-Glass.Critical Ethnography at the Margins of Europe.* Cambridge University Press. Cambridge, New York.

Herzfeld, Michael. 1997. *Cultural Intimacy. Social poetics in the nation-state.* New York/ London.

Hirschon, Renée. [1989]1998. *Heirs of the Greek Catastrophe. The Social Life of Asia Minor Refugees in Piraeus.* Berghahn Books. New York/Oxford.

Hobsbawm, Eric and Terence Ranger (eds.). 1983.*The invention of Tradition.* Cambridge University Press. Cambridge.

Hobsbawm, Eric. 2001. *Wieviel Geschichte braucht die Zukunft?* Deutscher Taschenbuch Verlag. Frankfurt/Main.

Hockenos, Paul. 2003. *homeland calling. Exile Patriotism and the Balkan Wars.* Cornell University Press. Ithaca and London.

Hofbauer, Hannes (ed.). 1999. *Balkankrieg. Die Zerstörung Jugoslawiens.* Promedia Verlag. Wien.

Hofstadter, Richard. [1952] 1967. *The Paranoid Style in American Politics and other Essays.* Random House. New York.

Humphrey, Caroline. 2003. *Stalin and the Blue Elephant: Paranoia and Complicity in Post-Communist Metahistories.* In: West, Harry G. and Todd Sanders. 2003. *Transparency and Conspiracy. Ethnographies of Suspicion in the New World Order.* Duke University Press. Durham and London: 175- 203.

Huxley, Aldous. [1932]1998. *Brave New World.* Perennial. London.

Jančar-Webster, Barbara. 1999. title? In: Ramet, Sabrina (ed.) *Gender politics in the western Balkans. Women and Society in Yugoslavia and the Yugoslav successor states*: The Pennsylvania State Universtity Press. University Park, Pennsylvania: 71.

Jansen, Stef. 1998. *Homeless at Home: Narrations of Post-Yugoslav Identities.* In: Rapport, Nigel and Andrew Dawson. *Migrants of Identity. Perceptions of Home in a world of movement.* Berg Press. Oxford, New York: 85-110.

Judah, Tim. 2000. *The Serbs. History, Myth and the Destruction of Yugoslavia.* Yale Nota Bene, Yale University Press. New Haven, New York.

Kaldor, Mary. 2000. *Neue und alte Kriege. Organisierte Gewalt im Zeitalter der Globalisierung.* Frankfurt/Main. (American edition: *New and Old Wars. Organized Violence in a Global Era.*1999)

Kapferer, Bruce. 1988. *Legends of People, Myths of State. Violence, Intolerance, and Political Culture in Sri Lanka and Australia.* Washington/London.

Kaplan, Robert. 1993. *Balkan Ghosts: A Journey through History.* Vintage Books. New York.

Keeley, Brian L. 1999. *Of Conspiracy Theories.* Journal of Philosophy 96 (3): 109-126.

Kerby, Anthony Paul. 1991. *Narrative and the Self.* Indiana University Press. Minneapolis.

Kojčve, Alexandre. 1975. *Hegel.* Suhrkamp Verlag. Frankfurt a. Main.

Krašteva-Blagoeva, Evgenija. 2003. *Who are we? Types of collective Identities in contemporary Bulgaria.* In: Ethnologia Balkanica, Vol. 7: 89-106.

Lazić, Mladen and Liljana Nikolić (eds.). 1999. *Protest in Belgrade. Winter of Discontent.* Central European University Press. Budapest.

Lévi-Strauss, Claude. 1962. *Das Wilde Denken.* Suhrkamp. Frankfurt (Main).

Libal, Wolfgang. 1996. *Die Serben. Blüte, Wahn und Katastrophe.* Europaverlag. München. Wien.

Linke, Uli. 1999. *Blood and Nation. The European Aesthetics of Race.* University of Pennsylvania Press. Philadelphia.

Lowenhaupt Tsing, Anna. 1993. *In the Realm of the Diamond Queen. Marginality in an Out-of-the-way place.* Princeton University Press. Princeton. New Jersey.

MacDonald, David Bruce. 2002. *Balkan holocausts? Serbian and Croatian victim-centered propaganda and the war in Yugoslavia.* Manchester University Press. Manchester.

Malkki, Liisa. 1992. *National Geographic: The Rooting of Peoples and the Territorialization of National Identity among Scholars and Refugees.* In: Cultural Anthropology 7 (1): 24-43.

Malkki, Liisa. 1995. *Purity and Exile. Violence, Memory, and National Cosmology among Hutu Refugees in Tanzania.* The University of Chicago Press. Chicago, London.

Malkki, Liisa. 2000. *Figures of the Future: Dystopia and Subjectivity in the Social Imagination of the Future.* In: JCAS Symposium Series 14.

Marcus, George (ed.). 1999. *Paranoia within Reason. A Casebook on Conspiracy as Explanation.* The University of Chicago Press. Chicago.

Marcuse, Herbert. [1964] 1998. *Der eindimensionale Mensch. Studien zur Ideologie der fortgeschrittenen Industriegesellschaften.* Deutscher Taschenbuchverlag. München.

Martin, David (ed.). 1978. *Patriot or Traitor. The Case of General Draža Mihailović.* Hoover Publication 191.

Melley, Timothy. 2000. *Empire of Conspiracy. The Culture of Paranoica in Postwar America.* Cornell University Press. Ithaca and London.

Merlino, Jacques. 1993. *Les Vérités Yougoslaves Ne Sont Pas Toutes Bonnes A Dire.* (The Truth from Yugoslavia is not being reported honestly). Editions Albin Michel S.A.: Paris.

Meštrović, Stjepan, Letica, Slaven, and Goreta, Miroslav. 1993. *Habits of the Balkan Heart. Social Character and the Fall of Communism.* Texas A&M University Press. College Station.

Meštrović, Stjepan G. 1994. *The Balkanization of the West. The Confluence of Postmodernism and Postcommunism.* Routledge. London and New York.

Meyerhoff, Barbara.1992. *Remembered Lives. The Work of Ritual, Storytelling, and Growing Older.*The University of Michigan Press. Ann Arbor.

Mikić, Dejan and Erika Sommer. 2003. *„Als Serbe warst du plötzlich nichts mehr wert." Serben und Serbinnen in der Schweiz.* orell füssli Verlag AG. Zürich.

Ninić, Ivan (ed.). 1989. *Migrations in Balkan History.* Narodna Biblioteka Srbije. Belgrade.

Nordstrom, Carolyn and Antonius C. G. M. Robben (ed.). 1995. *Fieldwork under Fire. Contemporary Studies of Violence and Survival.* University of California Press. Berkeley/Los Angeles/London.

North American News Analysis Group. 1994. *The Violent Dissolution of Yugoslavia. Truth and Deceit. 1991-1994. One Hundred Irrefutable Facts. The Yugoslav Mirror.* San Francisco.

Ochs, Elinor and Lisa Capps. 1996. *Narrating the Self.* In: Annual Review of Anthropology 25: 19-43.

Ong, Aihwa. 1999. *Flexible Citizenship. The Cultural Logics of Transnationality.* Duke University Press. Durham & London.

Orwell, George. [1949]2000. *1984.* Penguin Books. New York.

Padgett, Deborah. 1979. *Settlers And Sojourners: A Study of Serbian Adaptation in Milwaukee, Wisconsin.* Unpublished Ph.D. Dissertation. The University of Wisconsin. Milwaukee.

Parenti, Michael. 2000. *To kill a nation. The attack on Yugoslavia.* Verso. London, New York.

Paris, Edmond. 1961. *Genocide in Satellite Croatia. 1941-1945.* The American Institute for Balkan Affairs. Illinois.

Pekić, Borislav. [1978] 1994. *The Houses of Belgrade.* Northwestern University Press. Evanston, Illinois.

Perec, Georges and Robert Bober. 1997. *Geschichten Von Ellis Island. Oder Wie Man Amerikaner Macht.* Verlag Klaus Wagenbach. Berlin.

Petritsch, Wolfgang, Kaser, Karl und Pichler, Robert 1999. *Kosovo-Kosova: Mythen, Daten, Fakten.* Klagenfurt.

Procter, Nicholas. 1999. *Serbian Australians in the Shadow of the Balkan War.* Ashgate. Aldershot, Burlington USA, Singapore, Sydney.

Ramet, Sabrina Petra. 1996. *Balkan Babel. The Disintegration of Yugoslavia from the Death of Tito to Ethnic War.* Westview Press. Boulder, Colorado.

Rappaport, Joanne. 1990. *The Politics of Memory: Native Historical Interpretation in the Colombian Andes.* Cambridge University Press. Cambridge.

Ricoeur, Paul.1998. *Das Rätsel der Vergangenheit. Erinnern – Vergessen – Verzeihen.* Wallstein Verlag. Essen.

Rosaldo, Renato. [1989] 1993. *Culture and Truth. The Remaking of Social Analysis.* Beacon Press. Boston.

Roth, Klaus. 1988. *Wie „europäisch" ist Südosteuropa? Zum Problem des kulturellen Wandels auf der Balkanhalbinsel.* In: Nils-Arvid Bringeus et al. (ed.). *Wandel der Volkskultur in Europa*, Band 1, Münster 219-231.

Roudometof, Victor. 2000. *Transnationalism and Globalization: The Greek orthodox Diaspora between Orthodox Universalism and Transnational Nationalism.* In: Diaspora. A Journal of Transnational Studies (9:3): 361-397..

Roudometof, Victor 2001. *Nationalism, Globalization, and Orthodoxy.The Social Origins of Ethnic Conflicts in the Balkans.* Greenwood Press. Westport, Connectitut. London.

Said, Edward. [1994] 2001. *Reflections on Exile and other essays.* Harvard University Press. Cambridge, Massachusetts.

Schierup, Carl-Ulrik and Aleksandra Ålund. 1986. *Will they still be dancing? Integration and Ethnic Transformation among Yugoslav immigrants in Scandinavia.* University of Umea, Sweden.

Schierup, Carl-Ulrik. 1995. *Former Yugoslavia: Long Waves of International Migration.* In: Cohen, Robin (ed.). The Cambridge Survey of World Migration. Cambridge University Press. Cambridge.

Schiffauer, Werner. 2000. *Die Gottesmänner. Türkische Islamisten in Deutschland.* Suhrkamp Verlag. Frankfurt am Main.

Schlögel, Karl. 2006. *Im Raume lessen wir die Zeit. Über Zivilisationsgeschichte und Geopolitik.* Fischer Taschenbuch Verlag. Frankfurt/Main.

Schmitt, Carl. [1932] 1996. *The Concept of the Political.* The University of Chicago Press. Chicago and London.

Seierstadt, Åsne. 2001. *Mit dem Rücken zur Welt. Titos Erben.* Merlin Verlag. Gifkendorf.

Sekulić, Duško, Massey, Garth and Randy Hodson. 1994. *Who were the Yugoslavs? Failed Sources of a Common Identity in the Former Yugoslavia.* In: American Sociological Review (59/1): 83-97.

Serbian Unity Congress Bulletin. 1993. *Introductory Issue.* No. 42, 12/26/93.

Shain, Yossi. 1999. *Marketing the American Creed Abroad. Diasporas in the U.S. and their Homelands.* Cambridge University Press. Cambridge, New York, Melbourne.

Silber, Laura and Alan Little. 1996. *The Death of Yugoslavia.* TV Books. New York.

Simić, Andrei.1978. *Winners and Losers. Aging Yugoslavs in a changing world.* In: Andrei Simić and Barbara G. Meyerhoff (ed.) *Life's Career – Aging. Cul-*

tural Variations on Growing Old. SAGE Publications. Newbury Park, London, New Dehli: 77-106.

Simić, Andrei. 1999. *Machismo and Cryptomatriarchy: Power, Affect, and Authority in the Traditional Yugoslav Family.* In: Sabrina Petra Ramet (ed.). *Gender Politics in the Western Balkans.* The Pennsylvania State University Press. University Park: 11-29.

Simić, Andrei. 2000. *Nationalism as Folk Ideology.* In: Joel M. Halpern and David A. Kideckel (ed.) *Neighbors at War. Anthropological Perspectives on Yugoslav Ethnicity, Culture, and History.* The Pennsylvania State University Press: 103-115.

Simić, Andrei. 2002. *Nationalism, Marxism, and Western Popular Culture in Yugoslavia: Ideologies, Genuine and Spurious.* In: Anthropology of East Europe Review, Vol. 20/2: 135-146.

Simić, Andrei and Maria Budisavljević Simić. 2004. The Children of Lazo's Grove. Documentary. A Byzantia Production. Scottsdale, Arizona.

Simić, Andrei and Joel H. Halpern. 1997. *Serbs.* In: David Levinson and Melvin Ember *American Immigrant Cultures. Builders of a Nation.* Vol. 2. New York: 785-791.

Simmons, Anne. 1995. *The beginning of the End.* In: Carolyn Nordstrom and Antonius C.G.M. Robben *Fieldwork under Fire. Contemporary Studies of Violence and Survival.* University of California Press. Berkeley, Los Angeles, London: 42-61.

Skrbiš, Zlatko.1999. *Long-Distance Nationalism. Diasporas, homeland, and identities.* Ashgate: Aldershot, Brookfield USA, Singapore, Sydney.

Smith, Anthony D.. [1986]1989. *The Ethnic Origins of Nations.* Basil Blackwell. New York.

Spradley, James P. 1979. *The ethnographic interview.* Holt, Rinehart and Winston Inc., Orlando, Florida.

Strauss, Anselm, and Juliett Corbin. 1990. *Basics of Qualitative Research. Grounded Theory Procedures and Techniques.* SAGE Publications. Newbury Park, London, New Dehli.

Sundhaussen, Holm. 1982. *Geschichte Jugoslawiens 1918-1980.* Verlag W. Kohlhammer. Stuttgart, Berlin, Köln, Mainz.

Tanner, Marcus. 2001. *Croatia. A Nation forced in war.* Yale Nota Bene, Yale University Press. New Haven and London.

Taussig, Michael.1992. *The Nervous System.* Routledge: New York, London.

Terzić, Zoran. 2004. *Von Phantomkulturen und nationalen Logiken – 4 Thesen zur postjugoslawischen Befindlichkeit.* Unpublished article. Berlin.

Thompson, Mark. 1992. *A Paper House. The Ending of Yugoslavia.* Pantheon Books, New York.

Thurow, Roger and Tony Horwitz. 1992. *Paranoid and Vengeful, Serbs claim their war is to right old wrongs.* Wall Street Journal. Sept. 18th: A1.

Tišma, Aleksandar. [1985]1998. *Das Buch Blam.* Deutscher Taschenbuch Verlag: München.

Tölölyan, Khachig. 1991. *The Nation State and Its Others: In Lieu of a Preface.* In: Diaspora. A Journal of Transnational Studies: 3-8.

Todorova, Maria. 1997. *Imagining the Balkans.* Oxford University Press. New York, Oxford.

Tomashevich, George Vid. 2000. *Portraits of Serbian Achievers.* Serbian Literary Company. Toronto.

Tomasevich, Jozo. 1975. *The Chetniks: War and Revolution in Yugoslavia, 1941-45.* Stanford University Press. Stanford.

Trouillot, Michel-Rolph. 1995. *Silencing the Past. Power and the Production of History.* Beacon Press. Boston.

Tudjman, Franco.1996. *Horrors of War. Historical Reality and Philosophy.* M. Evans and Company, Inc. New York.

Tweed, Thomas.1997. *Our Lady of the Exile: Diasporic Religion at a Catholic Cuban Shrine in Miami.* New York: Oxford University Press.

Udovički, Jasmina and James Ridgeway (eds.). [1997] 1999. *Burn this house. The Making and Unmaking of Yugoslavia.* Duke University Press. Durham and London.

Ugrešić, Dubravka. 1994. *My American Fictionary.* Suhrkamp Verlag: Frankfurt (Main).

US Department of Justice. Immigration and Naturalization Service. 1999.

Van de Port, Mattjis. 1999. *'It Takes a Serb to Know a Serb': Uncovering the Roots of Obstinate Otherness in Serbia.* In: Critique of Anthropology, Vol. 19/1: 7-30.

Van der Veer, Peter. 1995. *Introduction: The Diasporic Imagination.* In: Peter van der Veer (ed.). *Nation and migration: the politics of space in the South Asian Diaspora.* University of Pennsylvania Press. Pennsylvania: 1-16.

Verdery, Katherine. 1996. *What was socialism, and what comes next?* Princeton University Press. Princeton, New Jersey.

Verdery, Katherine. 1999. *The Poltical Lives of Dead Bodies. Reburial and Post-socialist Change.* Columbia University Press. New York.

Verne, Markus. 1999. *Alltägliche Zauberei. Über Sinn und Symbolik magischen Handelns bei den Hausa in Nigeria.* Rüdiger Köppe Verlag. Köln.

Vlajki, Emil. 2001. *Demonization of Serbs. Western Imperialism and Media War Criminals.* Revolt. Ottawa, Ontario, Canada.

Vrga, Djuro J.. 1975. *Changes and Socio-Religious Conflict In An Ethnic Minority Group: The Serbain Orthodox Church In America.* Unpublished Master's Thesis. San Francisco.

Vucinich, Vladimir Nicholas. 1983. *From the Adriatic to the Pacific. Serbs in the San Francisco Bay Area.*Unpublished Master's Thesis. University of California. Santa Barbara.

Wachtel, Andrew Baruch. 1998. *Making a Nation, Breaking a Nation. Literature and Cultural Politics in Yugoslavia.* Stanford University Press. Stanford, California.

Werbner, Pnina. 1997. *Introduction: The Dialectis of Cultural Hybridity.* In: Pnina Werbner and Tariq Modood. *Debating Cultural Hybridity. Multi-Cultural Identities and the Politics of Anti-Racism.* ZED BOOKS. London & New Jersey: 1-28.

West, Richard. 1994. *Tito and the Rise and Fall of Yugoslavia.* Carroll & Graf Publishers Inc. New York.

West, Barbara A. 2002. *The Danger is everywhere! The Insecurity of Transition in Postsocialist Hungary.* Waveland Press, Inc.. Prospect Heights, Illinois.

West, Harry G. and Todd Sanders. 2003. *Transparency and Conspiracy. Ethnographies of Suspicion in the New World Order.* Duke University Press. Durham and London.

Winland, Daphne N. 1995. *„We are now an actual nation": The Impact of National Independence on the Croation Diaspora in Canada.* In: *Diaspora. A Journal of Transnational Studies* 4: 3-30.

Woodward, Susan. 1995a. *Balkan Tragedy. Chaos and Dissolution after the Cold War.* The Brookings Institution. Washington.

Woodward, Susan. 1995b. *Socialist Unemployment. The Political Economy of Yugoslavia, 1945-1990.* Princeton University Press. Princeton.

Živković, Marko 1996. *Too much Character, Too little 'Kultur': Serbian Jeremiads 1994-1995.* Paper read at the *CASPIC MacArthur Scholars' Conference,* 5-6 October 1996, Chicago.

Živković, Marko. 1998. *Serbia's place in European geopolitical imaginings.* Unpublished article. Chicago.

Živković, Marko. 2000. *Telling Stories of Serbia: Native and Other Dilemmas on the Edge of Chaos.* In: Hermine G. De Soto and Nora Dudwick (ed.). *Fieldwork Dilemmas. Anthropologists in Postsocialist States.* The University of Wisconsin Press: 49-68.

Zograf, Aleksandar (with an introduction by Terry Jones). 1999. *Bulletins from Serbia. E-Mails and Cartoon Strips from beyond the Front Line.* Slab-o-Concrete. New York.

Forum Europäische Ethnologie

hrsg. von Dorle Dracklé, Thomas Hauschild, Wolfgang Kaschuba, Orvar Löfgren, Bernd Jürgen Warneken und Gisela Welz

Thomas Hauschild;
Bernd Jürgen Warneken (Hg.)
Inspecting Germany
Internationale Deutschland-Ethnographie der Gegenwart
Die internationale Ethnologie hat Deutschland entdeckt. Seit der deutschen Vereinigung forschen zahlreiche ausländische Wissenschaftlerinnen in einem Land, dessen Verwicklung in eine völkische Vergangenheit und Entwicklung zu einer multikulturellen Gesellschaft sie mit ethnographischen Nahaufnahmen beizukommen versuchen. Der Band "Inspecting Germany" dokumentiert die erste Regionalkonferenz dieser neuen kultur- und sozialanthropologischen Deutschlandforschung. Er versammelt 26 Beiträge von Forscher/innen aus 14 Ländern, die sich kritisch-prüfend mit deutscher Hundeliebe, deutschen Müttern, deutschem Karneval, aber auch deutschen Türken, Russen und Antirassisten beschäftigen.
Bd. 1, 2003, 568 S., 30,90 €, br., ISBN 3-8258-6123-6

Pipo Bui
Envisioning Vietnamese Migrants in Germany
Crime reports, immigrant origin narratives and partial masking
Ethnic stigma is the worst-case scenario for a migrant group, but migrants cope with origin narratives and partial masking – two novel concepts introduced in this book. Parallel to the national narratives of natives, immigrant origin narratives by Vietnamese in Germany invoke and retrench the histories of East & West Germany and North & South Vietnam. By partially masking their identity as Chinese or Asian, Vietnamese entrepreneurs circumvent ethnic stigma and use their physiognomy to market exotic goods.
Bd. 3, 2003, 240 S., 19,90 €, br., ISBN 3-8258-6917-2

Michi Knecht
Zwischen Religion, Biologie und Politik
Eine kulturanthropologische Analyse der Lebensschutzbewegung
Als zeitgenössische Protestbewegung ist die Lebensschutzbewegung in der BRD in kollaborative wie antagonistische kulturelle Strömungen eingebettet. Die Untersuchung rekonstruiert die Anfönge der heutigen Bewegung aus der Perspektive ihrer Protagonistinnen und Protagonisten und analysiert, wie die Politisierung von Religion, die Sakralisierung von Biologie und eine moralische Rekonstruktion von Geschlechterverhöltnissen zusammenwirken. Sie versteht diese Dimensionen als Elemente einer *Kosmologie in Aktion*, die auf die Transformation von Individuen und Gesellschaft im Feld emergenter biosozialer Phänomene gerichtet ist.
Bd. 4, 2006, 328 S., 24,90 €, br., ISBN 3-8258-7007-3

Alexa Färber
Weltausstellung als Wissensmodus
Ethnographie einer Repräsentationsarbeit
Wissen in der Spätmoderne ist problematisch geworden, folgt es deshalb auch neuen Produktionsmodi? Die Expo 2000 in Hannover ist in dieser ethnographischen Untersuchung der Schauplatz für die Thematisierung und Problematisierung von Wissen. Am Beispiel des marokkanischen Nationenpavillons und der Arbeit der Künstlergruppe BBM in der Themenparkausstellung „Wissen – Information – Kommunikation“ wird dargestellt, wie im Kontext der Weltausstellung Wissen als Ressource, als Modell und im/als Transfer hergestellt wird und wirkt. Darüber hinaus geht das Buch der Frage nach, wie sich ethnographische Wissensproduktion in diesem institutionellen Umfeld positioniert. Dabei verknüpft diese Studie drei Felder der Repräsentationsarbeit miteinander: Politik, Kunst und Wissenschaft.
Bd. 5, 2006, 336 S., 24,90 €, br., ISBN 3-8258-8139-3

Elsbeth Kneuper
Mutterwerden in Deutschland
Eine ethnologische Studie
Eine Studie, die die besonderen Qualitäten ethnographischer Forschung demonstriert: „Mutterwerden“ als Prozess, dessen „Natürlichkeit“ angerufen wird, um kulturelle, soziale, technologische Eingriffe zu legitimieren. Ein Prozess, der durch Geltungsansprüche konkurrierender Wahrheitsregimes charakterisiert ist und an dem sich zentrale Elemente westlicher Kosmologien (Leitunterscheidungen, Leitwidersprüche) aufdecken lassen. Welches Wissen wird von wem wann wie mobilisiert, um eine spezifische Form der Körperlichkeit, der Subjektivität und sozialen Identität, die der Mutter nämlich, herzustellen?
Bd. 6, 2005, 320 S., 19,90 €, br., ISBN 3-8258-8114-8

Jana Binder
Globality
Eine Ethnographie über Backpacker
Durch intensive Befragung, Beobachtung und Begleitung von Rucksacktouristen aus der ganzen Welt war es Jana Binder möglich eine Ethnografie über in die Praxis Backpacking anzufertigen. Entlang des vielfältigen empirischen Materials wird

gezeigt, wie sich junge Menschen durch diese Praxis distinktiv von anderen sozialen Akteuren ihrer Herkunftsgesellschaften absetzen: Sie produzieren Reiserepräsentationen, die beweisen sollen, dass sie sich in Globalisierungsprozesse einschreiben können. Dadurch erwirtschaften sie wichtiges kulturelles Kapital: globality. Zum ersten Mal wird Backpacking zu aktuellen Transformationsprozessen moderner Gesellschaften in Beziehung gesetzt und als Thematik begriffen, die entlang der Konzepte Transnationalisierung, Netzwerke und Medialitätzur Theorieentwicklung der internationalen Sozial- und Kulturanthropologie beiträgt.
Bd. 7, 2005, 248 S., 29,90 €, br., ISBN 3-8258-8686-7

Elisabeth Tauber
Du wirst keinen Ehemann nehmen
Fluchtheirat und die Bedeutung der Toten bei den Sinti Estraixaria
Inmitten der zuweilen vernichtenden nation-state-Dynamiken Mitteleuropas überlebten die Sinti als kleine, in ihrem kulturellen Erscheinungsbild unsichtbare Gruppen. Ihr Überleben gehört bis heute zu den ungeklärten Phänomenen der europäischen Geschichte. Die vorliegende Ethnographie zeichnet die zentralen Momente nach, die für die Fortführung einer von Außen selten erkennbaren kulturellen Kohäsion bedeutsam sind. Diese ist geprägt von den großen Themen des Lebens - Liebe und Tod -, die während und nach der Fluchtheirat der Sinti für einen kurzen Augenblick sichtbar werden.
Bd. 8, 2007, 296 S., 19,90 €, br., ISBN 3-8258-8816-9

Ethnologie: Forschung und Wissenschaft

Wim van Binsbergen;
Peter L. Geschiere (Eds.)
Commodification: Things, Agency, and Identities
(*The Social Life of Things* revisited)
The empirically rich and analytically provocative contributions to this volume focus on Africa and on the process through which commodities come into being. Commodifcation is shown to be a powerful tool towards understanding the modern world, especially South economies and South-North interactions today. It greatly illuminates the three central concepts things, agency, and identities, and thus is conducive to the much-needed dialogue between anthropology and economics. In the book, some of the original contributors of A. Appadurai's edited collection from 1986 *The Social Life of Things: Commodities in Cultural Perspective* meet with today's prominent names in the field (Jean & John Comaroff, Paul & Jennifer Alexander, R. Dilley, M. Rowlands, and award-winning N. Rose Hunt) and with scholars of the next generation: B. Weiss, R. van Dijk, J. Roitman, J. Leach, and I. Stengs. Together with W. van Binsbergen and P. Geschiere, this team explores the dynamics of Commodification.
Bd. 8, 2005, 400 S., 34,90 €, br., ISBN 3-8258-8804-5

Eveline Dürr
Identitäten und Sinnbezüge in der Stadt
Hispanics im Südwesten der USA
Die Studie, die auf ethnographischer Feldforschung basiert, untersucht kollektive Identitäten, Repräsentationen und interethnische Beziehungen in zwei hispanischen Vierteln von Albuquerque, New Mexico (USA). Während im pittoresken Stadtteil Old Town Identitäten durch symbolische Praktiken öffentlich gemacht werden und zur Aneignung des Raumes dienen, sind im sozial schwachen Viertel Barelas kollektive Identitäten wesentlich weniger ausgeprägt und präsent. Die Studie geht den Gründen für diese Unterschiedlichkeit nach und stellt historische Entwicklungen, strukturelle Merkmale und räumliche Bedingtheiten in den Mittelpunkt der Analyse. Neben theoretischen Diskussionen liefert das Buch auch umfassende Daten zur Geschichte und Gegenwart von Albuquerque.
Bd. 9, 2006, 248 S., 19,90 €, br., ISBN 3-8258-9041-4

Julia Reuter; Corinne Neudorfer;
Christoph Antweiler (Hg.)
Strand Bar Internet
Neue Orte der Globalisierung
Strände und Straßen in Afrika, indonesische Internetcafés und laotische Bergdörfer gelten bislang nicht als die zentralen Schauplätze der Globalisierung. Kritiker und Befürworter der Globalisierung schauen lieber auf das Treiben an internationalen Finanzmärkten oder in die Chefetagen multinationaler Konzerne. Materielle Infrastruktur oder gänzlich informalisierte, transnationale Räume werden hier weitgehend ausgeblendet. Der Band wirft einen Blick auf diese neuen Orte der Globalisierung, deren Bewohner ihren eigenen Umgang mit globalen Themen gefunden haben: Sie entwickeln Strategien, um die Lebensbedingungen vor Ort zu verbessern, ihre (Minderheiten-)Identitäten zu vernetzen oder weltweiten Protest zu organisieren. Neben empirischen Fallstudien gelingt es den Beiträgen aus Soziologie, Ethnologie und Politik die neuen Orte unter Zuhilfenahme postkolonialer, praxistheoretischer und weltsystemtheoretischer Argumente auch theoretisch zu ‚verorten'.
Bd. 10, 2006, 218 S., 19,90 €, br., ISBN 3-8258-9294-8